THE RISE OF THE BRITISH TREASURY

THE RISE OF THE BRITISH TREASURY

Colonial Administration
in the Eighteenth Century

by DORA MAE CLARK

ARCHON BOOKS 1969

© 1960 by Yale University Press
Reprinted 1969 with permission
in an unaltered and unabridged edition

SBN: 208 00788 1
Library of Congress Catalog Card Number 69-16613
Printed in the United States of America

Acknowledgments

As THIS BOOK GOES to press I naturally recall the many friends and acquaintances who have contributed to its progress. I wish that I could adequately express my thanks to them.

First is the late Charles McLean Andrews, who originally gave me the incentive to start this long quest. The memory of his many kindnesses has often lightened my spirits when the going was a little rough. On numerous occasions in more recent years Robert Livingston Schuyler, Leonard Woods Labaree, and the late Godfrey Davies have come to my assistance with encouragement and welcome advice.

Less personal but indispensable has been the aid given by directors, librarians, and their staffs in the various centers where I have carried on my research. It seems invidious to single out a few for particular mention. Special thanks are nevertheless due two libraries in this country: the Henry E. Huntington in San Marino, California, and the William L. Clements in Ann Arbor, Michigan. I am grateful to both institutions for permission to reproduce certain items in their collections, and to their late directors for exceptional courtesies. Because of the extended periods of time which I spent in the Public Record Office and the British Museum I have special reason for remembering the considerate attention received there. Without it, and similar assistance of the staffs at the London Custom House Library and the General Post Office, this study would have been impossible.

A quite different kind of obligation prompts an acknowledgment to the owners of private papers. I owe special thanks to Earl Fitzwilliam and the Trustees of the Wentworth—Woodhouse Settled Estates for permission to use and quote manuscripts now housed in the Sheffield Public Library, as well as gratitude to the librarians there. I am glad to have this occasion to thank the Duke of Grafton for permission to use his collection. I am also greatly indebted to Miss Joan Wake of the Northamptonshire Record Society for originally obtaining permission for me to examine the Grafton papers, and more recently for securing assurance that I might publish information gathered from those papers.

Financial aid and the encouragement such assistance brings have come from the Social Science Research Council on two occasions, from the Huntington Library, and from the Eleanor Warfield Fund administered by the faculty of Wilson College. The President and Trustees of Wilson College, I might add, have been generous in granting leaves of absence so that I might have free time for research.

Finally, the editors of the Yale University Press have given their invaluable advice and technical assistance in such a friendly spirit of cooperation that it has been a pleasure to work with them.

Chambersburg, Penn.   D.M.C.
January 1960

Contents

Acknowledgments   v

Abbreviations   IX

1. The Treasury and the Plantations in the Early Eighteenth Century   1

2. The Age of Walpole   39

3. The Treasury under the Pelham Brothers, 1743–1762   76

4. Grenville's Administration: a Turning Point in British–American Relations   108

5. A Brief Interlude: the Administration of the Marquis of Rockingham   146

6. The Treasury and the Loss of Thirteen Colonies: the Administrations of the Duke of Grafton and Lord North, 1766–1776   165

7. In Brief   198

Bibliographical Notes and Lists of Selected Sources   203

Index   219

Abbreviations

For data on publication of manuscripts and their present location see the Bibliography at the end of the volume.

Add. MSS	Additional Manuscripts, British Museum. Because the folios of the Martin Papers, Add. MSS 41,346 ff., and the Correspondence of John Calcraft with the Earl of Chatham, Add. MSS 43,771, had not been numbered when I used them, I have designated individual letters by dates.
Adm.	Admiralty Papers, PRO. Adm. 1, In-Letters; Adm. 2, Out-Letters
AHR	*American Historical Review*
AO	Audit Office, PRO. AO 1, Declared Accounts; AO 3, Accounts Various
APC, Col.	*Acts of the Privy Council, Colonial Series*
BM	British Museum
BT, *Journal*	*Journal of the Commissioners of Trade and Plantations.* The Commissioners are usually called the Board of Trade
CHOP	*Calendar of Home Office Papers*
CJ	*Journals of the House of Commons*
CO	Colonial Office Papers, PRO
CSP, Col.	*Calendar of State Papers, Colonial Series, America and West Indies*
CSP, Dom.	*Calendar of State Papers, Domestic Series*
CTB	*Calendar of Treasury Books*
CTB & P	*Calendar of Treasury Books and Papers*

E	Exchequer, PRO. E 351, Declared Accounts of the Pipe Office
GD	Chatham Papers, PRO
GPO	General Post Office, a repository for many postal records
HC	House of Commons
HEH	Henry E. Huntington Library
HM	Huntington Manuscripts, Huntington Library
HMC	Historical Manuscripts Commission
LJ	*Journals of the House of Lords*
Md. Arch.	*Archives of Maryland*
N.J. Arch.	*Documents Relating to the Colonial . . . History of . . . New Jersey*
N.Y. Col. Doc.	*Documents Relative to the Colonial History of the State of New York*
PC	Privy Council, PRO. P.C. 2, Register of the Privy Council
PRO	Public Record Office, London
SP	State Papers, PRO
Stock	Leo Francis Stock, ed., *Proceedings and Debates of the British Parliaments Respecting North America,* Washington, D.C., Carnegie Institution, 1924—
T	Treasury, PRO. T1, In-Letters; T11, Out-Letters Customs; T27, Out-Letters General; T29, Minute Books; T38, Accounts Departmental; T52, King's Warrants; T53, Warrants Relating to Money; T54, Warrants Not Relating to Money; T60, Order Books; T61, Disposition Books; T64, Miscellaneous, including Blathwayt Journals. In cases where the numbering of folios in T1 was not clear, designation has been indicated by date or otherwise.
WLC	William L. Clements Library, Ann Arbor, Michigan

1.

The Treasury and the Plantations
in the Early Eighteenth Century

IN 1776 WHEN THE American colonies declared their independence, they were revolting against a set of policies devised by the British Treasury and the methods by which those policies were enforced. In the seventeenth century the Treasury would have been unable to wield such a fateful influence in colonial affairs, but during the course of the eighteenth century it became the most powerful of all the departments under the Crown. The head of the Treasury acquired a pre-eminence among the royal counselors that made him extraordinarily influential wherever colonial policies were discussed; and finance, which had originally been of minor consideration in colonial administration, finally came to be of major concern. As a consequence of these developments the Treasury, more than any other branch of the British Government, was responsible for the loss of the American colonies.

In principle the Treasury adhered to the fundamental tenets that had come to govern colonial administration. In the early eighteenth century, at least, there was no dispute over the theory that the plantations were royal domain or the policy of strengthening and extending crown control of their governments. Trade was considered the principal advantage to be derived by the mother country from her colonies, and it was the business of Parliament to regulate trade. If necessary, England should defend her colonies against foreign attack but, emergencies aside, the colonies should be self-supporting. Differences of opinion arose over methods of implementing and enforcing these principles and over their relative importance. The head of the Treasury was influenced by his responsibility for protecting both the royal treasure and public funds appropriated by Parliament for the armed services. He frequently resisted expenditures, whether from crown dues or public funds, which other officials believed necessary to carry out some of the above aims. In short, while other officials might have a colonial policy, the policy of the Treasury was essentially financial, and the principle it normally emphasized was that the colonial governments should be financially self-sufficient.

In a period like that of Queen Anne's reign, which very nearly coincided with the War of the Spanish Succession, there were unusual demands for military aid for the colonies, and the Treasury was hard pressed to carry out its policy of colonial self-sufficiency. In spite of the extraordinary power Anne entrusted to the head of her Treasury and his consequent influence on colonial policy, new precedents were established for grants of military assistance. Such grants increased the administrative functions of the Treasury in the colonial field. This period, therefore, is peculiarly suitable for an introductory study of the Treasury in both its political and administrative capacities, and for an examination of its special role in colonial affairs. Although later years produced new characters in somewhat different settings, developments in the Treasury under Queen Anne and in its relation to colonial problems formed the background for events which culminated in the American revolt of 1776.

Unlike her predecessor, William III, the Queen gave precedence among her counselors to the head of her Treasury. She conferred the white staff, symbol of the office of Lord High Treasurer, first upon Sydney, Earl Godolphin, and then, following an interval when the Treasury was "in commission" (under the management of a board), upon Robert Harley, Earl of Oxford and Earl Mortimer.[1] Both Godolphin and Oxford enjoyed extensive patronage

---

1. During the period of the commission, John, Earl Poulet, was First Commissioner; but Harley, who was Chancellor of the Exchequer, was the most influential member of the Board. In her last moments the Queen placed the white staff in the hands of Charles, Duke of Shrewsbury.

and as a rule controlled the issue of funds—the two foundation stones of political authority. In both cases, however, there were natural limits to their independence of action.

The continued support of the Queen was the first requirement for political success, and political power was a prerequisite for administrative strength. But the whole governmental framework limited the freedom of the Lord High Treasurer. This framework included the other great officers of state, who were competitors for the Queen's favor, the various councils of the realm, and Parliament. The officer most likely to challenge the authority of the Treasury in colonial affairs was the Secretary of State for the Southern Department, so-called because he was primarily responsible for relations with the southern part of Europe. He normally included the colonies in his jurisdiction although the Secretary for the Northern Department occasionally intervened in American matters. Like the Lord High Treasurer, the Secretary of State was a member of the Cabinet, which at this time was a small and intimate group. He also enjoyed the privilege of approaching the Queen directly. His functions were not restricted to civil administration, but included problems of defense.

The most dramatic conflict between the Lord High Treasurer and the Secretary of State occurred when Oxford was head of the Treasury. In 1711 Henry St. John, although Secretary for the Northern Department, secured the Queen's approval for a grandiose scheme for the conquest of Canada, a scheme that ended in complete disaster. Oxford later asserted that he had opposed the plans.[2] Whether he objected from the outset is doubtful, for early in 1711 the Treasury was authorizing the use of colonial revenue for the expedition.[3] Nevertheless, the procedure was a blow to his pride because the Queen had permitted the Secretary of State to

2. Henry St. John, Lord Viscount Bolingbroke, *Letters and Correspondence Public and Private During the Time He Was Secretary of State to Queen Anne,* ed. Gilbert Parke (4 vols. London, 1798), *1,* 253. HMC, *Portland MSS, 5,* 464. HEH, Stowe 57, *5,* 120-21. The Paymaster General's accounts of this expedition are in Stowe 8, *5,* passim.

3. T54:21, p. 187.

handle the contracts, a function that normally belonged to the Treasury. Such was the nature of the Queen's Government, however, that Oxford did not resign but swallowed his chagrin and remained in office until nearly the end of the reign.

The Privy Council, of which the great officers of state were members, issued the orders that formed the basis of colonial government; but in the last years of the reign of William III, the Council came to rely on the advice of a new agency, the Commissioners of Trade and Plantations, commonly called the Board of Trade, rather than on its own committee. While the head of the Treasury and other principal ministers were members of the Board, *ex officio,* they seldom attended. William's Treasury had by no means always approved the Board's suggestions for spending money in the colonies, but lacked sufficient prestige to do more than protest. The Board, moreover, had become so aggressive that it tended to assume administrative as well as advisory functions, sometimes stepping on the toes of other governmental agencies, including the Treasury.

During Queen Anne's reign there began a definite decline in the power of the Board, for which the Treasury was at least partly responsible. The attitude of the Treasury toward the Board's recommendations now carried much more weight because of Godolphin's political standing. In various ways the Treasury was able to influence policies before the Board sent its recommendations to the Council. Godolphin could name members, as they knew, and in the course of his administration he made several changes in personnel. He warned the Board sharply against what he considered unnecessary expenditures and extravagant plans.[4] He put it in its place by prohibiting direct correspondence with the Commissioners of the Customs, an agency responsible to the Treasury. As a result the Board was less able to counteract the natural tendency of the Treasury to emphasize costs and revenues in relation to colonial administration. Even policies for strengthening crown control of the colonial governments were sometimes sacrificed if they were at the expense of the Exchequer. The full impact of the

4. PRO, Index 4630, pp. 269, 313. This register of treasury minutes occasionally contains more information than the minutes themselves.

growing weakness of the Board was not felt immediately; but its decline and the rise of the Treasury were to have a profound effect upon England's relation to her colonies.

The tenure of the Lord High Treasurer was in the hands of the Queen, but his success in colonial as in English affairs was also dependent upon satisfactory relations with Parliament. Public officials were beginning to look to Parliament not only for the regulation of trade and grants of funds for the armed services, but also for statutes on affairs once left entirely to the Crown. For example, the Post Office Act of 1711 brought the colonial postal system within the scope of English law, although it had originally been under a private monopoly granted by William III.

Both Godolphin and Oxford recognized the importance of a sympathetic majority in the House of Commons, where money bills originated. They knew something of the strategy of timing elections and of the methods of influencing votes, whether at the polls or on the floor of the House of Commons. But as a member of the House of Lords, Godolphin had to depend on others to manage the Commons. After 1711 Oxford was under a similar disadvantage. Of the two men Oxford was the better politician. He knew how to secure popular support and realized the value of the press. When still a commoner and Secretary of State, he strengthened Godolphin's administration. The two men were then friends, or at least, political colleagues. But with his following in the House of Commons as well as his growing favor with the Queen, Harley was able to undermine the Administration, and eventually supplanted Godolphin at the Treasury. A young politician of the time—Robert Walpole, for example—could probably have learned more about politics from Oxford than from Godolphin. But he might have observed that Oxford's problems multiplied after he accepted the earldom, and he might have profited from that observation.

If Oxford better understood the game of politics, Godolphin was the administrator par excellence. Long years at the Treasury under William III had given him a thorough knowledge of government finance and of the institutions through which it was managed. As Lord High Treasurer he acquired the authority to strengthen and centralize the department of finance. While he was in office, there occurred a notable expansion of the financial aspects of colonial administration, partly as a consequence of the circumstances already mentioned, partly as a result of Godolphin's own attention to details. As one might expect, then, after Oxford came to power political considerations assumed more importance in making appointments to administrative offices, and administrative routine suffered somewhat from neglect.

In the execution as in the formulation of colonial policies it is clear that the personality and the character of the head of the Treasury had a far-reaching effect. Nevertheless, this official was only part of a well-established organization using methods and forms dating in some cases from the far-distant past. Knowledge of this machinery is necessary to understand how the Treasury functioned in the colonial phases of its business, and to appreciate the administrative problems it encountered in trying to enforce its policies. The pages immediately following, therefore, will describe those parts of the treasury organization involved in colonial administration in the early part of the eighteenth century.

Except for a brief interval, Queen Anne, as mentioned, followed the practice of concentrating power in a Lord High Treasurer, to whom she granted a patent for the office of Treasurer of the Exchequer as well as the white staff of political significance. Second in authority in administration of finance was the Chancellor of the Exchequer, who also held a patent naming him Under-Treasurer. His chief duty as Chancellor of the Exchequer was to officiate at the declaration of accounts. Godolphin apparently consulted with the Chancellor frequently, but Oxford had the reputation for acting alone.

When the Treasury was in commission, five men sat as a board to carry out the duties of Treasurer of the Exchequer. The member whose name appeared first in the patent was known as the First Lord. He presided at their meetings and represented them in official relationships. The second name in the patent was that of the Chancellor of the Exchequer and Under-Treasurer. The other three members were known as Junior Lords. A quorum of three was required for official business.[5] General letters of privy seal and general letters patent dormant, addressed to the Treasury, were issued at the beginning of each reign. The former authorized payments for public or particular services, according to royal warrants. The latter directed the Treasury to make payments of the customary fees and salaries of civil officials.[6]

As long as treasury officials held the Queen's favor they had tremendous power, for she seldom took part in their deliberations,[7] the head of the Treasury consulting her in private and securing her signature on the necessary papers.

The headquarters of the Treasury were located in the Cockpit, not far from the houses of Parliament. There were rooms where the officers sat in formal session to receive petitions, hold hearings, and make decisions. There were quarters for secretaries and clerks, provision for storing numerous books and papers accumulated throughout the years, and waiting rooms for those who came on business.

Under Godolphin the treasury staff consisted of one secretary and about eight clerks. In addition there were servants, including messengers, a doorkeeper, and a housekeeper. William Lowndes, originally appointed by William III, was one of the most capable and distinguished secretaries in the history of the office. He served as long as he lived. When Oxford became Lord High Treasurer he appointed his cousin, Thomas Harley, as joint secretary. Harley was often absent on official business for the Lord High Treasurer, however, and retired when Oxford fell from power. Both Lowndes

5. At the first meeting of the new Board the secretary read the commission. The opening of the commission marked the beginning of official acts. But a minister had political authority from the time he kissed hands. A Lord High Treasurer and a Chancellor of the Exchequer took special oaths of office. I have found no evidence that members of the Board, aside from the Chancellor of the Exchequer, had any prescribed oaths.

6. BM, Add. MSS 29,445 (1760), "The Method of Business at the Treasury," pp. 1-3. Salaries not thus provided for were paid on the basis of particular letters of privy seal or letters under the great seal.

7. When the Treasury was in commission the members were to meet with her on Wednesday if she wished (T29:17, p. 177).

and Harley were members of Parliament, and helped to promote treasury policies there. In their administrative capacity they prepared business for the Lord Treasurer or the Board, took minutes of decisions, put them into effect as far as they could, and carried on correspondence with officials at home and abroad.

The clerks, who were under the supervision of the secretaries, were on permanent tenure. The four who were most experienced were known as chief clerks. They had correspondingly important and confidential duties, and directed the under-clerks. One branch of the clerical work was that of preparing accounts of the revenue, especially the customs. Most of the clerks, however, were employed in preparing the necessary forms for the payment of money or the appointment and instruction of officials subordinate to the Treasury. One of the secretaries presented such papers to the Lord High Treasurer or the Board for the required signatures.[8] The clerks copied such documents, dockets of papers from other offices needed for reference, and letters going out of the office into volumes which were kept as a permanent record.

The Lord High Treasurer or members of the Board and the Chancellor of the Exchequer received salaries from the civil list; and the revenue clerks, payment from the customs. The secretaries and most of the clerks received varying amounts from the fee fund and from New Year's gifts. A fee was collected for each document prepared in the office whether for the benefit of a private individual or for another government office. The income from this source

8. Issues from the Exchequer might require, in addition to letters under the privy seal or letters patent under the great seal, a royal warrant (T52); a treasury warrant (T53); an order (T60) or debenture prepared at the Exchequer, requiring in the case of the former the signature of treasury officials; and finally a letter of direction (T61) from the secretary to the Treasury for actual payment by one of the tellers. Fewer steps were necessary to authorize certain payments, such as the fees and salaries of civil officials in the central offices of government. Issues by receivers and cashiers for the expenses of managing the revenues were made on the basis of treasury warrants. Payments for other purposes, made by receivers of the revenue, and payments by public officials who had received issues from the Exchequer required royal warrants countersigned by the Treasury.

varied with the extent of business, increasing greatly in time of war. The system had its drawbacks, though it was less demoralizing in its effect on the recipients than one might expect. Yet it was a cause of delay, expense, and consequent annoyance for clients, and occasioned some controversy among the clerks.[9] The staff took for granted that those who constantly did business at the Treasury would present "gifts" of definite amounts at the beginning of each New Year.[10] Through their shares of fees and gifts the secretaries were handsomely rewarded, and the chief clerks received adequate compensation. The under-clerks lived largely on expectation.[11] Nevertheless, even these lesser posts were much sought after. The clerks might obtain sinecures for themselves and favors for their friends. And there was the prospect of regular promotion as vacancies occurred in the higher ranks.

Attached to the Treasury was a special solicitor who prosecuted those who failed to pay their debts to the Crown, followed cases in the Court of Exchequer, and defended revenue officials against private charges when the occasion warranted it. He prepared legal documents, seeking the advice of the Attorney General on difficult points of law. When requested by the Treasury, he solicited the passage of government bills through Parliament. In this connection he paid witnesses for appearing before committees and obtained copies of pertinent papers.[12]

Although the Treasury had a great variety of administrative functions with respect to the American colonies, they all might be classified under the following heads: authorizing payments for colonial purposes from the Queen's civil list and English public funds; supervising parliamentary, crown, and local revenues raised

9. Documents used for colonial purposes were listed separately in fee tables of later dates, at least, and were more expensive than any other documents except contracts (T1:338).

10. T1:174, fol. 24 (1714), a list with "arrears."

11. T1:85, fol. 24; T1:88, fol. 54; T38:438. Existing records for this early period do not usually make clear how much the under-clerks received.

12. There were other subordinates of the Treasury who were responsible for particular branches of the revenue. These and their functions will be discussed below in connection with the revenues.

in America; and auditing accounts. In practice the lines suggested by this classification of funds were not always clearly drawn, as two examples will show. At the beginning of each reign Parliament set aside particular revenues for the royal household and the civil government of the kingdom—that is, for the civil list. But the sovereign occasionally used hereditary or crown revenues from the colonies to supplement the civil list. The second illustration of overlapping of funds occurred because for some years Parliament failed to appropriate the public revenue arising from the Plantation Act of 1673. The Queen, therefore, treated the income from this source as if it were part of the hereditary dues. But in spite of such inconsistencies, there is a significance in the classification which makes it useful in a study of the administrative functions of the Treasury.

Payments from the civil list were at the discretion of the Crown without interference by Parliament. It was the business of the Lord High Treasurer to advise the Queen as to the desirability of a particular payment and whether she could afford it, though he might be overruled. Queen Anne's own religious and philanthropic instincts made her much more likely than her successors to succumb to such requests.[13] Among her larger expenditures was £25,000 for caring for the poor Palatines en route to America.[14] In addition, there were grants for a chapel for Indians in New York and pensions for a minister in Boston and another at Albany. In another class was £1,000 advance payment to William Penn for the proposed surrender of his government. Oxford was less successful than Godolphin in resisting new items. It was almost impossible for either to break with the precedents that had been established in earlier reigns. Among these were regular payments to the Governor of Bermuda and the Attorney General of New York. Newly appointed governors usually acquired appurtenances for the royal chapel, such

13. There is evidence, for instance, that she favored the establishment of colonial bishops in the colonies, which would certainly have been a drain upon her civil list; but she declared her opinion too late for action to be taken during her reign (T1:181, fol. 31).

14. T29:18, p. 3.

as Bibles and Prayer Books. Some governors received gifts to pay the fees for their new commissions and the cost of their own equipment. When the decision had been made in favor of these expenditures from the civil list, it was then the function of the Treasury to follow the routine steps in such extraordinary payments, from obtaining the Queen's signature on the royal warrant to the secretary's letter of direction to the teller of the Exchequer when the Lord High Treasurer decided there was money available for the purpose.

From every point of view, military expenditures for the defense of the colonies formed a much more important item than the miscellaneous charges on the civil list. No matter how powerful the Lord High Treasurer might be or how much bent on economy, he could not risk the actual loss of the American plantations by opposing the experts in the military field. Consequently, during the War of the Spanish Succession grants from the public funds for colonial defense increased. And at the end of the war the acquisition of American territory, especially the frontier outpost of Nova Scotia, added new items to the peacetime budget.

Military expenditures fell under three heads: army, ordnance, and navy. While the establishment of regular troops in the colonies and rather extensive grants of stores were comparatively novel, naval defense had been almost a matter of course from the period of earliest settlement. Annual estimates of the need of each of the three services formed the basis for parliamentary appropriations. The Treasury directed the Secretary at War and the Ordnance Office to prepare their respective estimates and refer them to the Treasury. When the latter had approved, representatives of the two offices submitted their estimates to the House of Commons, where the Treasury in a limited sense was responsible for what was recommended. The Admiralty did not refer its estimates to the Treasury. What influence the Treasury may have had in this field was exerted in the Cabinet and the Council, where the numbers of the sea-service were fixed.[15]

15. PC 2:75, p. 4, for an earlier example of order to Commissioners of the Admiralty to prepare estimates for a certain number of men.

Just how much influence the Treasury had on the army and ordnance estimates is difficult to say. Probably it had very little effect on the actual number of troops in America.[16] On the other hand, it tried to reduce the necessity for parliamentary appropriations for this part of the service by securing grants from the colonial assemblies. During the war, Jamaica, for example, had made a contribution to the expenses of the regiment stationed there but was loath to support "a standing army in time of peace."[17] Nevertheless, the Treasury permitted the House of Commons to adjourn without making provision for revenue to cover the supply already voted for the forces in Jamaica.[18] Oxford made particular inquiries as to how the companies in Nova Scotia could be supported "without increasing the charge on the publicque," but found that hope for a colonial revenue for this purpose was largely illusory.[19] The common practice of asking Parliament for less than would be required in the ensuing year necessitated later grants to cover extraordinaries not previously provided for. In the meantime payments were often postponed. Partly as a result of these procedures English soldiers in such out-of-the-way places as Newfoundland and Nova Scotia, to say nothing of New York, were likely to go hungry and in rags.

One of the routine functions of the Treasury with respect to the army was to authorize the Paymaster General to draw from the Exchequer funds appropriated by Parliament. In an attempt to eliminate fraud in distributions from that point on, Godolphin established the Comptrollers of the Accounts of the Army. But the responsibility of the Treasury did not stop there. As time passed, the Treasury assumed more and more of the functions connected with supplying the armed forces in America instead of

16. Near the close of Anne's reign the peacetime estimates for the army included four independent companies each for Nova Scotia, Newfoundland, and New York; one company for Bermuda; and two regiments for the West Indies.

17. *CSP, Col.,* July 1712–July 1714, §492.

18. Ibid., §413.

19. T29:19, p. 127. HEH, Blathwayt 127, 12 Oct. 1711.

relying on the officers in command. Under Queen Anne direct intervention was rare. Godolphin, however, arranged for a transfer of funds from the Paymaster General to the Treasurer of the Navy so that the Victualling Board could send supplies to the forces in Newfoundland. He also arranged a credit in Massachusetts in case the commander was obliged to send to New England for food.[20]

Lack of experience, ignorance about conditions in the New World, the difficulty of communicating with commanding officers stationed at such great distances from the London offices, and lack of adequate funds led to many unhappy situations, for which the Treasury was partly responsible. When funds for the army were not available in the provinces, royal governors sometimes pledged their own credit, only to discover later that the Treasury had refused to accept their bills of exchange or approve the accounts which they submitted in support of their expenditures.[21] Technically the Treasury was justified in its refusal if such expenditures had not been authorized by the Crown or Parliament. Moreover, strict accountability was necessary to prevent fraud. On the other hand, the fundamental reason for such irregular methods was the treasury failure to secure adequate supplies from Parliament.

Estimates for the Ordnance Office, like those for the army, were insufficient to provide for colonial needs. In the period under review they covered the cost of two or three engineers stationed in the colonies to advise the colonists about fortifications, but not the stores actually sent to America. The Board of Trade had long recommended making such definite provisions; and after repeated disappointments in getting the colonial assemblies to pay for what they received from England, the Ordnance Office at last came to the same conclusion. The Treasury did not agree, but preferred to rely upon finding some means of making the colonies more nearly self-supporting and less dependent upon the English government.[22]

---

20. *CTB, 17,* 242.

21. For one example of the latter see Godolphin's comment on Governor Stapleton's accounts (*CTP,* 1702–07, p. 144).

22. *CSP, Col.,* 1711–12, §§69, 313; 1712–14, §349.

It is interesting that among the self-sufficient or nearly self-sufficient colonies were those of which the Board of Trade complained most bitterly on other grounds: Connecticut, Rhode Island, Massachusetts, and Pennsylvania.[23]

For some years the principal item in the estimates for the navy, expressly designed for the colonies, was the salary of a "surveyor of the woods," who was to train the colonists in producing tar and turpentine for the English navy. On the basis of a report by the House of Commons in 1714, the Navy Board dismissed this officer as useless.[24] The action created interdepartmental complications, for the Treasury had prepared his commission and the Board of Trade had not only drafted his instructions but was still very enthusiastic about the project.

In the light of the rising tide of expenditures for colonial purposes and the policy of making the colonies self-supporting, one might think that the Treasury would have recommended radical changes in revenue policies. There is no evidence, however, that the Treasury was responsible for the bill which, if passed, would have levied a tax on New York.[25] Nor was there any statute passed by Parliament in this period for the express purpose of raising a revenue in America, unless one includes the Post Office Act discussed below. The most important aspects of the revenue, therefore, were administrative.

The following classification of colonial revenues according to the authority under which they were collected forms a useful basis for their consideration: those resulting from acts of Parliament; hereditary revenues of the Crown, depending upon the prerogative; and taxes raised by acts of assembly in the royal provinces. This classification had a definite significance in the eighteenth century, although contemporary officials were not always consistent

---

23. *CTP*, 1708–14, p. 573.

24. Leo Francis Stock, ed., *Proceedings and Debates of the British Parliaments Respecting North America* (Washington, D.C., Carnegie Institution, 1924–), *3*, 330.

25. Add. MSS 33,028, fols. 22 ff.

in its use, as suggested above. Lack of precise definitions as well as changing concepts of the respective authority of the Crown and Parliament were largely responsible for blurring the lines between parliamentary, crown, and local revenues. Nevertheless, the various terms represent actual differences.

Before the close of Queen Anne's reign, Parliament had authorized the collection of two types of revenues in America: export duties and postal rates. The former, at least, were not expected to produce a significant revenue in the colonies, but were devised as a means of regulating colonial trade in the interests of the mother country. Nevertheless, when in the latter part of the eighteenth century the Treasury decided to raise a revenue in America, the customs system was available for that purpose. In the meantime, there was a growing number of customs officials in the colonies. Because the system covered the corporate and proprietary colonies as well as the royal provinces, the Treasury was more widely represented in America than were other administrative agencies of the Crown. Outside the royal provinces Americans were likely to come into contact with few crown officials. The mercantile classes, however, were well acquainted with customs officials, and probably formed their opinion of the English Government largely from these contacts.

In the royal provinces the governor and his deputy, the naval officer, had duties in the regulation of trade that preceded the establishment of the customs officers. The differentiation of functions was never clarified; on the contrary, there was duplication and overlapping of duties, resulting in considerable interjurisdictional strife, with adverse effects upon colonial administration in general. For all these reasons the colonial customs system as it had evolved by 1714 deserves rather careful examination.

The system was the result of the act of 1673,[26] which required that anyone exporting certain specified commodities from a colonial port should pay duties if he had not given bond to carry such commodities to England, Wales, or Berwick-on-Tweed, and to no

26. 25 Charles II, c. 7.

other place.[27] The act was intended to prevent a particular kind of law evasion. After giving bond in a colonial port to carry the enumerated commodities either to England or to another plantation, as the law permitted, some merchants had been accustomed to sail to another plantation merely to secure a certificate to show that they had technically complied with the terms of the bond, and had then carried their cargoes to a foreign port, contrary to the intent of the law.[28] The payment of customs duties when the goods were first put on board ship was supposed to discourage that practice.

For many years revenue was incidental to the main purpose of the law, which was to keep English colonial trade out of the hands of foreigners and assure Englishmen a monopoly of the enumerated commodities. The new customs officials were law enforcers rather than collectors of revenue. The act of 1696 left no doubt that they were to enforce all the acts of trade and navigation and not just the act of 1673.[29] The shipper must now obtain the collector's signature on papers once signed by the naval officer alone. Consequently one officer was a check on the other, and many of their records were duplicates. The customs officers took bonds, gave certificates, examined ships' papers on entry, and authorized clearance. They made seizures and brought suit for violations of the law. In short, the effectiveness of the law now depended primarily upon the customs officers.

The London Customs Board, an agency subordinate to the

27. The act of 1660 (12 Charles II, c. 18) had enumerated sugar, tobacco, cotton-wool, fustic and other dye-woods, and cocoa nuts as goods to be brought either to England or to one of the English plantations. Rice, molasses, and naval stores were added by 3 and 4 Anne, cc. 3 and 9. The act of 1696 (7 and 8 Wm. III, c. 22) clarified the point that the shipper was to give bond even if he had paid the duty in the colonial port, and in various ways strengthened the administration of the laws.

28. For a more thorough analysis of the statutes and their administration see Charles McLean Andrews, *The Colonial Period of American History* (4 vols., New Haven, Yale Univ. Press., 1934—38), Vol. 4; and Lawrence A. Harper, *The English Navigation Laws*, New York, Columbia Univ. Press, 1939.

29. 7 and 8 Wm. III, c. 22.

Treasury, had the immediate management of the colonial customs system.[30] It issued deputations to the principal officers in America on the basis of warrants from the Treasury. The latter often exercised actual patronage; but Godolphin, at least, referred names to the Board to see if the candidates were properly qualified.[31] The Board submitted the semi-annual salary bill for America to the Treasury for approval. It gave general instructions to the officers, disciplined them when necessary, granted leaves of absence, and allowed the collectors' accounts. The Treasury might intervene between the Board and the officers to grant special privileges, but this was not customary in the early eighteenth century. During this period there are evidences that the Treasury encouraged higher standards through such measures as preliminary training, promotion on merit, and the requirement that the collector should give security for his place.[32] One serious defect in the system resulted from the possibility that an officer might appoint a deputy either to act in his stead or to assist him in the outlying districts. This practice tended to weaken the Board's control of the customs officers.

Official personnel in the colonies varied in rank from the surveyor general to the men who manned the boats. At the close of Queen Anne's reign there were three surveyors general: one for the northern part of the Continent; a second for Pennsylvania, the southern colonies, the Bahamas, and Jamaica; and a third for the other islands of the West Indies and Bermuda. In each of the forty-two smaller districts, including Newfoundland, there was at least one officer. There was a collector in each of thirty-two main landing places, and in outlying areas there were so-called "preventive of-

30. The Board had a patent from the Crown, conferring authority in England, but its right to manage the plantation duty was derived from the statute of 1673. In addition to a staff consisting of a secretary and clerks, one of whom was known as the western and plantation clerk, there was a receiver general, a solicitor, an inspector of imports and exports, and a stationer, all of whom had some business with the colonies. Godolphin's brother, Charles, was both first commissioner and inspector of imports and exports.

31. T11:15, p. 297.

32. T11:14, p. 406. Although these were rules of general application, which may have been more difficult to enforce in the colonies, they set a standard.

ficers" bearing the title of surveyor or searcher. In a few of the more important ports there was a comptroller or surveyor or both, as well as a collector. The comptroller examined the collector's accounts and added his signature to that of the collector on various documents. He might combine this office with that of surveyor of the port. In the larger ports one would find lesser officers, such as tidesmen or waiters and boatmen.

There were four different ways of making salary payments. In the islands where the Crown's own duty of four-and-a-half per cent was imposed, the same set of officers collected this duty and the regular customs and received their salaries from the former fund, thus relieving the customs of the charge. This fact created an important difference between these islands and other parts of America in the opinion of English officials. Officers in Jamaica and Bermuda took their salaries out of their own receipts. The receiver general in England paid the salaries of the principal officers on the mainland from the English revenue.[33] And finally, the remuneration of certain personnel, known as "incidental officers," who were not on the regular establishment and whose appointment was not subject to treasury approval, came from the revenue of the district. The Board gave permission for such payments by the collector under the head of "incidents."

In addition to other sources of income the officers received fees for all kinds of business. There was no uniform system. In many cases the only basis was an informal agreement between merchants and customs officers or even an arbitrary decision by the customs officers themselves. In others, the local government fixed the fees. In later years, with the increase in the number of forms, the fees became a source of great irritation and expense to the merchants. Some officials also accepted gratuities for conniving at illegal trade.

With the approval of the Customs Board the receiver general paid many of the incidental expenses of the ports, such as rent for a customhouse, the cost of a boat and men, and compensation for injuries received in the course of duty. The Board supplied such

33. This annual salary bill was about £3,470, falling slightly in the last two years of the reign (T11:15 and 16, passim).

things as a customhouse jack, printed acts of Parliament, a book of rates, all kinds of forms, paper, and so forth.[34]

In spite of all these contributions from the English revenue, including many salaries, few of the collectors were able to remit a surplus to the receiver general, for the principal business of many districts was mainly preventive. Except for the year 1699 Parliament did not consider it worth while to appropriate this revenue. Consequently the Crown treated it as part of the royal dues, and made various grants for colonial purposes.[35] Even in this early period crown officials realized the possibility of using the revenue to finance military exploits. In 1711 the Treasury authorized Col. Francis Nicholson to take receipts from the collectors of seven colonies for the contingent charges of forces under his command.[36] Because so much of the revenue was retained in America, deposits in the Exchequer were even smaller than one might expect. The largest deposit in this period was £5,420 for the year 1710, but this was more than twice as much as had been deposited in any previous year in the century.[37]

The customs system reveals the lack of effective centralization and coordination in England's management of colonial affairs. Although the Treasury was primarily responsible for the customs as a branch of the revenue, two other administrative departments shared in the enforcement of the acts of trade: that of the Secretary of State and the Admiralty. The former was concerned in the first place because the secretary was the governor's superior. Furthermore, even in this early period, English consuls abroad were ex-

34. William H. Browne, ed., *Archives of Maryland* (Baltimore, 1885–1912), *23*, 362-63.

35. William III had made a permanent grant of the net receipts of Maryland and Virginia to the College of William and Mary (*CTB, 9*, Pt. IV, 1408). It was also customary to make a gift for a Pennsylvania divine and schoolmaster (*CTP*, 1697–1702, pp. 241, 417). Before 1710 the governor and council of New York had used the receipts for local purposes (*CSP, Col.*, 1710–11, §487).

36. T54:21, p. 187.

37. WLC, Shelburne, *104*, 4-5. In 1713 deposits amounted to only £525. Duties on prize goods brought into the colonies were collected temporarily and reported separately.

pected to report on evidences of illegal trade.[38] Ships of the Royal Navy, acting under admiralty orders, gave some assistance on the coast of America in apprehending smugglers.[39] Vice-admiralty courts, under commissions from the High Court of Admiralty in England, tried cases arising under the acts of trade.

The laws under which these various officials acted were far from precise, and many disputes and inefficiency resulted. In theory the Queen-in-Council could coordinate the work of all three departments of government, but as time passed the Council became less effective as a centralizer of colonial administration, and eventually the head of the Treasury increased his own authority over other ministers. One of the great problems in the enforcement of the customs system, however, was to achieve cooperation among crown officials in America, responsible to different superiors in England.

Unlike the colonial customs system, the post office was expected to produce a revenue. This objective influenced most administrative decisions. And the fact that the system failed to result in a surplus was a disappointment to all concerned. Neither Thomas Neale, to whom William III had granted a private monopoly to erect and develop a postal system in America, nor his creditors to whom he made over the rights in his patent were able to make a profit. Nevertheless, encouraged by growing receipts, the Postmaster General recommended to the Treasury that the Crown should accept the surrender of the patent, compensate the holders, and undertake administration of the office.[40] This was done.

In 1707, therefore, the Postmaster General acquired authority over the American office similar to that exercised in England.[41]

38. Harper, *The English Navigation Laws,* pp. 93-94.
39. Ibid., pp. 177-79.
40. T1:60, fol. 286. *CTP,* 1702—07, p. 488.
41. The office of Postmaster General actually had two incumbents but was customarily referred to in the singular. For a detailed study of the administration of this office see Kenneth Ellis, *The Post Office in the Eighteenth Century,* London, Oxford Univ. Press, 1958. As Ellis states (p. 24), "the Secretary gradually became the real director of the office."

With respect to patronage and other non-revenue aspects of administration, the Postmaster General was considerably more independent than was the Customs Board. On the other hand, he was obliged to secure the approval of the Treasury for all financial decisions. He named a deputy to manage the post office on the Continent of North America and authorized him to name the postmasters for the local offices. In this period the system did not extend beyond New England and the middle colonies,[42] though some of the southern colonies had their own offices.

At first, local laws, varying from colony to colony, provided a very inadequate and uncertain legal basis for the collection of rates.[43] In 1711, however, Parliament included the plantations in a general act to increase the postal revenue, and attempted to establish uniformity in both inland and transatlantic rates, but did not create an effective government monopoly.[44] In fact, although many difficulties lay in the path of providing a satisfactory postal system for the colonies, the principal obstacle was the belief that it should produce a revenue.

The government packet system, introduced soon after the outbreak of war in 1702, came to an end in 1711 in financial failure. Both the Board of Trade and merchants trading to America had recommended such a service, for the slow-sailing vessels which normally carried communications between England and her colonies were likely to be seized by the enemy. With the approval of the Treasury, therefore, the Postmaster General made the necessary

42. John Hamilton, the American manager, estimated that the extension of the post into Virginia would cost £500 a year (T1:60, fols. 291–92).

43. In New Hampshire and Pennsylvania the laws were allowed to lapse; in Massachusetts the law was disallowed by the Crown; and New Jersey apparently had no law until 1709. The lack of central offices in Rhode Island and Connecticut may explain why their laws dealt only with free passage on the ferries.

44. 9 Anne, c. 10. The act set specific rates between the principal towns; and for distances of 60 miles, and not exceeding 100 miles, from these centers. There were three transatlantic rates: one for letters between London and the West Indies; a lower rate between London and New York; and a still lower rate between New York and the West Indies.

arrangements for a regular run to the West Indies.[45] In the period before the passage of the act of 1711, transatlantic rates were fixed by royal warrant. A schedule of 1705 provided for higher charges on letters from the West Indies than on those originating in England, "putting a further Tax upon them in the Plantations over and above what they pay here," in the words of the Postmaster General.[46] He named deputies for most of the islands to handle letters and packets.[47] In the rather narrow view of the Treasury the experiment was a failure because it was not even self-supporting. The Treasury, therefore, refused to extend the service to the mainland of North America.

With the abandonment of the West Indian packets the Government and public again resorted to the use of merchant vessels. The return of peace made this method sufficiently safe. Under the act of 1711 anyone, captain or passenger, who had letters in his charge, was supposed to deposit them at the post office in the port where the ship landed. The captain was to receive a penny per letter for his pains. Presumably the intent of the law was that the captain should also receive letters through the post office rather than through private hands. As a matter of fact, many letters were carried privately, with a consequent adverse effect upon the revenue.[48]

The American office, serving the northern and middle colonies, continued without interruption. From the point of view of the Treasury it too was a failure, for the receipts did not cover even the salary of the deputy postmaster general, to say nothing of supplying

45. The terms of the contract varied from time to time (T1:87, fols. 136, 149; T1:89, fol. 64; *CTP, 1702–07,* p. 278; T54:20, p. 88). Originally the Post Office carried the risk; under later agreements Edward Dummer, the contractor, assumed the responsibility. He was forced into bankruptcy (*CTP, 1714–19,* pp. 208-9).

46. T52:22, pp. 365–66; T1:89, fol. 64. This assumed that the sender would pay the fee. The act of 1711 required this practice for letters going by ship, although for inland mail it was customary for the recipient to pay the postage. The object of the difference seems to have been to increase correspondence.

47. *CSP, Col.,* 1704–05, §886; 1706–08, §§816, 1330.

48. 5 Geo. III, c. 25, described the earlier requirement as "ineffectual."

revenue for the British Exchequer. Years passed before an increase in population, extension of routes, and various reforms made a surplus possible.

According to the classification of colonial revenues used in this survey of treasury functions, the second branch was that of the hereditary, crown dues. After the revolution of 1689 English sovereigns apparently owed their rights to such dues to a grant of Parliament, although in the past they were based upon prerogative.[49] Definitions of these various dues and explanations of their origin may make the later discussion of their administration clearer.

Crown revenues were of two sorts: those that were fairly constant and dependable, and others, sporadic and occasional in their nature. Theoretically, rents, often a mere token, payable by the great landed proprietors like William Penn, Lord Baltimore, and the proprietors of the Carolinas, Jerseys, and Bahamas, belonged to the first class. Actually their payments were both uncertain and of small financial importance.

Other, more constant revenues were the ordinary quit rents and the four-and-a-half per cent export duty levied in Barbados and the Leeward Islands. Quit rents were dues that the proprietor of the soil was entitled to receive from those who held land under him. In the seventeenth century the sovereign had reduced the potentiality of royal revenue from this source by tremendous grants to proprietors or corporations with accompanying rights to rents. At the end of Queen Anne's reign there were only three royal provinces in which quit rents were of any practical importance: Jamaica, New York, and Virginia.

The four-and-a-half per cent duty in the islands was the result of an agreement between Charles II and the assemblies when the islands came under crown control following a settlement of the proprietary claims. The King validated the individual titles without reservation of quit rents. The assemblies in return passed an act providing a permanent revenue of export duties on the chief com-

49. HC, "Return of Public Income and Expenditure," *Accounts and Papers* (1868–69), *35*, Pt. II, 456.

modities of the islands, of which sugar was by all odds the most important. During the War of the Spanish Succession, when England conquered the French half of St. Christopher, customs officers began to collect the duty there. Exporters protested and appealed to England. The Attorney General decided that the local act, which had authorized collection in the English section, did not apply to the part of the island formerly under French sovereignty.[50] He advised the Queen, however, that she could make laws binding on conquered territory. The Privy Council approved this procedure, and the Treasury took the necessary steps to procure a great seal to impose the duty on the former French area.[51]

In addition to the quit rents and four-and-a-half per cent duty, there was a miscellaneous classification of crown dues known as the "casual" revenues. With rare exceptions they occurred only in the royal provinces or at sea.[52] Even contemporaries found it difficult to list them all. In the long run, sales of land formed the most remunerative source of the casual revenues on shore. Other miscellaneous sources included fines, forfeitures, penalties, amerciaments, escheats, costs of suit in court, royalties from mines, waifs and strays, and treasure trove. Many of these dues resulted from decisions in the common law courts. Fines and forfeitures for illegal trade caused considerable difficulty, for they might be claimed by both customs collectors and royal receivers.

Admiralty droits were distinguished from the foregoing crown dues largely by place of origin. They included prizes, such as ships and goods seized from the enemy in war or from pirates; wrecks, flotsam, jetsam, and lagan; great fish; and deodands. Claims to such items were usually settled in courts under admiralty jurisdiction.

For the supervision of crown revenues other than the four-and-a-half per cent and the admiralty droits, the Treasury relied in the

---

50. *APC, Col.*, 2, 454. George Chalmers, ed., *Opinions of Eminent Lawyers on Various Points of English Jurisprudence, Chiefly Concerning the Colonies, Fisheries and Commerce of Great Britain* (Burlington, 1858), pp. 158-59.

51. T54:18, p. 165.

52. W. A. Whitehead et al., eds., *Documents Relating to the Colonial . . . History of . . . New Jersey* (1880–1949), Ser. 1, *3*, 108.

first place upon the surveyor and auditor general of His Majesty's plantation revenues. Under this title William Blathwayt supervised both the collection and the audit of American crown dues. According to his patent, which he held for life, he was to follow the instructions of the Treasury. The latter named the receivers, one for each of the royal provinces, who might be appointed by a patent under the great seal or by commission under the sign manual, and gave them instructions. In Barbados and the Leeward Islands, where there were no quit rents, the royal collectors were known as receivers of the casual revenues. Subject to the approval of the Treasury, Blathwayt appointed deputies to reside in the varoius royal provinces, check on the work of the receivers, and audit their accounts.

Great vigor characterized the administration of the crown revenues under Godolphin. There was close cooperation between him and Blathwayt. They promptly filled vacancies in the revenue offices and made unusual efforts to secure the payment of dues. They had some slight success with the great proprietors. The effects of their efforts were especially noticeable in the case of the Virginia quit rents. William Lowndes, secretary to the Treasury, made a particular study of revenue problems in Virginia, probably using a report from Governor Nicholson. One resulting improvement was the separation of the offices of receiver and deputy auditor, which had been held by the same man; and another was a new and more adequate rent roll or register of all the lands in that province subject to quit rents.[53]

In contrast to Godolphin, Oxford showed little interest in the administration of the crown dues under Blathwayt's supervision. According to Oxford's plan of business, the auditor general was to attend the Treasury only when summoned. Two years passed without any record of his attendance. He or his clerk wrote repeatedly of vacancies in the receiver's office and again and again requested approval of his nominees for the office of deputy auditor—only, it seems, to have these suggestions ignored.[54] Consequently, during

53. T64:89, pp. 265-66, 235-36.
54. T64:90, passim.

the last years of Anne's reign there was considerable neglect of the crown dues.

The Commissioners of the Customs managed the collection of the four-and-a-half per cent export duty in Barbados and the Leeward Islands. In 1709 Godolphin integrated the administration of this duty with that of the customs by abolishing the institutiton of subcommissioners and making port officers directly responsible to the London Board.[55] One set of collectors handled both duties. The practice of accepting payments in kind and shipping the produce to London necessitated special officers to handle the products on arrival in that port. The principal London officer was known as the husband. With the comptroller he sold the goods at auction and accounted for the money received. He either issued funds as directed by the proper warrants or paid them over to the receiver general of the customs for deposit in the Exchequer.

During the war, prizes were the principal source of revenue under the head of admiralty droits. William III had named a special commission to administer prizes taken during his reign, but these commissioners had been rather more dependent on the Admiralty than on the Treasury. As Lord High Treasurer, Godolphin brought this phase of the revenue more directly under his control by naming the commissioners and fixing their salaries. Nevertheless, they were still dependent upon the Admiralty for information and assistance.

As regards the revenue, there was no distinction between prizes taken in English waters and those taken off the coast of America. American waters were favorite hunting grounds, and many prizes were condemned in colonial admiralty courts, although the Admiralty would have preferred to have them all brought to England for trial.[56] In 1708 Parliament appeared to sanction this method of trial in the colonies.[57]

---

55. T11:15, pp. 219-20. At the same time a surveyor general was appointed for Barbados, the Leeward Islands, and Bermuda.

56. Adm. 1:3667, fol. 38. The Admiralty discouraged the establishment of special prize courts in the colonies.

57. 6 Anne, c. 64.

The Admiralty claimed jurisdiction over tenths of prizes, prizes taken under special conditions, and various minor dues.[58] It named special agents for the colonies; but the Commissioners of Prizes also had agents there. In many instances, fortunately, the same individual represented both agencies. Nevertheless, there was considerable confusion over the custody of prize goods.[59] Regular receivers of crown dues, especially the casual receivers, were adversely affected by the claims of the prize and admiralty agents. Governors discovered that the new appointees assumed some of the responsibilities they had exercised under their vice-admiralty commissions. As the home government failed to distinguish between the functions of the permanent officials and those with temporary grants, the collection of the casual revenue was in considerable confusion. Furthermore, there were suspicions of fraud. After a few years the Prize Office and the Admiralty sent special commissioners to America to investigate conditions and supervise their respective agents.[60]

Oxford made a direct attempt to create order out of chaos by the somewhat questionable procedure of appointing yet another commissioner, with the broad powers of recovering all revenue due the Crown and investigating many other phases of colonial administration.[61] Sir Francis Nicholson was employed for two years in this undertaking, with results that are very difficult to assess. While there was greater centralization of responsibility for admiralty droits in the Treasury during this period, there was no real solution for the fundamental problem of overlapping jurisdictions.

Although the Treasury arranged for the disposition of surplus

58. *CSP, Col.,* 1702–03, §1359.

59. Admiralty agents were accountable to the receiver general of the rights and perquisites of the Admiralty, who paid his receipts into the Exchequer, where they were subject to the direction of the Treasury, as was the revenue from prizes.

60. T54:19, pp. 117, 520. Adm. 1:3662; Adm. 2:1049, pp. 367-77.

61. The Commissioners of Prizes drafted his instructions with respect to prizes; and the Treasury, those for the recovery of other admiralty droits (T29: 20, p. 24; T52:25, pp. 3-6; T52:28, p. 230; CO 323:7, fol. 23).

crown revenues, its recommendations were subject to royal approval. Proposals or petitions for the use of these funds came from many sources, both private and official, and for a variety of objects, not merely colonial administration, although a great deal was spent for this purpose. As indicated below, policies with respect to the use of crown revenues varied from fund to fund. In any case the disposition of these revenues had great significance for relations between the English Government and the colonies. When the Crown used the hereditary dues from the colonies for such non-American purposes as pensions, for example, or permitted the local assemblies to gain control of these funds, it was effectively weakening crown officials in the seemingly inevitable struggle with the assemblies.

Receipts of dues from the great proprietors were comparatively insignificant. No one apparently objected, therefore, when the Queen assigned the dues from the proprietors of Carolina to Edward Hyde.[62]

Ordinary quit rents were far more important as far as their actual or potential value was concerned. In Jamaica, however, the assembly had assumed the right to appropriate these dues, and they were no longer under the control of the Crown. In New York the revenue from the quit rents was theoretically subject to disposal by the Crown, but the income was slight and was customarily combined with other funds used for the provincial government. Only in Virginia, exclusive of the Northern Neck belonging to Lord Fairfax, was there a considerable surplus. This was kept strictly under crown control. During this period the Queen authorized payments from this source for a variety of provincial objects, such as the salary of the commissary acting under the Bishop of London, an increase in the salary of the provincial attorney general, assistance in rebuilding William and Mary College after the fire of 1705, and stores of war supplied by the Ordnance Office in England.[63] More important, because of the principle thereby estab-

62. T64:89, pp. 107, 187, 420; T52:24, p. 27.
63. T64:89, passim.

lished, were the orders to have the balance of the fund sent to England to supplement the Queen's civil list. Both Godolphin and Oxford insisted on this practice over the objections of the provincial governor and Blathwayt, who declared that the balance "was always intended to be left in Virginia . . . to answer pressing occasions in the colony."[64]

The disposition of the four-and-a-half per cent caused greater controversy. The islanders contended that under the original agreement the surplus was to be used for the support of their government. The Crown claimed the right to dispose of it at will.[65] Parliament did not include it in Anne's civil list, as it had for William III. At the beginning of her reign the House of Commons proposed that the remainder of the fund, following the payment of annuities to the heirs and assigns of the Earl of Kinnoul, one of the claimants under the old proprietary grant, should be used for fortifications and other public needs in the islands. The Queen agreed. Throughout her reign, therefore, the Treasury respected the agreement, and followed specific recommendations of the Board of Trade and the Ordnance Office in directing issues of these funds.[66] The islanders had no control over appropriations.

In two cases provincial assemblies made successful inroads upon the casual revenues. In Jamaica the act of 1703 appropriated them as well as the quit rents through a general provision that all crown

64. *CTP,* 1708–14, pp. 8-9. During a period of six years, according to Blathwayt, sums amounting to £13,917.5.10 were sent to England (T64:90, pp. 61 ff.). Not all the payments have been traced, but one interesting item was a little over £2,000 for the Queen's promised share of the cost of the Elector Palatine's journey to Vienna in 1704 (T29:15, pp. 273-74).

65. The preamble of the Barbados Act of 1663 implied it was to be used in the island. In 1821 the Chancellor of the Exchequer defended the Crown's right, stating that the revenue was "for the sole use and benefit of the Crown in consequence of the renunciation of certain rights": "Return of Public Income and Expenditure" (above, n. 49), Pt. II, p. 463.

66. *CTB, 17,* 190, 195, 307. In 1714, following an investigation of the collectors' accounts, £12,000 was paid into the Exchequer, more than in any succeeding year until 1733 (HC, *Accounts and Papers,* 1809, *9,* 78-79).

revenues of the island should be used for the government there.[67] Since the Queen accepted this measure, the casual revenues of Jamaica were lost to the Crown for at least the twenty-one years that the act was to be in force. The assembly of Barbados appropriated £100 of such revenues for their own expenses. On the advice of the Board of Trade, the Privy Council also approved the measure.[68]

Of all crown revenues, prizes were potentially most valuable. The Queen, however, sought to encourage seizures by promising to the captors one-half to the whole value of prizes, exclusive of the admiral's tenths, the exact proportion depending on the circumstances of the capture.[69] Early in 1703 the Queen assigned her remaining shares to the public for the conduct of the war, as she had already done in the case of other admiralty droits.[70] In 1708 Parliament voted to assign the whole value of prizes to the captors.[71] Nevertheless, the combined value of prizes and admiralty droits deposited in the Exchequer before 1710 amounted to nearly £200,-000.[72] What part of this sum was derived from America it is impossible to say because no such distinction appears in the accounts. Small amounts were expended on American aid.[73]

A review of the various crown revenues during this period of the early eighteenth century shows that the Queen's rights and actual receipts were materially reduced. Factors contributing to the situation were the Queen's own generosity, pressure from the Commons in the case of the four-and-a-half per cent, and earlier encroachments of local assemblies with subsequent concessions

---

67. T64:89, p. 283. HEH, Blathwayt 347.

68. *CSP, Col.*, 1708–09, §§844, 862.

69. CO 323:5, fol. 28 (i). *CTB, 18,* 114, 466. *APC, Col., 2,* 519-20, 542.

70. T1:85, fol. 24. Adm. 2:1049, pp. 369-70. She reserved £2,500 for her own use.

71. 6 Anne, c. 64.

72. "Return of Public Income and Expenditure," Pt. I, p. 28.

73. For the "Distressed Inhabitants of Nevis and St. Christopher's" (T38:369, fol. 106, General Account of Prizes); and for guns for Boston Harbor (T64:89, p. 189).

by the Crown.[74] The Board of Trade was in favor of leaving crown revenues in the provinces for local uses. The favorite policy of the Treasury, on the other hand, was illustrated by the tight rein kept on the Virginia quit rents. The practice of using American crown dues for non-American purposes was typical of the failure to develop a consistent financial policy for the colonies. While objecting to supplying them from English funds, and stressing the importance of making them financially self-sufficient and at the same time dependent on the Crown, the Treasury diverted from America part of the revenue that might have served the purpose.[75]

In theory, of course, the provincial assemblies were to provide for the needs of their own governments by levying taxes. Receipts from such taxes formed the third branch of American revenues, according to our previous classification. British officials hoped to secure from each assembly a permanent grant for the local civil list. Before the close of the seventeenth century they had been at least partly successful in four provinces: Jamaica, Bermuda, Virginia, and Maryland while it was temporarily governed by the Crown.

A Jamaican grant was limited to a period of twenty-one years ending in 1704. To secure a renewal, even for the same limited time, the Queen relinquished control over all crown revenues in the province as well as the supplies voted by the assembly. Although Bermuda's grant made in 1698 was without limit of time it covered only a few specified items, excluding the governor's salary. Moreover, the act allowed for no control by the home government.[76] The assemblies of Virginia and Maryland had granted certain revenues in perpetuity, the chief of which in both cases was a tax

74. Barbados had previously used fines, forfeitures, and amerciaments for her own use (*CSP, Col.*, 1708–09, §844). In 1701 the Treasury had an opportunity to comment on a draft for a new revenue act for Jamaica, but had shown little interest (*CTB, 16*, 267).

75. In the very year in which the Queen agreed to apply the four-and-a-half per cent to the needs of the islands the Treasury used £1,000 previously deposited in the Exchequer to purchase cloth for the Swedish army (*CTB, 17*, 246).

76. T64:89, pp. 170 ff. *APC, Col., 4*, 230-31.

of two shillings a hogshead on tobacco exports.[77] In Maryland the governor received one-half of the receipts and the proprietor the other. In the case of Virginia the Crown retained control of these particular revenues by the requirement that payments should be made only on the warrant of the Queen or her governor. Because none of the permanent or long-term grants was sufficient to meet all provincial demands, the assemblies in these four provinces retained an important element of financial independence through making or withholding additional levies. In other parts of the colonial world the official policy of a permanent civil list failed completely.

To be sure, in theory all grants of the local assemblies, whether temporary or permanent, were subject to the same regulations as the hereditary dues. Instructions to the royal governors, though lacking in uniformity and full of inconsistencies, incorporated this principle and continued to express it long after the expression had become practically a dead letter.[78] Necessity dictated that officials should choose between local grants subject to the will of the assembly and none at all. In emergencies they chose the former, and by such precedents contributed to the determined independence of the assemblies.

The Crown had practically lost control over the temporary grants before Queen Anne's accession to the throne. A report by Blathwayt in the time of William III referred to revenues "raised annually in the Plantations by the respective Assemblys There under the Denomination of Country Revenues for which they appoint particular Treasurers with Directions, That those Revenues be not issued without Warrant from the said Assemblys and for which those Treasurers do not hold themselves accomptable to any other than the Assemblys who take to themselves the sole Cogni-

77. The Virginia duties included proceeds from a tax of 15*d*. per ton on all ships arriving in the colony except those of the inhabitants, and a 6*d*. head tax on immigrants other than mariners (*CTB, 16,* 358-59). No accounts of the Maryland duty were sent to Blathwayt (T64:90, p. 51).

78. Leonard W. Labaree, ed., *Royal Instructions to British Colonial Governors, 1670—1776* (New York, Appleton-Century, 1935), *1,* 173-76.

zance and Disposal of what is so raised . . . whereof no regular Accompt is returned from thence."[79] The lack of such records was keenly felt in later years when the Government was trying to estimate the cost of running the colonial governments.

Under Queen Anne neither the Treasury nor the Board of Trade was ready to accept the situation described by Blathwayt. Yet the Board felt obliged to allow exceptions to the governor's instructions in New York,[80] and following a report of the Attorney General, the Privy Council regretfully approved a local law of Barbados appointing a treasurer, because the assembly had long exercised this privilege.[81] So, yielding here and conceding there, the Crown was fast losing all possibility of controlling local grants.

In 1713 the Board of Trade made an acute observation on the difference between the political philosophy of the Crown and that of the assemblies, saying of the latter: "Some of them, particularly those of New York, pretend they have an inherent right to dispose of the money of the Freemen of that province and that such their right does not proceed from any commission, letters patent, or other grant from H. M., but from the free choice and election of the people."[82] In the early part of the eighteenth century, as one may readily see, the issue between the home government and the colonies was clearly understood. Up to this time, however, it was practically limited in its application to taxes levied by the local assemblies.

Failures in the Crown's financial policies for the colonies cannot be ascribed to the Treasury alone. The Board of Trade drafted the governor's instructions and the Privy Council approved them. Colonial legislation passed under the surveillance of these two agencies. The Secretary of State was the immediate superior of the governor. Nevertheless, the Treasury shared in the failure to enforce the governor's instructions with respect to funds raised by the assembly. The effect on the provinces was to harden the attitude

79. T1:85, fol. 22. *CTB, 16*, 357-62.
80. *CSP, Col.*, 1706—08, §86.
81. *APC, Col., 2*, 625.
82. *CSP, Col.*, 1712—14, §352.

of assemblies when they wished to resist other policies of the home government, especially if such policies depended upon the expenditure of money.

The audit, which the Treasury lost in the case of the assembly funds, was supposed to apply to all money raised or spent in the colonies, whether public or crown. Subordinates of the Treasury—the auditors of the imprests or the auditor general of His Majesty's plantation revenues—performed this function. The principal accounts prepared by the auditors of the imprests were those of public rather than crown funds, although some of the latter which were outside of Blathwayt's jurisdiction were also submitted to them.

During this period and for years to come, the receiver general's were the only accounts of the American customs submitted to the auditors of the imprests. The comptroller general's would normally have included all the accounts of individual collectors. It proved impossible, however, to get these accounts into the form required for the exchequer process, that is, the audit by the auditors of the imprests. With the approval of the Treasury, therefore, the Customs Board terminated such accounts, following inspection by the comptroller general.[83] Contemporary accounts of the American post office were not audited until a later date.[84] The auditors of the imprests prepared accounts of prizes and other admiralty droits for declaration as if those revenues were ordinary public funds.[85] Governors and military commanders who had occasion to spend public funds also submitted their accounts to the auditors of the imprests. And, of course, the accounts of the Paymaster General of the Forces, audited after considerable delay, included many items of expenditure for the colonies.

Briefly stated, the exchequer system of accounting was as follows.

83. William Molleson and John Lane, eds., *The Reports of the Commissioners for Taking and Examining the Public Accounts* (London, 1783—87), *3*, 71 (i). GD 32:38, pp. 338-39, for rules of 1677 observed in later years. The accounts of the receiver general are in the Declared Accounts of the Audit Office.

84. AO 1:183:2001.

85. Final accounts of prizes taken during this period were not passed until 1755 (T54:36, pp. 122 ff.).

The auditors examined the original accounts and vouchers supplied by the accountant, and arranged them in the accepted form for declaration before the Chancellor of the Exchequer. Many colonial accounts lacked the necessary vouchers. In such cases, if the omission were not too glaring, the auditors prepared a "state," as the summary was called, which they presented to the Treasury in advance of declaration. The Treasury might approve or make exceptions of particular items. If it approved an item for which the voucher was lacking, it might procure a privy seal for its acceptance. When the account was declared before the Chancellor of the Exchequer, he signed it, together with two other lords if the Treasury was in commission, authorizing the Pipe Office to grant the accountant his "quietus" showing that he owed nothing to the Crown, and that the account was "even and quit." If the account showed that the Crown was in debt to the accountant, the Treasury authorized the necessary payment from the Exchequer. If the account was final and not just an interim statement, as was often the case with the revenue, the Treasury directed the Queen's Remembrancer to return the bond which the accountant had deposited on his original appointment.

The procedure for handling the accounts of crown revenues under Blathwayt's supervision was usually simpler, although Godolphin at one time favored the more elaborate process.[86] In most cases the declaration before the Chancellor of the Exchequer was omitted because of the irregularity of such accounts. With the approval of the Treasury the auditor general of the plantation revenues terminated these accounts, thus relieving the accountant of later charges. The auditor general relied to some extent upon the audit in the colony and the oath of the accountant given before the governor and council in the province where the money was collected, but his examination was more than nominal.

The accounts of the four-and-a-half per cent presented exceptional difficulties. Before 1704 the Treasury held Blathwayt responsible for auditing these accounts, and he actually prepared

86. Index 4630, p. 30. T64:90, p. 51.

some of the earlier ones for declaration, in spite of the fact that the patent of the comptroller general directed him to submit such accounts to the auditors of the imprests.[87] Under new regulations of 1704, however, the auditors of the imprests were to receive such accounts. Blathwayt seems to have acquiesced readily in this change, later characterizing the four-and-a-half per cent "as being in the nature of an English Revenue."[88]

The receiver general could readily prepare his accounts for the exchequer process, but unless the comptroller general's accounts were available, the desired check on the former was lacking. And the comptroller general had the same difficulty in procuring proper accounts and vouchers for the four-and-a-half per cent as he did in the case of the customs. The Treasury apparently considered the situation more serious as regards the four-and-a-half per cent, presumably because of the greater emphasis on revenue as the one and only purpose of this duty. After beginning a prosecution against the comptroller general, the Treasury became convinced he was doing all that he could and put a stop to the process.[89] For some years, therefore, the accounts of the collectors were subject to examination only by the comptroller general and the Customs Board. The requirement for a formal audit, however, was not abandoned, as it seems to have been for the customs.

The personal attention which the Lord High Treasurer gave to the audit shows how important he felt this phase of treasury business to be. Godolphin in particular adopted more stringent rules, ordered long-outstanding accounts to be presented to the auditors, tried to keep the audit up to date, and prosecuted accountants who failed to respond.[90] Years after his death the Treasury continued to refer to precedents of his administration; for fifty years after the close of Queen Anne's reign there was never quite the same emphasis on the audit.

87. T1:280, fol. 1(a).
88. T64:90, p. 50.
89. T52:22, p. 49.
90. T29:16, p. 300. *CTB, 18,* 95.

An analysis of the political and administrative aspects of government at the time of Queen Anne's death in 1714 shows that the Treasury had secured for itself a position of unprecedented influence in the field of colonial affairs. Whether the successors of Godolphin and Oxford would enjoy similar power would depend upon factors comparable to those which had contributed to the rise of the Treasury under Queen Anne. But they would have the advantage of recent precedents and improvements in the machinery of administration.

Whether powerful or weak, new administrators at the Treasury would have more colonial problems on their hands than had been the case in the seventeenth century. More English money was being expended in the colonies. The Treasury under Anne had held disbursements from the civil list to a minimum. But the practical necessity of defending English territorial claims in America had led to the establishment of English forces on American soil and to supplying the colonists with ordnance for their own defense. It would be difficult if not impossible to hold back the rising tide of public expenditures.

The policy of making the colonies financially self-supporting and at the same time keeping them dependent upon the Crown had not been an unmitigated success. Revenues resulting from parliamentary statutes were negligible; and the customs, at least, were not intended for that purpose. At the beginning of the reign of George I the Crown was actually poorer with respect to the hereditary dues than it had been at the beginning of the century. Although a large part of the remaining dues was used for colonial purposes, the Treasury had persisted in applying the balance of the Virginia quit rents to the English civil list. Had the Crown succeeded in its general policy, the provincial assemblies would have raised funds needed for their own governments but would have left disbursements to the Crown. Far from being able to dictate expenditures from most of these funds, English officials lacked even a record of how they had been spent.

In brief, the Treasury had found no formula whereby it could make the colonial governments self-supporting and at the same time keep them dependent on the Crown. Whether a new king and a new Treasury would adopt new policies or, if they adhered to the old, would succeed where others had failed remained to be seen.

2.

The Age of Walpole

LITTLE MORE THAN A YEAR after the accession of George I, Robert Walpole became head of the Treasury. Thereafter, aside from an interval of four years, he continued to hold that office until his resignation in 1742.[1] More than any of his predecessors he was responsible for the character of his administration. Historians have naturally given his name to this age, which was as significant in colonial history as in that of England herself.

Walpole's administration was comparatively peaceful at home and abroad. Aside from the suppression of the uprising of 1715 to preserve the Hanoverian succession, and retaliatory action against Spanish ships to protect England's commerce, peace prevailed until nearly the close of the period. During these years the colonies, like the mother country, were prosperous. Walpole's colonial policy, if such it could be called, was one of relative inaction. Because the colonies considered the conditions of his administration normal and change both unwarranted and undesirable, the period was of the utmost significance for succeeding governments.

Walpole was no novice in public life. He had served his apprenticeship under Godolphin, lost office under Oxford, and was now ready for new responsibilities.[2] His former experience, to-

1. Charles, Earl of Halifax, 13 Oct. 1714–23 May 1715; Charles, Earl of Carlisle, to 11 Oct. 1715; Robert Walpole, to 15 Apr. 1717; James Stanhope, to 20 Mar. 1718; Charles, Earl of Sunderland, to 3 Apr. 1721; Walpole, to 16 Feb. 1742.

2. He entered the House of Commons in 1700. Under Godolphin he was Secretary at War and Treasurer of the Navy; and after Harley left the Government, he managed the House of Commons: William Coxe, ed., *Memoirs of the Life and Administration of Sir Robert Walpole, Earl of Orford* (London, 1798), *1*, 61, 64. John H. Plumb, *Sir Robert Walpole* (Boston, Houghton Mifflin, 1956), treats the early years.

gether with fortunate family connections, led to appointments by George I.[3] He was sworn of the Privy Council, named Paymaster General of the Forces, and entrusted with the management of the House of Commons. In the election campaign of 1715 he was practicing the arts that were to make him famous,[4] and within a few months of that election the King named him First Lord of the Treasury and also Chancellor of the Exchequer. After an interruption beginning in 1717, he was recalled in 1721 to save the country in the crisis resulting from the collapse of the South Sea Bubble. He was now stronger than ever, for he was considered indispensable. He remained at the head of the Government for twenty-one years.

One of Walpole's assets was his knowledge of psychology. In his most successful years he was extraordinarily patient with both high and low. He flattered the great, but also listened to the "little fellows."[5] He used to the best advantage the political currency of the time: honors, pensions, and places. Another characteristic was his willingness to let well enough alone. Far from stubborn, he knew when to make concessions. Using a combination of political acumen and administrative skills he made the Treasury even more important among the agencies of the Crown than it had been under his predecessors.

To discuss Walpole without referring to his younger brother would be to ignore an important factor in his administration. Horatio, commonly called Horace or in his later years "Old Horace," to distinguish him from his nephew, the man of letters, served his brother and the Government in many capacities. In the House of Commons he was frequently a speaker and member of committees, and always available to those who had petitions or complaints. He not only relieved his brother of some of his parliamentary burdens, but had a considerable share in shaping the

3. His brother-in-law was Charles, Viscount Townshend, Secretary of State.
4. Add. MSS 32,686, fol. 27, letter to Newcastle with regard to suitable candidates for Middlesex and Westminster.
5. Ibid., 32,853, fol. 253, Horace Walpole's advice to Newcastle in 1755, referring to his brother's practices.

policies and character of the Administration. Although his diplomatic career is better known, the part he played in colonial affairs was equally significant. A member of the Privy Council, active member of its Committee on Plantation Affairs, *ex officio* member of the Board of Trade, secretary to the Treasury, and surveyor and auditor general of His Majesty's plantation revenues, he influenced colonial affairs for many years.

As a day-by-day practitioner of the arts of politics and administration, Robert Walpole neglected none of the elements of which the English Government was composed. First among these was the King. Because of his tact, his maintenance of peace, and his ability to lighten the burdens of state for the sovereign without seeming to diminish the royal power, Walpole retained the confidence of both George I and his son, George II.

Walpole was first among the ministers. Of his principal competitors, Sunderland died in 1722; Carteret resigned in 1724; and even his brother-in-law, Townshend, left office in 1730. The Duke of Newcastle, who in 1724 became Secretary of State for the Southern Department, showed little or no evidence of the jealousy so characteristic of his later years.[6] He used his electoral strength on his vast estates in the service of the Administration.

The various councils of the realm continued to play their appropriate parts in colonial administration, but with significant differences. Early in the Hanoverian period the Privy Council reverted to the practice of referring plantation affairs to its own committee, whether or not the Board of Trade had first made its recommendation. Until 1730 Walpole was a faithful attendant at these committee meetings; in that year Horatio was sworn of the Council, became a member of the committee, and relieved his brother of constant attendance, although both were present for important business relating to the colonies.[7]

Walpole, of course, dominated the Cabinet or Cabinet Council,

6. He remained in office after Walpole's fall, however, refusing to admit joint responsibility.

7. PC 2:91, p. 281 and passim.

which included as many as twelve ministers in this period, as well
as the small group that met to plan business. Normally the Cabinet
considered the plantations only when they were involved in questions of defense or foreign affairs. It might, for example, approve
a letter to a colonial governor, advising him with respect to military
problems.

In 1721 the Board of Trade made a bold proposal that it should
have executive authority in its own field comparable to that of
the Treasury and Admiralty in theirs.[8] It failed. Moreover, it
never even recovered the prestige and power it had enjoyed in its
earlier years. Within two weeks of the time it made the above representation, Horace Walpole received *ex officio* membership by
virtue of his office of auditor general of the plantation revenues.[9]
As Robert Walpole was also a member *ex officio*, the Treasury was
adequately represented. But the Walpoles seldom found it necessary
to attend. Most business between the two boards was handled by
correspondence, although the secretaries to the Treasury occasionally appeared at the Board of Trade in person. Through his office
of auditor general Horace Walpole was in possession of considerable colonial information. The Treasury, therefore, was less
dependent upon the Board of Trade in this respect. Whereas in
the past individuals who wanted colonial matters taken up by the
Privy Council usually sought the support of the Board of Trade,
they now realized, whatever approach they made, that it was essential to have one of the Walpoles speak in their behalf.[10]

Both patronage and the issue of funds from the Exchequer were
in control of the First Lord of the Treasury. Candidates for office

8. E. B. O'Callaghan and Berthold Fernow, eds., *Documents Relative to the
Colonial History of the State of New York* (Albany, 1853–87), *5*, 630. Only 4
of 7 members signed the representation, however.

9. SP 44:360, p. 376.

10. Governor Mathew, wishing a favor, suggested Horace Walpole as one
to be "played" upon (HEH, Stowe Americana, William Mathew Correspondence, 27 Sept. 1721). The Duke of Chandos advised the Governor of New
York that either the Duke of Newcastle or Sir Robert Walpole might move the
King on his own authority, and preferred this course to one through the Board
of Trade; but the latter was followed (Stowe 57, *45*, 213, 256).

recognized him as the chief patron, although he showed his usual consideration for the King and the secretaries of state. A candidate for the office of colonial governor, for example, found it discreet to apply to Walpole as well as to the Secretary of State.[11] Colonial offices were increasing in number and political significance. The Treasury often took the initiative in making appointments in the customs system, and made at least one suggestion for a postmastership in the colonies. Horace Walpole exercised the patronage in connection with the crown revenues. As for that other accompaniment of power, the issue of funds, Walpole was more strict in protecting the rights of the Treasury than any of his predecessors.[12] Certain colonial revenues, however, were slipping from the Treasury's grasp, as will be explained below.

Favored by the King, first among the ministers, influential in all the councils of the realm, and comparatively secure in the handling of patronage and funds, Walpole also proved his superior skill in the management of Parliament. As Parliament was becoming more involved in colonial affairs, its management had greater significance in this field of legislation.

The first step in securing a tractable House of Commons was, of course, to obtain the desired election results.[13] In influencing elections the Government used as many different techniques as there were situations in the election districts at the time. In a few boroughs the Treasury, regardless of who was the head, could establish

11. Add. MSS 32,687, fol. 501.

12. Warrants for payments from the King's civil list, unlike those for public funds, might be countersigned by a secretary of state, especially for foreign service. The Privy Seal sent docquets to the Treasury for signatures. In 1716 Walpole ordered the clerks to record the name of the official who had countersigned the original (T29:22, p. 281).

13. There were four general elections after that of 1715 before Walpole fell from power: 1722, 1727, 1734, and 1741. Individual elections have been treated by Stebelton H. Nulle, "The Duke of Newcastle and the Election of 1727," *Journal of Modern History, 9* (1937), 1-22; Basil Williams, "The Duke of Newcastle and the Election of 1734," *English Historical Review, 12* (1897), 448-88; John B. Owen, *The Rise of the Pelhams* (London, Methuen, 1957), analysis of the House of Commons, 1741, and election of that year.

a political following because of government offices located there.[14] More numerous were the boroughs in which the interests of one or more important families were paramount. If the great landholders were friendly to the Administration they would use various means to secure the votes of their tenants for a candidate approved by the Treasury.[15] But even in places where family influence was strong, a good word from the ministers might be necessary to turn the tide.[16]

The counties presented somewhat different problems. Government funds and patronage, however, were useful in both types of election districts. And where money was an important factor, if only to furnish transportation for the voters, the odds were in favor of the Government, for the King was generous with secret service funds.[17] Under certain circumstances a county might be more dependable than a town with a large electorate.[18]

In spite of government influence upon elections, there was considerable evidence of independence on the part of the electorate

14. For example, in 1720 Chandos asked Sunderland for his support for a particular candidate in Weymouth if there was a vacancy: "the Court having a considerable interest in that corporation" (Stowe 57, *17,* 138-39).

15. Ibid., *30,* 182, and James J. Cartwright, ed., *The Wentworth Papers, 1705—39* (London, 1883), p. 471, for complaints that costs were increasing. The younger Pelham brothers established a club at Lewis where they drank with the members weekly (Add. MSS 32,688, fols. 567 ff.). Threats and actual evictions were not unknown (ibid., fols. 86, 96; 32,993, fol. 28).

16. In 1727 Chandos wrote that his kinsman had been ill-advised, in spite of family influence at Haslemere, to become a candidate without first securing Walpole's approval (Stowe 57, *30,* 218).

17. In 1734 Walpole boasted, so it was said, that the Crown would "tire the gentry out, for 100,000 1. a year spent by the Crown will in a little time drain the gentry's pockets" (HMC, *Diary of the First Earl of Egmont, 2,* 1734—38, London, His Majesty's Stationery Office, 1923, 39). In 1734 the King spent over £40,000 more for secret service than in the following nonelection year (Add. MSS 33,039, fol. 37). In 1741 the King spent only £80,116.8.5 for secret service, as compared with £117,145.19.0 during the year of the hard-fought election of 1734 (ibid.).

18. Having had trouble in Norwich in 1734, Walpole thought the county would be "a much more secure gamble" (ibid., 32,689, fol. 241).

and members of Parliament. The voters reacted to government policies, and occasionally instructed their representatives. Although Walpole had finally yielded to the opposition and had ceased to press for the passage of the Excise Bill, the following election of 1734 was the most hard fought of his career. Even placemen might be subject to the influence of their constituents as well as that of the Crown. Both Scrope, secretary to the Treasury, and his nephew voted to repeal the Test Act because they had been elected on that condition.[19] In 1742 Walpole resigned from his treasury offices because he was losing the support of the House of Commons.

Under these circumstances the methods used in promoting legislation were of the utmost importance. As long as he was in office Walpole chose to remain a commoner and manage the House of Commons himself. In meetings at the Cockpit he briefed his principal supporters on government plans for legislation.[20] The secretaries to the Treasury kept in touch with individual members and often sat on committees where bills were prepared. Rather than arouse opposition Walpole would permit an objectionable measure to pass the House of Commons with the understanding that it would be defeated in the House of Lords.[21]

Both houses of Parliament were interested in the colonies and frequently called for information; yet the amount of commercial legislation relating to the colonies is remarkably slight. The Treasury rarely took the initiative in proposing such measures, and legislation often started with some dissatisfied group asking for relief. But the influence of the Treasury is usually apparent and always to be taken for granted. If petitioners were wise, they consulted the Treasury before taking other steps. The Treasury then referred the question to the appropriate agency—the Board of Trade or the Customs Commissioners, as the case might be—to see if there were official objection. Walpole found it effective to an-

19. *Egmont Diary, 2,* 243.

20. Ibid., *1,* 1730–33 (1920), 365.

21. Ibid., p. 50, illustrates his trying to defeat a measure in the Commons because he could not then depend upon Townshend's influence in the Lords.

nounce to the House of Commons that one or the other of these agencies had been consulted. Two policies attributed to him illustrate his cautious nature: "he was always against repealing old laws, made for the benefit of trade, and breaking into the Navigation Act," and he characterized prohibitions as "dangerous for they often put other countries upon retaliation."[22]

This philosophy explains the attitude of the Treasury toward the most controversial colonial issue of Walpole's administration, the Molasses Act. The Privy Council and the Board of Trade had already been concerned with the problems of the sugar trade for some years when in 1730 the Barbadians petitioned the Council for relief. Their chief complaint was that the northern colonies traded with the French islands and so deprived the British islands of their natural market. Among their suggestions was one for completely prohibiting this trade.[23]

The Duke of Chandos, whose ear was close to the ground, wrote to his friend John Ashley in Barbados that England was "too closely engaged with the French" to lay a duty that would amount to a prohibition and ruin their trade.[24] Yet it was not Walpole's way to give a flat negative to a proposal that clearly had the support of many people; and everyone, so the Duke of Chandos said, thought something should be done for Barbados.[25] The Privy Council prepared to hold a hearing to which the Board of Trade was summoned, but in the meantime the petitioners, possibly discouraged by the attitude of the Council, decided to take their case directly to Parliament, partly to secure action, if possible, before the northern colonies could organize effective opposition.[26] The Council, therefore, gave them leave to withdraw their petition.

In the House of Commons in 1731 a large select committee in-

22. Ibid., pp. 173, 341.
23. PC 2:91, p. 285. It appears that officials were trying to evade responsibility by encouraging the colonies to pass restrictive acts (*CSP, Col.,* 1716—17, §§389, 393; Stock, *4,* 105).
24. Stowe 57, *35,* 242-43.
25. Ibid., *38,* 305.
26. PC 2:91, pp. 296-97, 322, 328, 353, 363. *Egmont Diary, 1,* 131.

cluding Walpole and all the merchants, as well as several other members, considered the petition. On the strength of their report leave was given to bring in a bill for encouraging the trade of the sugar colonies. Although a severe measure from the point of view of the northern colonies and contrary to Walpole's general principles, it passed the Commons. Walpole may have expected the House of Lords to defeat it. As a matter of fact, the session closed without its passage.[27] As Chandos explained, possibly parroting the Administration, there were many who thought "that the bill was more calculated for the good of Barbados than the benefit of England."[28] It seemed unreasonable, furthermore, to deprive the northern colonies of their export trade, as the bill would have done. The Duke, nevertheless, encouraged his friend to try to secure a modified measure the following session.

In 1732 Horace Walpole was a member of the committee appointed to examine a new petition.[29] The resultant bill, lacking the clauses interfering with the export trade of North America, was more acceptable than its predecessor. It passed the Commons, but again failed to pass the Lords before Parliament was prorogued.[30]

In the following year a third bill to encourage the trade of the sugar colonies moved swiftly and surely to its conclusion. From the beginning the Walpoles were apparently managing and directing its progress.[31] Instead of waiting for the Barbadians to introduce another petition, the Commons resolved to consider the state of the sugar colonies.[32] Horace Walpole and Scrope, secretary to the Treasury, were on the committee which brought in the bill. The former read the bill when it was reported. With government support the bill passed both houses of Parliament and became law.[33]

27. Stock, *4*, 110, 119, 120.
28. Stowe 57, *38*, 304-5.
29. *CJ, 21,* 802.
30. *LJ, 24,* 52, 107, 157.
31. Charles Dunbar later spoke of the Walpoles as the "parents" of the bill, and personally claimed credit for helping to secure the passage (T1:328, 5 Apr. 1747).
32. *CJ, 22,* 38.
33. 6 Geo. II, c. 13.

The Molasses Act was a compromise measure. It was not the out-and-out prohibition demanded by the planters, although the sixpenny a gallon import duty on foreign molasses would probably have amounted to a prohibition if the act had been strictly enforced. Since the act contained no clause of appropriation the Government may not have expected to secure much revenue from this source. It was a departure from earlier practices, for, aside from the prize duties, it provided the first import duty levied in the colonies by act of Parliament. Largely neglected by Walpole's administration, it was to become one of the major sources of trouble in later years.

Discovering that the Molasses Act did not solve their problems, the sugar planters soon renewed their pleas for effective legislation, but the Treasury avoided further interference with the North American trade. In 1739 Parliament attempted to appease the islanders by permitting them to send their sugar south of Cape Finisterre, if laden in British-built ships.[34]

Other commercial laws of the period also had the effect of liberalizing the acts of trade in the interests of particular colonies.[35] One might describe Walpole's views, illustrated in this legislation, as those of a liberal mercantilist. Positive encouragement was given to the production of certain products.[36] In promoting the production of naval stores, for example, Walpole agreed with the Board of Trade rather than the Admiralty, which considered premiums on this article as wasted. But premiums were reduced.[37] A few pro-

---

34. 12 Geo. II, c. 30, later extended to all ships of His Majesty's subjects residing in Great Britain (15 Geo. II, c. 33).

35. 3 Geo. II, c. 28, permitting rice to be shipped from the Carolinas to points south of Cape Finisterre, extended to Georgia by 8 Geo. II, c. 19. 13 Geo. I, c. 5; and 3 Geo. II, c. 12: permitting Pennsylvania and New York, respectively, to import salt directly from Europe.

36. 5 Geo. II, c. 24, for growth of coffee. 10 Geo. I, c. 16; and 12 Geo. I, c. 27: exempted whale fins from duties. 8 Geo. I, c. 15, reduced the duties on beaver skins.

37. 2 Geo. II, c. 35.

posed restrictions failed to pass;[38] more were successful.[39] The islands and the southern provinces were more affected by relaxation of the laws, and the northern colonies by the added restrictions. This differentiation of treatment became more pronounced in later years.

There was no set pattern for drafting these commercial laws. A petition to the Treasury often started the movement. Limited evidence suggests that the secretaries to the Treasury occasionally prepared the actual drafts, later presented as the work of a committee of the House of Commons.[40] Scrope, at least, was fully competent. On other occasions the Customs Commissioners or the Board of Trade performed the task with treasury approval.[41] Consideration of such measures by the treasury officials was usually informal and not reported in their minutes.

Quite aside from the traditional role of Parliament in regulating various aspects of trade, there was a growing tendency to use an act of Parliament to state colonial policies previously declared by royal instructions to the governors. The act for the more easy recovery of debts and another to prevent the establishment of land banks, for example, incorporated the principles of earlier instructions or orders. As a result of policies of this period, therefore, Parliament

38. The manufacture of iron and issues of paper currency (Stock, 5, ix, xvii).

39. 8 Geo. I, c. 18, enumerating copper. 8 Geo. I, c. 12; and 2 Geo. II, c. 35: restricting the cutting of white pine. 14 Geo. II, c. 37, making land banks illegal. 5 Geo. II, c. 22, curbing the manufacture of hats. 7 Geo. I, c. 21, for forfeiture of East India goods carried to plantations unless first landed in Great Britain. 5 Geo. II, c. 7, for more easy recovery of debts. 15 Geo. II, c. 31, defining the condition of plantation bonds. Laws for the transportation of felons and extending Greenwich Hospital dues to America became subjects of controversy.

40. There is evidence that Scrope drafted the prize bill (T11:21, pp. 401-2; 13 Geo. II, c. 4).

41. The bill to encourage the growth of coffee followed a petition to the Privy Council, a report of the Board of Trade, and reference by the Treasury to the Customs Commissioners, requiring a report in a matter of hours (PC 2:91, pp. 584, 589; T27:25, p. 94). The Board of Trade was asked to draft a bill restricting the cutting of white pine (T29:25, p. 280).

was becoming more deeply involved in colonial affairs, internal as well as strictly commercial.

No development of the period, however, represented a greater divergence from past policies than the growing investment of Parliament in the colonies. In 1729, according to an act of Parliament, the Government accepted the surrender of the Carolinas from seven of the eight proprietors who had originally derived their title from the Crown.[42] And Parliament appropriated the money to purchase the proprietary rights. A committee of the Council had already considered the proprietors' proposals and approved the price. It then referred to the Treasury the matter of financing the purchase.[43] The Treasury approved of the surrender, but added: "we cannot propose any Method or Fond for accomplishing & perfecting the same without the Aid and Assistance of Parliament."[44]

Walpole therefore assumed responsibility for the policy of applying to Parliament rather than using funds from the King's civil list, as Oxford had planned to do in the case of Pennsylvania. At the request of the Treasury the Attorney General and Solicitor General drafted the bill for the purpose, using the terms proposed by the Council,[45] and the text of the act was ready when the House of Commons ordered these same law officers and Scrope to bring in a bill for an agreement with the proprietors.[46]

In this period Parliament also accepted a limited obligation in connection with the settlement of Georgia—but in the guise of charity or a defense of the frontier, for which there were prece-

---

42. 2 Geo. II, c. 34. Charles C. Crittenden, "The Surrender of the Charter of Carolina," *The North Carolina Historical Review, 1* (1924), 383-402. Lord Carteret retained his share, undivided for the time being, but lost all control of the government.

43. *APC, Col., 3,* 177.

44. T54:31, p. 64.

45. T29:26, pp. 182-87. The price was £17,500 plus £5,000 for quit rents due.

46. Stock, *4,* 44. Proceedings for the purchase of the Bahamas were not completed until 1787, although the proprietors lost their rights of government in 1717 ("Bahamas," *Encyclopaedia Britannica*, 1956; WLC, Shelburne, *61,* fols. 305 ff.).

dents. In the first place Walpole opposed a suggestion that Parliament grant the charter to the trustees, being unwilling, so it was said, that "the colonies should depend on Parliament for their settlement."[47] He did, however, consent to a petition to Parliament for financial assistance, announcing, as was customary in such cases, that the King had no objection to a grant for the purpose. And he advised the trustees on parliamentary procedure. He also arranged to have the appropriation made from funds already in the Exchequer, proceeds from the sale of land on St. Christopher, in origin crown revenue but transferred to the public by the King. Horace Walpole seconded the motion and spoke in its favor. In 1733, as a result of these carefully laid plans, Parliament voted £10,000 to aid in the settlement of Georgia, assuming an obligation without actual precedent, for in the seventeenth century private individuals had always raised the capital for such enterprises.[48]

In spite of growing opposition Parliament continued until 1742 to make annual grants for the young colony, but always in response to a petition and under the appearance of philanthropy, and with the underlying object of providing defense against Spanish aggression. A proposal that the Government present an annual estimate, thus putting the colony on a regular establishment, must have met with an unfavorable response.[49] Toward the end of Walpole's administration the question of aiding the Georgia settlement became more controversial because of clashes of opinion with respect to policies toward Spain. Using a now common technique, Robert Walpole withheld his full support for parliamentary grants, but permitted Horace to second the motion for appropriation.[50]

Before Walpole left office, he brought to Parliament the King's positive recommendation for aid to sufferers from a fire in South Carolina.[51] In earlier years the King's bounty might have been drawn upon in such an emergency.

47. *Egmont Diary, 1,* 157.
48. Stock, *4,* 215-17, 219.
49. Add. MSS 35,909, fols. 74 ff. *Egmont Diary, 2, 390.*
50. Stock, *5,* 89.
51. Ibid., p. 94.

In addition to these various grants that were primarily civilian, Parliament gradually increased its appropriations for colonial defense. No matter how attractive the theory that the colonial assemblies should provide additional funds for this purpose, they were not to be relied upon. One of the most disturbing items brought to the attention of Parliament was that of the debt remaining from the unfortunate Canadian expedition of the previous reign. In 1717 Parliament finally provided for the settlement of claims of merchants who held bills of exchange drawn on the Treasury but not accepted because of lack of funds for the purpose.[52] The greatest increase in military obligations, however, came from additions to the regular forces stationed in America. Even before the outbreak of war in 1739 these had nearly doubled.[53]

In this survey of legislation dealing with the colonies, the growing stake of Parliament in their affairs is evident. What is not so clear is whether Walpole had a deliberate policy, for his methods were extremely subtle. Commercial legislation suggests that he adhered to the main tenets of mercantilism but that his approach was practical rather than academic. Several changes in the acts of trade modified earlier restrictions, giving the colonies greater freedom. Where colonial interests were in conflict, as in the case of the Molasses Act, he secured a compromise. During his administration enforcement of the act was somewhat less than enthusiastic.

The growing tendency to use parliamentary grants for colonial purposes demands other explanations. The increase in funds for defense grew out of sheer necessity. The reasons for parliamentary

52. T29:19, p. 105. Stock, *3,* 390.

53. In 1715 there was a regiment in the Leeward Islands, 4 companies in N.Y., 4 at Annapolis Royal, 4 at Placentia, 1 in Bermuda, and 2 in Jamaica, in addition to garrisons at Annapolis and Placentia (Stock, *3, 349,* n. 4). Estimates in 1717 added a company in the Bahamas; 1718, a regiment formed by combining companies at Annapolis and Placentia; 1721, a company in the Carolinas; 1732, an additional garrison at Canso; 1735, 6 additional companies in Jamaica; 1738, a regiment in Georgia (Stock, *3 and 4,* passim). The costs had increased from over £34,000 to over £61,000, omitting in the latter case expenses incurred but not provided for.

appropriations for other purposes are not so obvious, but limited evidence suggests that Walpole may have concluded that if Parliament did not supply the necessary funds, he would have to draw on the King's civil list, intended for the English Government and royal household and already burdened. He might have had to ask Parliament for an addition to the civil list, which probably would have been more dangerous politically than to seek specific appropriations; for the civil list, once established, was beyond the control of Parliament. But whatever the reason may have been, the continuing movement toward greater parliamentary responsibility in the colonial field would eventually have a profound effect upon relations between England and her colonies.

As the political and legislative activities of the Treasury increased, there was a comparable development in administration. Treasury functions with respect to the colonies were becoming more numerous and more significant from the point of view of either the colonies or the mother country. Larger sums of money were involved in colonial administration, and touched the colonists in a greater variety of ways than ever before. Precedents were followed or new ones established which would affect all future administrations, whatever their policies might be.

Years of peace and prosperity combined with good management resulted in giving to Walpole's administration, especially after 1721, a very different financial character from that of the years of Queen Anne's reign.[54] For example, whereas the salaries of government officials had once been years in arrears, most of them were now brought up to date. Formerly it had been customary to encourage someone to proceed with a project for the Government on the assumption that he would be rewarded when the job had been completed. Too often no money would be available when the time came for payment. Walpole was more ready to provide credit for an undertaking which he approved in principle. Although his

54. Hubert Hall, "The Sources for the History of Sir Robert Walpole's Financial Administration," *Transactions of the Royal Historical Society,* Ser. 3, 4 (1910), 40-41.

enemies could find occasions for criticism, his administration was more modern and more business-like than that of his predecessors. Aspects of colonial government dependent upon spending felt the difference.

The Hanoverian kings took even less part in the actual management of the Treasury than had Queen Anne.[55] At the same time, by combining the offices of First Lord and Chancellor of the Exchequer in one man George I created a position which under Walpole became more powerful than had been the place of Lord High Treasurer under Godolphin or Oxford. Walpole held these offices for a generation. On the other hand, there was a fairly rapid turnover in the places of the four Junior Lords. Walpole undoubtedly made most of the policy decisions—subject in some cases, of course, to the King's approval. The Board met much less frequently than under less experienced or less powerful leaders. The secretaries and clerks were competent to handle routine business.

Horace Walpole became joint secretary on his brother's first appointment to the Treasury, left office with him in 1717, returned in 1721, and remained until the summer of 1730. Edward Walpole, son of Sir Robert, succeeded his uncle, contributing far less to the success of the Administration. He retired in 1739. On the death of William Lowndes in 1724, Walpole was fortunate in securing for what one might call the permanent post John Scrope, trained both in the law and in public finance, having served as Baron in the Scottish Court of Exchequer.[56] Considering the character of the times the management of the treasury office was business-like, dis-

55. The minutes give no evidence that either George I or George II used the King's chair that was kept in the boardroom as a symbol of the royal presence. From time to time the Board sat at the royal residence, more for Walpole's convenience than for the King's. A plan of 1733 called for one meeting a week at Hampton Court, but practice was irregular (T29:27, p. 204 and passim).

56. Stephen Fox and Henry Bilson Legge followed Edward Walpole in succession. John Taylour, a former clerk, served 3 Nov. 1714–12 Oct. 1715. Charles Stanhope was secretary while Walpole was out of office.

cipline was strict, and ethical standards were high.[57] Walpole increased the number of clerks by three, doubled their pay, and respected the principle of permanent tenure.[58]

Turning to the Treasury's actual influence upon colonial affairs through the management of English funds, one finds that Walpole was averse to drawing on the civil list for American purposes, although he followed the few well-established precedents. In effect he closed the door upon the possibility that the civil list might in time serve the needs of both the English and colonial governments. In two significant instances in this period the Treasury failed to proceed with projects already begun or contemplated, which would have required expenditures from the civil list. When Halifax was still at the Treasury the Society for the Propagation of the Gospel presented to the Privy Council its plan for the establishment of bishops in America and asked for financial aid. The Council referred the papers to the Treasury, where they were read; but neither Halifax nor any of his successors ever made a formal report, as far as the records show.[59] In the other case, Walpole refused to complete the purchase of Pennsylvania, thus defeating a basic policy of the Board of Trade. Although the cost was not the only objection the Treasury may have had to these projects, it was presumably an important factor.[60]

57. From time to time the Board itself gave directions for more meticulous handling of treasury business. It once labeled as "vile and pernicious" a private arrangement between a former clerk and his successor for sharing the income (T29:24, Pt. II, p. 152).

58. Warrants for payment, T53:24, 25, passim; and orders for admission, T29, passim. New offices were ready for occupancy in 1736, having convenient connection with 10 Downing St., which the King in 1731 had permanently assigned to the First Lord (*London Topographical Record, 7,* London, 1912, pp. 50-55; T29:27, pp. 195, 205).

59. PC 2:85, p. 107. T1:181, fols. 31(a), 32. In 1721 the Council ordered the omission from governors' instructions of a clause introduced in 1718 that would have permitted "some other bishop," i.e. other than the Bishop of London, to license American schoolmasters (PC 2:91, pp. 219, 222, 228).

60. T29:26, p. 77. *N.Y. Col. Doc., 5,* 603, representation of the Board of Trade.

Unlike expenditures from the civil list, those from public funds grew steadily. Administrative problems increased accordingly.

Difficulties in assuring an adequate supply of funds for the regular forces in America were likely to arise whether agents drew bills of exchange on the Paymaster General in England or the Treasury engaged contractors to furnish specie. Two successive agents for companies in Jamaica and the Bahamas became bankrupt while heavily in debt to the forces. As legal proceedings instituted by the Treasury failed to recover what was due, it was necessary to apply to Parliament to make good the loss.[61] When contractors were employed, the rate of exchange was an essential feature of the agreement. In the case of the expeditionary force destined for Carthagena, the rate was £120 Jamaican currency for £100 sterling, permitting the contractors to make a handsome profit at the expense of the troops. After receiving protests, the Treasury raised the rate to £125.[62] The Committee of Secrecy later charged that the rate should have been nearer £140 of currency to £100 sterling, and held Walpole personally responsible for the terms of the contract and the failure to advertise for bids.[63]

Uncertainties connected with such unpredictable items as recruiting for new companies in the colonies interfered with financial planning. Arrangements for raising recruits for the Carthagena expedition on the outbreak of war with Spain were somewhat haphazard. It didn't appear feasible to prepare an establishment in advance because the date of recruitment would vary from man to man. Colonel Blakeney, therefore, received permission to draw bills of exchange as necessary to cover his expenses. The cost was greater than expected because Spotswood, who was also engaged in recruiting, had promised more than the sixpence per day Blakeney had expected to pay. These expenses were later included in the extraordinaries of the war.[64]

Walpole's Treasury found no real solution for the many prob-

61. T52:37, p. 346; T29:28, pp. 123-354, passim. Stock, *5*, 110.
62. T29:28, p. 350.
63. Stock, *5*, 153 ff.
64. T29:28, pp. 231, 248. *CTB & P*, 1739—41, p. 258.

lems of financing English forces in America. On the other hand, conditions were scarcely worse than in certain later periods of the eighteenth century. Closely connected with finance was the necessity of providing the army with food. Under Walpole the Treasury made definite improvements in handling this function.

The expense of food varied according to the location of the forces. The Treasury took this fact into account in deciding whether the whole cost should be deducted from the soldiers' pay or covered in part by an additional appropriation by Parliament. Consequently there were several different arrangements.[65] Those that were less satisfactory from the point of view of the soldier contributed to unrest and danger of mutiny. Later arrangements were more generous than those at the beginning of the period.

Neither the practice of leaving responsibility for procuring food to the commanding officer or employing the Victualing Board proved satisfactory in the case of the northern garrisons. Therefore, the Treasury made arrangements with a private contractor to supply the garrisons of Nova Scotia and Newfoundland. The Comptrollers of the Accounts of the Army prepared the draft of the contract and instructions for the commanding officers and the commissaries with regard to receiving and accounting for the provisions.[66] The Treasury also used the contract method for supplying Oglethorpe's regiment in Georgia and the independent com-

65. If covered in part by appropriations, it was possible to include provisions in the estimates, as was done eventually for the garrisons at Nova Scotia and Newfoundland, and still later for Oglethorpe's regiment in Georgia and the independent company in the Bahamas (Stock, *5*, passim). On the other hand, the cost of provisions might be submitted later with other extraordinaries. In the case of the Carthagena expedition the Victualing Board of the Navy supplied provisions which were included with the debt of the Navy (ibid., p. 97, n. 93). Normally the amount deducted from the soldiers' pay was 4*d*. per man per day, and Parliament made up the total daily cost of about 7*d*. (ibid., *3*, 392). But Oglethorpe's men suffered a deduction of only 2*s*. a week during the siege of St. Augustine, and 9*d*. at other times (ibid., *5*, 181). Before Parliament appropriated funds for Nova Scotia, the soldier's food cost him 6*d*. a day *(CSP, Col.,* 1714–15, §411).

66. T27:23, pp. 84, 90; T52:30, pp. 385-86.

panies in Jamaica. The comparative lack of criticism leads one to conclude not only that this system worked far better than the other methods, but also that it was more satisfactory in this period than in later administrations when the Treasury assumed more direct responsibility for supervising the contracts. As contrasted with the beginning of the period, there was improved morale in the garrisons, resulting from a combination of better victualing and the fact that deductions from the soldiers' pay were smaller.

Increased demands for ordnance naturally accompanied the expansion of the armed services and especially the outbreak of war. The regular estimates included fixed amounts for the garrisons. Repairs of the fortifications and new barracks, on the other hand, required extraordinary grants. The Privy Council considered requests for additional engineers or arms and ammunition for the colonial militia, and gave orders as it saw fit. Although the Ordnance Office continued to protest against this irregular procedure, it failed to obtain advance estimates for this purpose.

In dealing with colonial projects dependent upon naval funds, the Treasury appeared to have more sympathy for the policies of the Board of Trade than for the point of view of the Admiralty. The Treasury often found it necessary to act as arbitrator between the other two agenices. For instance, the Board of Trade recommended, but the Admiralty opposed, reimbursing the Governor of Nova Scotia for a sloop he had fitted out to defend the coast. The Treasury ordered the Treasurer of the Navy to pay this bill.[67]

The most controversial issue concerned the surveyor general of the woods. Shortly after Bridger's dismissal the Board of Trade secured his reinstatement, although the Admiralty still thought the office useless.[68] A new appointee, named by Sunderland after he became First Lord of the Treasury, remained in England, and two years passed before his deputy arrived in America. During this time Bridger continued to act, though superseded. After Walpole

67. T29:25, p. 96.
68. T52:27, pp. 168-69, commission. *CSP, Col.*, 1716–17, §11, for Admiralty's order to stop his salary.

returned to office in 1721, Bridger received compensation for the full time he had acted.[69] Walpole removed the official incumbent and appointed David Dunbar, giving him additional powers, including that of hiring assistants at a definite rate, and eventually making an allowance for traveling expenses.[70] By direct correspondence with the surveyor and by recommending stricter laws on the cutting of white pine, the Treasury showed its genuine concern for the protection of the King's rights.

This interest of the Treasury was reflected in the activity of Dunbar and his deputies, who were not only busily marking the trees to be reserved for the navy but also prosecuting the colonists who failed to respect these claims. When they lost a case in the vice-admiralty courts in America, they appealed to England. Here again they met with more encouragement from the Treasury than from the Admiralty, which tried to avoid responsibility for prosecuting an appeal on the ground that any award to the plaintiff would accrue in part to the King and not at all to the Admiralty.[71] In the history of relations between England and her colonies Walpole's policy of protecting the King's claims in American forests and woodlands had a special significance: he was running counter to his usual instinct for avoiding controversy. In this case he was arousing deep-seated antagonism, for in these claims and counterclaims lay fundamental differences of opinion with respect to property rights.

In the light of the increased public expenditures for defense and appropriations for various civil purposes, one might expect more emphasis on the collection of American revenues, especially the customs, now appropriated to the aggregate fund from which part of the civil list was drawn. Yet this was not a period of outstanding development in the customs system. In administering the laws Walpole not only adhered closely to the traditional view that American duties were levied for the purpose of regulating trade, but permitted considerable laxity in their enforcement. The fact is that en-

69. T52:31, pp. 233-34.

70. T52:35, p. 343; T52:36, pp. 121-23, 127; T29:27, pp. 137, 234; T27:25, p. 200.

71. Adm. 2:1053, 15 Dec. 1731. T29:27, p. 90.

forcement of the acts of trade, which had once been stimulated by Edward Randolph and nurtured by the Board of Trade, had no equally determined advocates in this administration.

The normal expansion of population called for the addition of five new ports of entry on the mainland: one in New Hampshire and four in the Carolinas. In the older ports, however, only four officers were added to the regular establishment. The Treasury thought that the Molasses Act might require additional officers, but as the Customs Commissioners had recently reduced the force in America, the net increase was slight.[72]

Walpole made extensive use of the patronage, unquestionably for political purposes. The Treasury now required lists of vacancies from the commissioners. It also acted quickly in cases of expected vacancies of which it learned from candidates or their patrons, forestalling nominations by the commissioners. In some cases the Treasury even wrote to the surveyor general in the colonies to name such and such a person to the first vacancy. Occasionally, but less frequently, it created a vacancy by dismissing the incumbent for cause or superseding him without reason.[73] In making such appointments, the Treasury seems to have ignored the question of qualification and training upon which Godolphin had placed so much emphasis.

The use of deputies had an unfavorable effect upon the system, for as a rule the deputy received only a fraction of the income and was therefore an easy prey to corruption. There is little evidence that Walpole had any positive views on the question of deputies in the colonial customs system, although he had objected to having the surveyor of the woods act by deputy. The Treasury granted numerous leaves of absence, which necessitated the use of deputies, but there was not such gross abuse of this practice as under later

72. T11:20, pp. 207, 257, 391-93.

73. Richard Fitzwilliam, who was collector on the Lower James, lost his office, was reinstated although warrants involving two other people had to be recalled, was advanced to the position of surveyor general though it was necessary to remove the incumbent, and then after a few years was again superseded (T11:17 and 18, passim; T29:27, p. 59; T27:25, p. 14).

administrations. The only formal provision for a deputy occurred when Walpole transformed the collectorship at Philadelphia into a patent office for the benefit of William Erdman Fox, who acted by deputy.[74] Evidence suggests that Walpole was ignorant of the most objectionable, subrosa arrangement whereby the actual office-holder paid most of the income from his place to his patron.[75]

Although the Treasury exerted little pressure on the Customs Commissioners, the latter did not neglect the colonies. The surveyors general received new instructions, and the subordinate officers were disciplined if they were absent from duty without leave or failed to send home their accounts, lists of shipping, and other records. The commissioners asked the Treasury to help them secure more accurate shipping lists from the governors and naval officers.[76]

The officers in America must have been fairly efficient, for the Treasury received a good many protests against their strictness and appeals for relief from the penalties of the law. The Treasury complied when there was evidence of misunderstanding.[77] On a rare occasion it intervened directly to urge the Governor of Massachusetts to secure justice for an officer who had been injured in a riot.[78] All in all, however, the records give the impression that the Treasury was comparatively casual in its attitude toward the customs system. At least, the administration of the law at this time failed to prepare the colonies for the more meticulous enforcement that characterized Grenville's administration a generation later.

Considering the purpose of the acts of trade, as interpreted by Walpole, and the character of their administration, it is not surprising that little revenue ever reached the British Exchequer from

74. T11:19, p. 264.

75. HEH, William Mathew Correspondence, 10 June 1720; 21 July, 12 and 19 Aug. 1721.

76. Custom House Library, Notes and Extracts, 2, passim.

77. Case of captain carrying Palatines from Rotterdam to America who did not land their possessions in England en route (T11:17, pp. 432-33). In another case the Treasury allowed a premium on imports, although the importer had unintentionally failed to give the required oath (T11:21, pp. 56-57).

78. T27:24, p. 5.

this source. Annual statements of gross receipts and the costs of administration paid in the ports are not available.[79] Yet this much is clear: deposits in the Exchequer under the head of the enumerated commodities were considerably less than the annual salary bill paid by the receiver general.[80] The receipts from the Molasses Act were negligible; at least, there were no deposits from this source in the Exchequer during this period.[81] Parliament made no appropriation of the revenue from this act until long after Walpole's day. Yet because the theory persisted that the purpose of American duties was to regulate trade, no one criticized the colonial customs system for its failure to produce a profit.

Unlike the plantation duties, the American postal system was supposed to earn a revenue.[82] So far it had been a disappointment, for there had been a constant deficit, borne by the British Exchequer. But in 1721 the Postmaster General, with the approval of the Treasury, made a new contract relieving the Exchequer of all costs of administration.[83] A few years later Alexander Spotswood accepted the office of American deputy, also under a con-

---

79. They were not included in the general accounts but were audited separately by the commissioners (Notes and Extracts, *2*, passim).

80. Deposits were seldom over £1,000 a year and often much less (WLC, Shelburne, *104*). The annual salary bill paid in London ranged from about £3,400 at the beginning of this period to £3,700 toward the close (T11:17, and 11:21, passim). Other costs included salaries paid in the plantations, £2,798.2.6, and charges of management paid there "by a medium about £1,600," making a total of about £7,798 (T1:236, fol. 164). Bermuda was placed on the establishment in this period (T29:26, p. 329), but Jamaican officers continued to be paid in the island.

81. The receipts averaged about £20 a year while Walpole was in office (T1:430); but in 1758 deposits in the Exchequer were £10,742, probably the accumulation of many years (Shelburne, *104*).

82. 3 Geo. I, c. 7, made the act of 1711 perpetual. 6 Geo. I, c. 21, explained that certain privileges with regard to enclosures did not apply to the dominions.

83. T53:30, p. 33. Previous to this time the American deputy postmaster general had received a salary from the English receiver general. In 1722 John Lloyd was named deputy for both North America and the West Indies (*CSP, Col.*, 1722–23, §169).

tract that prohibited any charge to the British Exchequer.[84] Spotswood extended the system to Virginia and made plans for carrying it into North Carolina.[85] Nevertheless, there was no profit for the British government.

Soon after the outbreak of war there was a demand for a revival of the packet system. A report from the Post Office on the service in Queen Anne's time was, of course, financially discouraging and was probably responsible for Walpole's failure to restore this service.[86]

In contrast to the growing sense of imperial responsibility evident in parliamentary legislation and the liberal attitude of the Treasury in the management of the customs, a narrow, proprietary interest prevailed in the administration of the crown dues. Both Godolphin and Oxford had had a tendency in this direction, counteracted to some extent by the Board of Trade and Blathwayt, who favored using crown dues in the colonies. The decline of the Board of Trade and the succession of Horace Walpole to the office of auditor general weakened the opposition to treasury policies. In fact, the auditor general seems to have been the strongest adherent of these policies.

As early as 1715 Walpole received the reversion of the profitable place of surveyor and auditor general of His Majesty's plantation revenues.[87] In 1717, when Blathwayt died, the Walpoles were out of office, but after 1721 when they returned to the Treasury, the office of auditor of the plantation revenues was practically a branch of the Treasury, whereas during most of Blathwayt's tenure it was

84. T98:2, 2 Jan. 1729; T27:24, p. 421. The contract was for ten years, with permission to draw a salary of £300 a year plus 10 per cent of the net profits.

85. *N.J. Arch.*, Ser. 1, *11*, 289. *The Virginia Historical Register, 1* (Richmond, 1848), 67. When Spotswood resigned in 1739, he was succeeded by Head Lynch, who held the office until his death in 1743 (Ruth Lapham Butler, *Doctor Franklin, Postmaster General,* Garden City, N.Y., Doubleday, Doran, 1928, p. 34).

86. T27:25, p. 523. In 1716 a privy seal relieved Dummer's estate from all charges for the earlier packet system (T52:28, pp. 39-41).

87. T52:27, p. 78. Index to the Patent Rolls, *38*, 55.

closely connected with the Board of Trade or its predecessor.[88]
The Treasury relied upon Horace Walpole to make decisions with
respect to the crown revenues. Peter Leheup, a treasury clerk, acted
as his deputy until 1742, when Robert Walpole resigned. After
1730, when Horace Walpole gave up his place as secretary, he seems
to have given his deputy less close supervision.[89] Leheup proved
faithless, and the revenue suffered. Toward the end of his administration Sir Robert may have become suspicious, for in 1741 the
Treasury undertook an investigation of crown revenues—too late
to achieve results in this period.[90]

The early effect of Horace Walpole's admission to the office of
auditor general, however, was a renewed vitality in its affairs, for
Blathwayt had recently been out of close touch with the London
offices. On the other hand, Walpole lacked the experience and interest in general problems of colonial administration that had
characterized his predecessor. Whereas Blathwayt had agreed with
the Board of Trade, of which he was long an influential member,
that crown dues should be used for the support of English policy in
America, Walpole begrudged payments from crown revenues even
for colonial salaries and still more for other purposes. When he
agreed, he wished there were some other source.[91] He seemed even

88. Sometime before 1726 Walpole was occupying offices very close to the
Treasury (T29:25, p. 134). In that year he asked for a grant of office space in
part of a house adjoining the Tennis Courts, probably the place already in
use (PRO, Index 4624, Reference Book of the Treasury, p. 234), and received
a fifty-year lease at a rent of £2.10.0 per annum (T52:34, p. 390). In 1729 the
Crown purchased the vault under the office for £185 of Virginia quit rents
(*CTB & P*, 1729–30, p. 36).

89. Yet even when Walpole was in Europe, the Treasury occasionally consulted him on the crown dues (T29:27, p. 341).

90. *CTB & P*, 1739–41, p. 446.

91. T52:38, pp. 160-70. He added to the salary and perquisites which
Blathwayt had enjoyed £100 salary from the Carolina quit rents, £150 per
annum from the Virginia quit rents for the incidents of his office, and, by
making good his claim to audit the four-and-a-half per cent, the fees for that
function. Although he secured the right to audit accounts of the revenue from
prizes taken in American waters, there were no such accounts in his day.

more interested than Blathwayt in his personal income from office. This attitude, however, led to a determined effort to increase collections from the quit rents, the four-and-a-half per cent, and the casual revenues, and to protect the Crown's interest in them.

Possibilities for increasing the quit rents resulted from the purchase of proprietary rights in the Carolinas and Agatha Campbell's seigneury in Nova Scotia.[92] Plans to collect both quit rents and the four-and-a-half per cent duty in the neutral islands was contrary to the custom elsewhere, and illustrates the emphasis placed on revenue in this period.[93]

Treasury policies were directed toward securing more complete rent rolls in the old as well as the newer provinces, reducing the period in which new grants were free from rents, resisting local tendencies to exempt landholders from payment of their arrears, and even raising the rate of payments on new grants—all intended to increase the revenue. The enforcement of these policies depended, to some extent at least, on persuading the local assemblies to pass satisfactory laws, for the prerogative alone was no longer a sufficient basis for the collection of quit rents. The Treasury, the Board of Trade, and the Privy Council all cooperated in an attempt to secure such laws. Yet it was unrealistic to suppose that the assemblies, made up of landholders, would support the rights of the Crown at their own expense unless they had some control of the revenue or received other compensation. As a matter of fact, throughout this period it proved impossible to obtain legislation that really satisfied the Crown.

The Board of Trade proposed that Parliament pass a law regulating land grants in New York, a step toward improving quit rents in that province.[94] But evidently the Walpole administration did not take kindly to this proposal, any more than it approved the suggestion that Parliament should confirm the grant of Georgia

92. Although Parliament had provided the money for the former, surprisingly enough it assumed no other rights over the revenue than to ask for accounts (T27:25, p. 567, 17 Feb. 1741).

93. Labaree, *Royal Instructions*, 2, 604-5.

94. *N.Y. Col. Doc.*, 5, 654.

to the trustees. By thus protecting the prerogative against parliamentary interference, Walpole may have prevented the development of an important source of colonial revenue independent of local control. Such a revenue might have been used to strengthen colonial administration. On the other hand, of course, Parliament might have appropriated this fund for noncolonial purposes as it did most of the money from the sale of land in St. Christopher, discussed below. In either case the colonists might well have objected, and the quit rents might have become a major cause of the American Revolution.

Without satisfactory legislation the Treasury did the best it could with administrative measures. For example, it pensioned the old receiver in New York and appointed a new officer.[95] It gave Walpole's deputy in the Carolinas exceptional powers of inspection and control, and combined his office with that of land surveyor.[96] As conditions in the Carolinas remained unsatisfactory, it later sent Henry McCulloh to investigate and supervise the collection of quit rents in those provinces.[97] Collections remained below expectations, but there was some improvement everywhere. Receipts in the former proprietary provinces, however, never compared favorably with those in Virginia.

Small as the revenue was, it nevertheless served a useful purpose. Somewhat grudgingly the Treasury agreed to use the income from the quit rents in North Carolina for the local civil list, as in the time of the proprietors, and part of the revenue in the other provinces for a limited number of officials, making the recipients comparatively independent of the local government and, therefore, more responsible to the Crown.[98] At the same time it insisted on retaining in England final authority over issues from these funds. As far as New York was concerned, recent practice had violated

95. T27:23, p. 95; T29:24, Pt. II, pp. 56, 61.
96. T54:31, pp. 375-76; T52:37, pp. 179-80.
97. T29:28, pp. 89, 166; T52:40, pp. 281 ff.
98. T52:38, pp. 166-70, the civil list of N.C. T52:39, pp. 36-37, salary for the chief justice of S.C. T52:34, p. 128, for secretary of Indian affairs in N.Y. *CTB & P,* 1731—34, p. 387, addition to salary of attorney general of Va.

this policy. The receiver in that province had handled both crown dues and grants of the assembly, and had been accustomed to issue both on warrants from the governor and council. He now received a stern warning to make no payments from crown dues other than for the cost of management, except by royal warrant.[99]

From a practical point of view, Virginia was the only province in which the quit rents produced enough to make control of the revenue an issue of great importance. It was significant, therefore, that shortly after Walpole's original appointment as First Lord, the Treasury refused a petition of the Governor of Virginia, supported by the Board of Trade, that the quit rents should be left in the province to be used in an emergency at the discretion of the governor and the council.[100] The annual establishment approved by the Crown was only £850, and the larger part of this sum was an annuity for thirty-one years, granted when Stanhope was First Lord.[101] From time to time the King authorized payments from this fund for special colonial purposes; but he ordered the receiver to send the greater part to England, payable in most cases to a secretary or clerk of the Treasury for the King's special service, thus avoiding the routine of the Exchequer.[102]

From the beginning the four-and-a-half per cent export duty, unlike the quit rents, had been based upon local legislation, except in the case of the recently acquired French section of St. Christopher. But any amendment or repeal, of course, would have been subject to confirmation by the Crown. In 1729 the Privy Council approved a local act extending the duty to the former French area, so that it no longer depended upon the royal prerogative.[103] From

99. T52:34, pp. 125-27.

100. T1:192, fol. 7. PC 2:85, p. 281. T27:22, p. 19. Horace Walpole later admitted to the Board of Trade that the Treasury had not reported to the Council, but said it was a standing order that quit rents should be issued only by order of the Crown (BT, *Journal*, Nov. 1718—Dec. 1722, p. 279).

101. *CSP, Col.*, 1717—18, §422.i(c).

102. T52, passim.

103. PC 2:91, pp. 14, 36.

the accession of George I Parliament left the disposal of this revenue to the discretion of the King. The revenue not only bore its own costs of administration and those of the customs in the islands where the four-and-a-half per cent was collected, but returned a sizable surplus.[104] From almost every point of view, therefore, this was the most satisfactory of the crown dues.

These circumstances, together with the fact that Horace Walpole made good his claim to audit these accounts, caused the Treasury to give particular attention to this revenue. Soon after Robert Walpole's return to office in 1721 the Treasury noted that there had been neglect in examining the collectors' accounts. New instructions to the Customs Commissioners required that collectors should submit their accounts to the auditor general's deputies in the islands before sending them to the commissioners in London. The auditor general was to have duplicates. According to the plan, after the accounts had been stated by the comptroller and approved by the commissioners they were to be audited and passed by the auditor general.[105] It proved impossible, however, for the comptroller general to prepare an account incorporating the accounts of the individual collectors which could be audited according to accepted procedures.[106] Walpole, however, took over the audit of the accounts of the receiver general, previously handled by the auditors of the imprests.

In examining the collectors' accounts Walpole discovered, as he thought, evidences of fraud in weighing casks of sugar. Investigations followed. Although his suspicions do not appear to have been entirely justified, the collectors probably became more care-

104. Although there was a decline in the revenue during 1714–24, the net deposited in the Exchequer during 1724–41 ranged from £4,000 to £14,000 (Shelburne, *104*). T38:372, pp. 16, 126, averages for 1734–39 and 1739–44.

105. T27:23, p. 315; T11:18, p. 15.

106. T1:305, fol. 54, report of comptroller general. No accounts had been declared since 1684. After long consultations, the Treasury in 1741 decided that the auditors of the imprests should take the accounts before 1721, and Walpole those after that date. The auditors were to draft appropriate warrants for passing these accounts in spite of their defects. T29:38, pp. 359, 363-64.

ful in every particular.[107] The investigations may have been partly responsible for the improvement in receipts which occurred during the latter part of this period.

In spite of the fact that Parliament and the Board of Trade had encouraged the policy of using the surplus of the four-and-a-half per cent for the defense of the islands, under Walpole such payments ceased. The Treasury continued to draw on the fund for salaries of the governors and lieutenant governors in the islands where the revenue was collected, and also for salaries of officials in other dependencies.[108] A few miscellaneous items, including a pension to a former governor of Massachusetts Bay, were also charged to this fund.[109] These latter uses were contrary to the principle often expressed by the Board of Trade, the islanders, and even the governors located there. On the other hand, most of these payments, like similar ones from the quit rents, helped to accomplish another aim of the Administration—that is, to make officials independent of the local government.

Like other crown dues the casual revenues attracted the attention of the auditor general as soon as he came into office. Although individually most of these revenues seemed unimportant, they might have produced a rather significant total had they been efficiently collected and faithfully accounted for. Occasionally there was a real windfall, as was the case with the sale of land on St. Christopher. Although Walpole was sincere in his attempts to improve the various branches, a real revolution would have been required to achieve important results.

Among Walpole's attempts to improve the situation were the following. To avoid further encroachments by local assemblies the Treasury directed the Board of Trade to refer to that office all

107. Collectors had allowed an arbitrary amount for wastage, instead of weighing each cask (T11:21, pp. 123-27). As merchants later complained of delay, instructions were modified (T29:27, p. 321; T11:21, pp. 123-27).

108. These included the captain general of the Bahamas, the governors of Bermuda, Mass., S.C., and the island of Jersey.

109. T29:27, p. 29. Commission for settling case of Mohegan Indians and Connecticut (T29:28, p. 379).

local acts appropriating revenues before making any representation to the Privy Council.[110] The Treasury now filled vacancies that had been neglected; made at least one change in personnel; issued new instructions to the casual receivers (but not to the other crown receivers), defining and extending their jurisdiction; and brought the receiver of the perquisites of the Admiralty under treasury regulations.[111] The last-named official finally resigned in disgust over the insufficiency of the income.[112] In general, the division of responsibility among various officials and the lack of clear and specific instructions to all concerned resulted in confusion, negligence, and consequent ill effects on the revenue.

One important exception to this criticism of the administration of the casual revenues was the method employed in handling the sale of lands on St. Christopher. Customarily in the American provinces the governor made grants of land under his seal, following instructions drafted by the Board of Trade. Income from the sale of rights to take up land was paid to the receiver general and often accounted for with the quit rents. The Crown sometimes made more extensive grants under the great seal of England.[113] But the situation on St. Christopher was exceptional. There were existing claims growing out of prior occupation and grants made by the governor subject to the royal pleasure. The demand for land was great. During the time Walpole was out of office the House of Commons had requested that the land should be sold and the proceeds used for public purposes.[114] The Board of Trade

110. *CTP,* 1720—28, p. 18.

111. The Customs Commissioners evidently planned to make instructions to collectors harmonize with those to casual receivers (T1:236, fol. 172). T54:34, pp. 141-42, appointment of Robert Byng as receiver of rights and perquisites of the Admiralty under the sign manual.

112. Adm. 1:3673, fol. 173; T54:38, pp. 113-14: appointment of his successor, Burrington Goldsworthy. His accounts went to the auditors of the imprests (E369:9), although the auditor general seemed to have a rightful claim.

113. 1730—31, Chandos had a scheme whereby he hoped to obtain a vast grant of vacant land in New York (Stowe 57, *35, 37-39,* passim).

114. *CJ, 18,* 600. T29:23, p. 128.

and the Treasury had considered various plans, and the Privy Council had approved the principle of sales to the highest bidder, but no action had been taken before Walpole returned to office.[115]

The Treasury now assumed full responsibility. Following a survey of available land it named commissioners to manage the sale, and the secretaries drafted their instructions.[116] The Treasury kept in touch with the commissioners until sales were completed and their accounts audited. No sales were final until approved by the Treasury.[117] By the end of two years after their arrival the commissioners had disposed of most of the desirable land.[118]

The net proceeds amounted to a little over £111,000.[119] Although the ministers, so it was said, considered the revenue "properly the King's," they evidently felt bound by the earlier request of the House of Commons. They secured the authority of Parliament before applying £80,000 as a marriage portion for the princess royal and £10,000 toward the settlement of Protestants in Georgia.[120] In 1740 Parliament appropriated the remainder toward the supply of that year.[121] Thus the King lost one more traditional source of crown revenue which might have been used either to supplement his civil list or to make better provision for the government of the provinces.[122]

115. T54:22, pp. 324 ff.; T1:181, fol. 25; PC 2:85, pp. 102, 208. Under one plan all land would have been sold to one buyer. Stanhope's Treasury had gone so far as to advertise for buyers (*CSP, Col.*, 1717–18, §§7, 156).

116. T29:25, p. 169. The Board of Trade had opposed sending commissioners, preferring to handle sales in England (T1:282, fol. 248).

117. All former grants made by the governor were void, but actual possessors were given the first option on terms agreed to by the commissioners. Otherwise land was auctioned in lots of 200 acres each (T52:34, pp. 168-72).

118. A single commissioner remained to complete sales and examine disputed claims (T29:27, p. 55).

119. Stock, *4*, 213, 219; *5*, 32.

120. Add. MSS 33,038, fol. 196. Stock, *4*, 213, 219.

121. Stock, *5*, 9, n. 49; 32.

122. This transfer to the public was a precedent for revenue from the Ceded Islands after 1763. Elsewhere the governors normally granted land. Horace Walpole audited these accounts for a fee of 2.5 per cent of the net balance (E351:1566, 1567; T52:40, pp. 163-67).

The Walpoles discovered very early that the assembly grants had a background of treasury failure unmatched in the case of any other colonial revenues with which they had to deal. Yet they appeared undaunted. Their major purpose here, of course, was to develop this source of revenue to avoid the charges on crown dues and lighten those on funds supplied by Parliament. To achieve this result it would have been necessary to reverse the strong trend toward financial independence on the part of the assemblies, and to substitute crown control. The Treasury soon encountered serious obstacles. To be sure, in 1728 Jamaica passed its first permanent revenue act; but this was a victory more in name than in fact. The law lacked most of the provisions which the Treasury had insisted were essential.[123] It established the independent authority of the local government in making appropriations from the revenues, including crown dues, and authorizing issues therefrom; failed to provide for the royal forces; and made the receiver, though a royal appointee, accountable to the assembly. Although the receiver might continue to send his accounts to the auditor general, the assembly retained the real authority. The Treasury enjoyed the patronage, and could obtain useful information from the accounts. In most important respects, however, the act limited the power of the Crown forever. Nevertheless, the Privy Council confirmed this act. The taxes were insufficient to cover all the needs of the province, leaving the Crown dependent upon the will of the assembly for further grants.

Having lost this battle, Horace Walpole refused to approve defense items in the accounts of the Virginia permanent revenue known as the two-shillings-a-hogshead, as they had not been authorized by the King. The Governor protested that this revenue was raised and appropriated for the defense of the country as well as the support of the government, and that the governor with the advice of the council "had always been allowed the proper Judge of

123. T27:23, pp. 287-88; T27:24, p. 13; T54:29, pp. 357-58. Agnes M. Whitson, *The Constitutional Development of Jamaica, 1660–1729* (Manchester Univ. Press, 1929), pp. 152-53.

the measures necessary for that purpose."[124] The Treasury finally approved the items, but procured a king's warrant for the purpose, maintaining the principle of royal check on expenditures from this fund as well as from the quit rents.[125] The advantage gained in the case of Virginia, however, was exceptional.

The auditor general's experience with the New York assembly was more typical. Soon after coming into office Horace Walpole was shocked to learn that the assembly had transferred its funds from the crown receiver to a treasurer of its own choosing. Having brought this matter to the attention of Sunderland's Treasury, he was invited to draft appropriate letters and instructions for the officials in that province. The resulting letter to the local treasurer threatened him with prosecution if he failed to account with Walpole.[126] The Treasury also recommended to the Lords Justices that they instruct the Governor to defend the royal prerogative.[127]

As it happened, Walpole's fees, described by the Governor as "extravagant," were at stake in this dispute. With Robert Walpole again in office, the Treasury gave the Governor a severe reprimand for his attitude and ordered him to see that the accounts were sent to the auditor general, and that in the future all revenue was placed in the hands of the King's own receiver.[128] But this was not the end of the assembly's defiance in the matter of fees, nor of the larger issue of Crown versus assembly in the control of funds granted by the latter.[129]

The tendency of the governors to sympathize with the local point of view, as illustrated in Virginia and New York, is significant in the development of England's relation with her colonies. The

124. H. R. McIlwaine, ed., *Executive Journals of the Council of Colonial Virginia* (Richmond, Virginia State Library, 1925–45), *4*, 298.

125. T52:38, pp. 205-7.

126. T54:26, p. 37. Walpole's memorial to the Treasury, T1:221, fol. 191. Treasury reply, T27:22, p. 430.

127. T27:23, p. 94.

128. T54:27, pp. 139-41.

129. Discovering a shortage of funds, the assembly later prohibited their treasurer from paying these fees (*N.Y. Col. Doc.*, *6*, 94).

Treasury, for its part, seemed to place little more confidence in the governor than in the assembly. Its objective was direct management of this branch of colonial finance; but it made little headway against determined opposition. As a result of its activities, the governors corresponded more frequently with the Treasury than had been customary, and often enclosed copies of local accounts. The assemblies, however, continued to grow in financial independence.

When Sir Robert Walpole left the Government in 1742, he had presided at the Treasury for more than twenty consecutive years. During that time he had made a deep and lasting impression upon colonial administration. Although one might debate endlessly the motives for his actions, there is no doubt that what he did and also what he failed to do had a profound effect upon succeeding governments.

Under Walpole the Treasury became far more important in the colonial field; and the financial aspects of colonial administration received greater emphasis than in the past. One of the most significant developments that can be attributed to the First Lord of the Treasury was the increased investment by Parliament in the colonies, laying a foundation for more interference in a field of government previously left to the Crown.

Another important characteristic of this period was in part at least a result of the Treasury's rather casual attitude toward the customs duties and hence the enforcement of the acts of trade. During most of these years the colonies were peaceful, prosperous, and comparatively content. They were bound, therefore, to view later attempts at stricter enforcement of the laws as an unwarranted innovation.

The failure of the Walpoles to develop an efficient system for the collection of crown dues and their hesitancy to use these revenues for the provincial governments, least of all for defense, necessitated reliance upon other sources of revenue to defend America and carry out crown policies there. As the assemblies were both unreliable in the matter of raising money and independent of the Crown in the use of these funds which they considered their own, the one recourse of the English Government in case of an emergency was to call upon Parliament.

Succeeding war years increased Parliament's responsibility for the colonies. Only time would tell how long Parliament would be willing to appropriate English funds for colonial purposes without demanding larger contributions by the colonies themselves. This question, hardly formulated in 1742, was nevertheless the principal inheritance of England and the colonies from the Walpole administration.

3.

The Treasury under the Pelham Brothers,

1743–1762

WAR, OR THE DANGER of war, hung over England and her colonies for twenty years after Walpole's resignation. The war of the Austrian Succession came to a close in 1748, but six years later fighting began again in America, introducing the French and Indian War. Peace was finally concluded in 1763.

During these two decades the Government tended to subordinate all other aspects of colonial policy to the one great object of winning the war. In discussions of military strategy the First Lord of the Treasury naturally played a secondary role. The defense of the colonies, however, placed an unprecedented burden on the British Exchequer. Treasury officials were given increasing responsibility for raising funds and handling expenditures. The effectiveness with which they performed these functions affected the course and outcome of the war, and influenced the lives and attitudes of American colonists.

For a year and a half after Walpole's resignation the Earl of Wilmington presided at the Treasury.[1] Then, on Wilmington's death, the King followed the advice of Walpole, now Earl of Orford, and summoned Henry Pelham, already experienced in government finance, to fill the place of First Lord.[2] In many respects "dear Harry," as Walpole had called him in earlier days, became

1. 16 Feb. 1742–25 Aug. 1743.
2. William Coxe, ed., *Memoirs of Horatio Lord Walpole* (2d ed. London, 1808), *2,* 52. Owen, *The Rise of the Pelhams,* p. 171, notes that he has found no evidence that Walpole was in communication with the King, but suggests this was not necessary, as the King knew his views.

the real heir of the great Prime Minister. On Pelham's death in 1754 his elder brother, the Duke of Newcastle, previously Secretary of State, moved to the Treasury, where he remained until 1762, with the exception of a few months in 1756 and 1757.[3] For nearly twenty years, therefore, one or the other of the Pelham brothers occupied the post of First Lord of the Treasury. Except for the first few months of his tenure, Henry Pelham was also Chancellor of the Exchequer. Unlike as were the two brothers personally, their colonial policies and their administrations were similar in so many respects that it seems best to treat them as a unit.

Although trained in Walpole's school of politics and generally skillful enough to maintain first place among the ministers, neither of the Pelham brothers achieved the political supremacy enjoyed by Walpole. The most obvious reason for this comparative failure was the military character of the times. But there are other explanations, some applying to only one brother, some to both.

Henry Pelham, sensitive and less ruthless than Walpole, was less likely to persist against opposition, especially when it was his brother as Secretary of State who resisted him. Newcastle, on the other hand, was always eager for power; yet as First Lord of the Treasury he lacked assurance and sought facts and advice from every source. His principal consultant was his friend, the Lord High Chancellor, the Earl of Hardwicke. Although diligent and conscientious, Newcastle failed to achieve the respect accorded to his younger brother or the recognition received by Walpole with considerably less show, and at the height of the war he had to concede to William Pitt the position of real leadership.

Yet in spite of these personal characteristics either of the brothers might have been more powerful had he had more influence with the King. In 1743 George II was far more experienced than when he ascended the throne in the midst of Walpole's administration. Although he was aware of the King's limitations in what was described as a balanced government, he learned how to use his personal

3. 18 Mar. 1754—15 Nov. 1756, when the Duke of Devonshire became First Lord; 2 July 1757—28 May 1762.

influence.[4] He undermined Pelham's authority by encouraging other ministers; and he crushed Newcastle by his criticism. As for George III, his devotion to Bute was an important factor in Newcastle's decline.

Without the complete support of the King, the First Lord of the Treasury found it difficult to resist the demands of other great officers, especially the secretaries of state. For this reason there is less justification for ascribing general colonial policies to either Henry Pelham or Newcastle during their respective treasury administrations than to Walpole in his day. Nevertheless, the First Lord was always a powerful minister and influential in the various councils where colonial affairs were discussed.

Many matters of colonial administration came before the Council's Committee on Plantation Affairs, where Pelham was a fairly regular attendant. Newcastle, however, seemed to feel his presence unnecessary, possibly because in his administration, with the rise of the Board of Trade under the Earl of Halifax, the committee was less important.[5] This Board, in actuality, had little to do with the formulation of broad policies.

The great and exciting questions of the day, which now often involved the colonies, were decided in the Cabinet Council or, more likely, the inner group which Newcastle called the committee of the Cabinet Council.

Patronage was, as always, one of the most powerful instruments of government. Pelham, however, never monopolized the privilege of distributing favors.[6] When Secretary of State, Newcastle as-

---

4. When Pelham found the King "in perfect good humour," he wrote: "I am certain he designs to make me do something that he knows I don't approve of" (Add. MSS 32,709, fol. 414).

5. Halifax was appointed in 1748. Through the order of 1752 the Board was more directly in touch with colonial governors (*APC, Col., 4*, 154-56; CO 5:216, pp. 16-17).

6. Army appointments were the special province of George II or the Duke of Cumberland. Pelham sent applications for the navy to Lord Anson, with whom it was said he had an agreement (HEH, Grenville, Political Papers, Box 100, Temple West to George Grenville, 11 Aug. 1753).

sumed the right to handle much of the patronage.[7] Even a member of the Treasury Board wrote to him concerning proposed changes in this department.[8] When he became First Lord of the Treasury, therefore, Newcastle was prepared to claim extensive rights of nomination.[9] Although Halifax expected to enjoy more colonial patronage than his predecessors at the Board of Trade, he felt bound to consult Newcastle about the more important offices.[10] After Pitt came into the Government, Newcastle arrived at an agreement with him on the subject of patronage,[11] but Pitt was never really interested in this branch of politics, and as a matter of practice left it largely to Newcastle.

The Treasury experienced more difficulty with regard to expenditures. This was understandable in time of war when economy had few supporters. But even after peace had been restored in 1748 Pelham was almost desperate in the face of demands for public funds. For example, the Duke of Bedford, recently appointed Secretary of State for the Southern Department, was able to secure the King's approval for reimbursing a colony for fitting out sloops in its own defense, even though Pelham protested.[12]

When Newcastle was in a position of financial responsibility, his reactions to demands for money were like those of his brother. As expenses increased the Cabinet was bitterly divided over war

7. Church livings were said to be under his "cognizance" (Add. MSS 32,708, fol. 369). He gave "commands" with regard to the Post Office (ibid., 32,709, fol. 263).

8. George Lyttelton offered his place on the Board and was willing to go to any foreign court, as he was tired of seeing his friends quarrel (ibid., 32,707, fol. 92). Nevertheless, he remained at the Treasury for nearly a decade.

9. The King protested against Newcastle's disposing of places in the royal bedchamber; but Hardwicke defended him, saying that the right to make recommendations was necessary for carrying on the king's business (ibid., 32,852, fols. 27-30, 63-65).

10. Newcastle assumed the right of nomination (ibid., 32,735, fols. 268-72). In 1761 the Board lost even its nominal right to appoint to the higher offices.

11. Ibid., 32,997, fol. 270, Sept. 1757.

12. T27:26, pp. 347, 359.

policies.[13] Newcastle grasped at straws in his desire for peace; but as long as war continued, the Treasury was obliged to find funds to support it.

For this purpose it was necessary to apply to the House of Commons. Parliaments elected in 1747 and 1754 showed a high degree of compliance, although Newcastle experienced more difficulties than his brother. Neither brother spared any pains to influence elections, while John Roberts, personal secretary to Pelham, and James West, who became secretary to the Treasury in 1746, were specialists in election management.[14] Funds for election purposes were presumably more limited than under Walpole.[15] But too many factors were involved in securing cooperation from the House of Commons to speak with assurance on the effectiveness of money, places, and pensions.[16] Newcastle resigned only a short time after the election of 1761, which he had so carefully managed.[17]

The actual test of loyalty came when Parliament met. In managing the House of Commons, Henry Pelham had a marked advantage over his brother, who had to act through a deputy. Short sessions and lack of controversy toward the latter part of Pelham's admin-

13. Even Lord Anson complained: "Mr. Pitt would cover the Seas with Ships" (Add. MSS 32,893, fol. 102).

14. When Newcastle succeeded his brother on the eve of the election of 1754, he found that the latter had made very careful preparations, including a list of candidates showing how much elections in particular constituencies would cost, and information as to promises of money and places (ibid., 32,995, fols. 63-66, 75 ff., 174-75; 32,857, fol. 590; 32,734, fols. 237-40).

15. The Pelhams regularly spent far less for secret service than Walpole, and in election years used only from £10,000 to £15,000 more than in normal years (ibid., 33,039, fol. 37). Lewis B. Namier, *The Structure of Politics at the Accession of George III* (London, Macmillan, 1929), *1*, 259, concludes that no money was issued from the Treasury under George III for the election of 1761.

16. One analysis estimated the government majority after the election of 1754 as between 140 and 189 (Add. MSS 33,034, fol. 171). But according to other calculations the Government gained only one to four seats (ibid., 32,995, fol. 221).

17. For a full treatment of this election see Namier, *England in the Age of the American Revolution*, London, Macmillan, 1930.

istration testify to his skill. Newcastle was less fortunate. In 1755 there was little doubt, as Sir Thomas Robinson implied, that the House of Commons was insecure. Newcastle found it necessary to bring first Fox and then Pitt into the Government, and could no longer claim to be sole leader.

Because of the political conditions described above, petitioners for legislation felt less necessity for applying directly to the Treasury than had been the case under Walpole. Under Halifax the Board of Trade appears to have taken somewhat more initiative with respect to commercial legislation; but there was often consultation with the Treasury.[18] The hand of the Treasury, however, is clearly evident in steps to protect the New Englanders against further interference with their foreign sugar trade. Under Pelham the Privy Council referred a petition from the sugar islands to the Treasury. From there it went to the Custom House, where it stayed until called for by the House of Commons.[19] This petition and another calling for complete prohibition of the foreign sugar trade were suppressed in committee.[20]

In 1754 Newcastle was prepared to resist the sugar lobby.[21] When the Treasury received a direct request to support an application to Parliament, it refused.[22] During the war, of course, all trade with the enemy was theoretically prohibited.

The Treasury eventually took a definite though more obscure part in promoting the act which prohibited the New England colonies from making bills of credit legal tender.[23] In 1744, however,

---

18. Among the statutes: for a premium on indigo (21 Geo. II, c. 30); importing potash duty free (24 Geo. II, c. 51); iron and silk acts (23 Geo. II, cc. 29, 20); extension to outports of privilege of importing iron duty free (30 Geo. II, c. 16); and freedom for Nova Scotia to import salt (2 Geo. III, c. 24). In some cases the solicitor to the Treasury helped to get the bills passed. A bill making the collection of duties for Greenwich Hospital perpetual applied to American seamen (2 Geo. III, c. 31).

19. T11:24, p. 53. Stock, *Proceedings, 5,* 469.

20. Stock, p. 460, passim.

21. Add. MSS 32,995, fol. 309.

22. T29:32, p. 276.

23. 24 Geo. II, c. 53.

a petition to the House of Commons from merchants trading to America failed to bring results.[24] In 1749 a bill introduced by Horace Walpole and the Board of Trade died in committee, probably because of opposition to a clause which seemed to give royal instructions the force of law.[25] Success came in 1751, when the Treasury considered a petition from certain Rhode Islanders referred to it by the Privy Council; it consulted the Board of Trade, and evidently gave its approval.[26] It may be significant that the treasury solicitor represented the Rhode Island group.[27] The actual bill was private, but the Americans understood that the Administration was behind it.[28]

Financing colonial defense was the chief responsibility of the Treasury during these years. Planned expenditures, based on estimates submitted to the House of Commons, increased with the declaration of war against France in 1744; declined somewhat with the announcement of peace; but reached what would once have been considered fantastic heights before the end of the Seven Years' War.[29] The peculiar conditions of war on the frontier made it impossible to foresee all needs; and as the war developed, commanders

24. Stock, *5*, 183, 187. In 1745 the Board of Trade appeared to favor such a measure but must have been advised against it (*Journal*, 1741/2—49, p. 104, passim).

25. Stock, *5*, 298 n. In vain the Speaker announced that the objectionable clause would be dropped (ibid., p. 361 n.). WLC, Sydney, *9*, 18 May 1749, letter to Pelham explaining opposition.

26. T27:26, pp. 481, 484; T29:31, p. 349; T1:345, 12 Feb. 1750/1.

27. BT, *Journal*, 1749/50—53, p. 161.

28. Stock, *5*, 467, 479; New York Public Library, William Smith Papers, *3*, 230, Robert Charles' statement that the bill carried "on the Face of it the Marks of an intended job."

29. Additions to the regular forces during the earlier war included 3 companies for S.C., 4 regiments at Cape Breton, officers for the garrison at Louisburg, and the Georgia rangers (dropped in 1747). The end of the war resulted in reducing forces to 3 regiments, 9 independent companies, and 4 garrisons. One regiment was added during the peace. During the later war the number of regiments grew to 20, and there were 8 battalions, 9 companies, several separate divisions, plus 3 regiments of foot on the Irish establishment. Figures are from Stock and *CJ*, passim. There were comparable increases for ordnance.

enjoyed considerable financial leeway. Consequently, estimates often bore little relation to the actual costs of war.

One type of demand that often followed the expenditure grew out of the practice of reimbursing colonial assemblies for funds raised for their own defense. In 1744 Governor Shirley laid the basis for this novel procedure when he raised troops for the war against France and when a year later, he encouraged New Englanders to undertake the expedition against Louisburg. The Treasury accepted his bills of exchange for the defense of Annapolis. On this occasion, however, it drew on the four-and-a-half per cent for the purpose.[30] When the New Englanders petitioned for payment of the expenses incurred in 1745, Pelham undertook to obtain the necessary funds from Parliament.[31]

The next request for reimbursement followed the fruitless project for a joint expedition against Canada in 1746. On this occasion the Treasury seems to have been taken by surprise. Newcastle, Secretary of State, had agreed to plans of the Admiralty when he and his brother were not on speaking terms. He had promised colonial governors that their troops would be in English pay. Although the plan was abandoned, the governors expected England to pay for the men they had recruited.[32] In 1750, without debate, Parliament granted compensation to the nine colonies whose accounts had been approved.[33]

In 1754 when the Government learned of French encroachments in America, one of the first questions was how to stimulate the colonies to undertake their own defense. There was no satisfactory answer, since no decision had been taken on how the cost could be met. When news of Braddock's defeat reached England, how-

---

30. *CTB & P,* 1742-45, pp. 667, 669.

31. Stock, *5,* 265. ff. PC 2:99, pp. 239, 450, 480, 512. Shirley's private letters to Pelham may have contributed to the decision to apply to Parliament (HEH, HM 9705, 9709, 9710). Somewhat comparable was the grant to pay bills of exchange drawn for the ill-fated Canadian expedition of 1711 (above, p. 52).

32. The affair can be followed in Add. MSS 32,707, 32,708; and HM 9718, Shirley's correspondence.

33. Stock, *5,* 414-18.

ever, the Cabinet swiftly decided to ask Parliament to reimburse the northern colonies for what they had already spent, in the hope of encouraging all of them to greater activity.[34] Nothing was then said of eventual repayment by the colonies. As a matter of fact, the bill for making reimbursement, as well as a later treasury reference, characterized this grant as "a free gift."[35] Every year as long as the war lasted Parliament made comparable appropriations.[36] Although there seemed to be no difficulty in obtaining parliamentary support for this policy, leading men in and out of Government were harboring thoughts of colonial taxation to relieve Great Britain of some of the burden of future payments.[37]

During Pelham's administration Parliament not only added to its military commitments for America, but began to make regular provision for the civil governments of Nova Scotia and Georgia. Until after the peace of 1748 the former was little more than a military garrison, but New Englanders advised the Government to encourage settlement there in order to hold this area against the French.[38] Both the Duke of Bedford and the Duke of Cumberland favored the plan,[39] and it became the favorite project of the Earl of Halifax when he was head of the Board of Trade. Although

34. Add. MSS 32,996, fols. 352-53. Fox had secured from the Board of Trade the figure of £120,000.

35. 29 Geo. II, c. 29. T27:27, p. 194.

36. The total appropriation was over £1,080,000 (30 Geo. II, c. 26; 31 Geo. II, c. 33; 32 Geo. II, c. 36; 33 Geo. II, c. 18; 1 Geo. III, c. 19; 2 Geo. III, c. 34; 3 Geo. III, c. 17).

37. Add. MSS 32,736, fols. 243-45, 508, 510-13; 32,996, fol. 265, views of Halifax and Charles Townshend. In 1756 Newcastle even placed a plan for extending stamp duties to America on the agenda for a cabinet meeting (32,996, fols. 243-44).

38. HEH, Stowe, Grenville Misc., "Proposals of Divers things to be Done for the Preservation of the English Colonies and Interests ... Made in Obedience to the Commands of his Grace the Duke of Newcastle and humbly submitted to his Consideration by Mr. Warren, Mr. Clark & Mr. Bollan," undated, but evidently sometime after Bollan's arrival in England in 1745.

39. John Russell, Fourth Duke of Bedford, *Correspondence,* ed. Lord John Russell (London, 1842-46), *1,* 563, 572.

Pelham postponed action, he must have yielded in the end:[40] from 1749 Parliament made regular appropriations for this settlement.

Pelham also objected to a regular establishment for Georgia,[41] but after the surrender of the charter in 1753 there was no alternative, for Georgia was not self-supporting.[42] These civil expenditures, added to those for military purposes, made the members of Parliament very conscious of the cost of the American colonies. Yet in spite of some pressure, neither Henry Pelham nor the Duke of Newcastle showed any inclination to tax the colonies.

The problems described above both increased and complicated the administrative work of the Treasury. Under Pelham, notwithstanding, it functioned smoothly. Unlike his brother, Newcastle was fussy and demanding, making the life of his subordinates unnecessarily hard. Like Walpole, both men were able to run the department with a minimum of board meetings. To be sure there was a disadvantage in this procedure: contemporaries in the latter part of the period sometimes complained of delays.[43]

Newcastle was obliged to work with a Chancellor of the Exchequer, whereas his brother had held this post as well as that of First Lord. Henry Bilson Legge who served as Chancellor of the Exchequer for several years under Newcastle was admittedly competent, but often differed with the First Lord on political issues.

Fortunately, the personnel of the office were mostly on permanent tenure, although Newcastle's over-riding concern with political patronage threatened this and other traditions of the office. During his administration doubt arose as to whether either secretarial post was secure against change if the First Lord went out of

---

40. Ibid., p. 572.

41. WLC, Sydney, *9*, 9 Jan. 1748.

42. The estimates for June 1761—June 1762 for Georgia were £4,057.10.0, and for Nova Scotia, £5,684.1.10 (*CJ*, *29*, 99).

43. Virginia State Library, Letter Book of James Abercromby, passim. Secretaries were sometimes obliged to send papers to the country houses of the members for their signatures (T27:27, p. 483), and to authorize a subordinate board like that of the Customs to proceed without formal papers (T11:26, p. 137).

office.[44] Newcastle's violation of tradition is even clearer in the case of the clerkships, which he manipulated for political purposes, in at least two cases violating the long-established custom of regular promotion according to seniority.[45] Resistance among the clerks, however, tended to discourage further violations.

One of the solicitors' places was now a sinecure and was held by Newcastle's private secretary. But this appointment had been made in 1744 by Pelham. As a consequence of relieving one incumbent of business, it had been necessary to name an assistant to the other.[46]

Parliamentary investigations did not touch these aspects of treasury management but had a good effect on others. In 1742 the House of Commons charged Nicholas Paxton, the solicitor, with failure to render accounts, causing his dismissal.[47] His successors submitted their accounts promptly.[48] Years later Peter Leheup lost his place as treasury clerk after being convicted of mismanaging a lottery for the benefit of the British Museum.[49] The Treasury was well rid of this fellow. Fortunately such incidents were not typical, although they reveal certain underlying weaknesses in the machinery.

The Treasury was able to handle its growing burdens because most of the personnel were loyal and responsible. The secretaries, especially, bore a burden that at times seemed almost intolerable.

44. The case of Samuel Martin, who hoped to fill a permanent post, is not entirely clear; but he felt ill-treated for not being reinstated in July 1757 (Add. MSS 41,356).

45. He brought Thomas Bradshaw from the War Office at Barrington's request, and made him a principal clerk, creating temporarily a fifth place of this rank (T29:34, pp. 206-7; T1:419, fol. 332). He also appointed a new clerk to a place above the lowest rank (T29:32, p. 466; T29:33, p. 2).

46. T29:31, p. 60.

47. T27:26, p. 54, appointment of John Sharpe in his place. In 1756 Philip Carteret Webb succeeded to the office (T27:27, p. 245).

48. AO 3:1102. These accounts are disappointing, for some of the most interesting work of the solicitor was evidently paid from funds issued "without account." In 1761 some of Paxton's accounts were still outstanding (Add. MSS 34,736, fols. 184-92).

49. T29:32, pp. 183, 332; T1:360, "The King against Leheup." Add. MSS 32,735, fol. 320; 32,584, fols. 385, 467-73. Horace Walpole now referred to him as "my former Black freind Peter" (32,735, fol. 489).

In addition to Scrope, who served until 1752, there were three outstanding secretaries in this period: James West, Nicholas Hardinge, and Samuel Martin. They helped to enhance the reputation of an office already considered one of the most responsible and desirable in the gift of the ministers. West and Martin, a remarkable team, contributed unstintingly of time and energy in the later and victorious years of the war.[50] Since the secretaries handled many kinds of colonial business, they were to a great extent responsible for the character of treasury administration of colonial policies.

Like Walpole, Henry Pelham and Newcastle kept payments from the civil list for colonial purposes to a minimum.[51] There were rare examples of payments for secret service in America, compensation to former prisoners of war, rewards for those who brought early news of American battles, and a grant to Dr. Mitchell for his controversial map of North America.[52] Those who wished to establish an American episcopate in America evidently continued their campaign, but again without success.[53]

Unlike expenditures from the civil list, those from the public funds continued to expand at an alarming rate, much of the ex-

50. The names and dates of the various secretaries: John Scrope, to 21 Apr. 1752; Henry Bilson Legge, 30 Apr. 1741–15 July 1742; Henry Furnese, 15 July 1742–30 Nov. 1742; John Jeffreys, 30 Nov. 1742–1 May 1746; James West, 1 May 1746–18 Nov. 1756, 5 July 1757–29 May 1762; Nicholas Hardinge, 22 Apr. 1752–9 Apr. 1758; Samuel Martin, 18 Nov. 1756–30 Apr. 1757, 31 May 1758–18 Apr. 1763.

51. From Nov. 1742 the salary of the Bermuda governor was paid from the four-and-a-half per cent instead of the civil list, but the attorney general of New York continued to receive his salary from the latter (*CTB & P*, 1742-45, p. 91; T52:50, pp. 255-56).

52. The original of the map is in PRO (MR 634), inscribed to the Earl of Halifax and other members of the Board of Trade. Hardwicke was alarmed when he first learned the map was to be published, for the ministers were then (Feb. 1755) thinking of a compromise with France and the map represented the extent of English possessions as greater than any he had seen (Add. MSS 32,852, fol. 505).

53. Sheffield City Library, Wentworth-Woodhouse Muniments, Rockingham Papers, American 7, "Present State of the Church of England in America, 1764." *APC, Col., 4,* 100.

pansion resulting from the war in America as the Administration departed farther and farther from the ideal of self-supporting colonies. Financial planning became essential. For their own use or for that of the First Lord, the secretaries prepared a kind of general budget, showing available funds, money promised and not paid, a digest of expenses for the current year, necessary expenditures for the following year, new taxes to be proposed, the rate of interest to be offered on loans, and so forth.[54]

Service estimates for a particular year, as we have seen, covered only part of the funds eventually provided. As far as possible, however, the Treasury insisted that the various armed services should be systematic in their plans.[55]

In handling finances for the campaigns of this period the Treasury had to make decisions that were not essentially different from those made by Walpole. The increasingly critical nature of the struggle, especially during the Seven Years' War, gave urgency and weight to old problems. The primary question for the Treasury was how to assure the army in America a steady flow of funds. The First Lord of the Treasury was in a delicate situation in this respect. If he failed to provide adequate resources, he would be answerable in the Cabinet and ultimately in Parliament. On the other hand, any error in judgment that resulted in loss or waste would result in embarrassing investigations in the House of Commons. Newcastle, who was in terror of such investigations, tended to err on the side of caution and economy, although he had previously harassed his brother by what seemed to the latter extravagant demands.

During Pelham's administration the most common method of supplying the forces with cash was to authorize certain officers to draw bills of exchange which, on warrant from the Treasury, were accepted by the appropriate government agency in London, usu-

54. Add. MSS 32,998, fols. 158 ff., 162 ff.; 33,040, fols. 336 ff.

55. Objections to Admiralty's asking for supplementary appropriations, T29:31, pp. 339-40, 359; demand that the Secretary at War should present estimates for new establishments in advance of raising the forces (T29:30, pp. 64, 170-93).

ally the Ordnance Office or the Paymaster General. Officers drawing such bills were accountable in the Exchequer. This method
was satisfactory if the rate of exchange was favorable and if, when
the bills reached England, there was no question as to the authority
of the drawer or the legitimacy of the service. If the bills were not
accepted, they had to be returned to America; and if they were
later accepted for payment, there was an extra charge for the re-
exchange. Pelham's immediate predecessor at the Treasury refused
to accept Oglethorpe's bills because there was no money appropriated for this express purpose, thereby risking the credit of the army.
Before Parliament could grant the necessary funds, the bills were
returned to America.[56]

Whenever or wherever there was likely to be a shortage of specie
in America, the Treasury resorted to the contract method. Pelham
found this system desirable at such remote points as Louisburg and
Nova Scotia.[57] He also approved the appointment of a deputy
paymaster to reside in Nova Scotia to facilitate the handling of
funds.[58] Nevertheless, it was still difficult to assure payment at such
great distances from London.

Throughout the French and Indian War Newcastle relied chiefly
on contractors. Commanders might still resort to drawing bills on
the Treasury or other appropriate offices, for the power to draw
bills in emergencies was "incidental to the Commission and authority of a Commander-in-Chief."[59]

The responsibility of the Treasury did not end with the signing
of a contract. On the contrary, it advised the contractors as to
whether their agents in the colonies could rely upon raising money
there by bills of exchange drawn on their London superiors or

56. T29:29, pp. 314, 325, 332, 375, 378; T29:30, p. 24.
57. Ibid., pp. 197, 238.
58. T29:31, p. 359.
59. T29:33, p. 94. In 1760 the Navy, which did not take orders from the
Treasury in these matters, returned bills drawn by Amherst for the cost of
transporting cattle up the St. Lawrence (T1:400, 21 Apr.), although it was
a legitimate charge. The Treasury designated a particular clerk to handle
bills coming to that office (T1:396, 20 Oct. 1759).

would require specie shipped from England, and in the latter case
how much should be sent.[60] If specie were required, the Treasury
tried to arrange for safe transportation and for its transfer from
deputy paymasters—who received it from the contractors' agents in
America—to the army, wherever it might be located. The last step
became most difficult as the army advanced through virgin territory
and farther from the port towns where the deputy paymasters were
located.[61]

General Braddock's experiences illustrate the dependence of the
army on the judgment and efficiency of the Treasury, and the misfortunes that might result from defects in methods of financing the
king's forces. Late in 1754, after some investigation, the Treasury
decided on a contract with Thomlinson and Hanbury. The contractors were to purchase gold and silver in either America or England and deliver it to the deputy paymasters then stationed at Williamsburg and Boston.[62] Although the personnel of the firm
changed, the terms of the contract remained fundamentally the
same throughout the war.[63]

Braddock had scarcely arrived in America in the spring of 1755
when he discovered that these plans for financing the army were
inadequate. In the first place he was short of small coined silver.[64]

60. Factors in the decision included the plan of the campaign, letters from
commanders to the Secretary at War and sometimes directly to the Treasury,
memorials of the Secretary at War to the Paymaster General and the latter's
request of the Treasury, and letters from the contractors' agents in America.

61. In 1756 the Treasury made elaborate arrangements for the army in
New York. Two deputies were to have headquarters in New York, but one was
to follow the army and receive orders for cash, and the other was generally
stationed in the city. They met at some half-way point for the transfer of
funds: the one with an escort from the army; the other with an escort supplied
by the governor: T52:47, pp. 321-22.

62. Although the Treasury did not advertise for bids, it received three
different proposals (T29:32, p. 252). The contractors received a commission
of 2 per cent; the Government paid for the original cost of the specie and for
its delivery (T54:36, pp. 109 ff.).

63. T54:37, pp. 79, 169.

64. The regimental paymasters had brought funds for immediate needs, but
only gold and Spanish dollars (Add. MSS 32,853, fols. 388-89).

Furthermore, the colonies had failed to establish the hoped-for fund on which he might have drawn for contingencies.[65] And because they contributed less food than expected, Braddock was obliged to purchase provisions at very high prices. The contractors' agent could supply only £4,000; yet Braddock declared that he must have an additional £10,000 before he could move his army from Fort Cumberland.[66]

Late in June, but probably soon after learning of Braddock's needs, the Treasury directed the contractors to send £10,000 in specie to Virginia immediately.[67] There is no doubt, it came too late to answer Braddock's primary need for funds to purchase food, wagons, and other supplies; and how much the fatal results of this expedition were due to delay no one can tell.[68] Nor is it possible to estimate how much the delay was due to lack of funds: Braddock, the only one fully competent to make such an estimate, lost his life before Fort Duquesne.

As time passed and the theater of war expanded, the Treasury became accustomed to making shipments of £50,000–150,000 at a time.[69] By 1759, however, England as well as America was feeling a shortage of cash. If there was actually plenty in the colonies, as some officials believed, it was not always available where and when it was needed.[70] On June 6, 1759, for example, General Wolfe who was then planning an attack on Quebec, wrote from the army transports in the St. Lawrence River: "This is one of the first sieges per-

65. Ibid., 32,854, fols. 183-85.

66. Letters passing between Braddock and the agent (T1:361; Add. MSS 32,853, fols. 388-89).

67. T52:47, p. 154.

68. Braddock left Fort Cumberland 10 June, and the battle took place 9 July. Winthrop Sargent, *The History of an Expedition against Fort Duquesne in 1755* (Philadelphia, 1855), p. 178, wrote of the expedition being "fatally delayed" for lack of stores, and declared (p. 179) "a Fortnight's earlier arrival on the Ohio would have given victory to his arms." Stanley Pargellis, "Braddock's Defeat," *AHR, 41* (1936), 253-69, deals only with strategy.

69. T52:48, p. 453; T52:49, pp. 51, 91.

70. William Pitt, *Correspondence When Secretary of State with Colonial Governors . . .*, ed. Gertrude S. Kimball (New York, Macmillan, 1906), *1*, 196.

haps that was ever undertaken without it."[71] Like Braddock before him, Wolfe failed to survive to tell the full story of his financial plight.

At home, Pitt was charging Newcastle with responsibility for the shortage of funds in America.[72] Newcastle in one of his most pessimistic moods expected to see both Bank and Exchequer close.[73] Victories were soon to bring money out of hiding, the Treasury would give the contractors more discretion with regard to remitting specie,[74] and for these or other reasons shortages never seemed so acute as they had in the summer of 1759. Nevertheless, officers often had to improvise methods of raising funds in an emergency, borrowing from colonial governments or even from ships' officers.[75]

Related to the basic task of supplying the army with funds were questions of policy settled at the Treasury or in consultation between treasury and other officials, such as the rate at which money should be issued to the soldiers on service in the colonies, and whether the English Government should assume the cost of recruiting or expect the colonial assemblies to accept this charge. After experimenting with variations in rates, the Treasury in 1757 settled on the standard ratio of 4s. 8d. to the dollar for all His Majesty's forces in America.[76]

71. T1:389, to Pitt.
72. Add. MSS 32,891, fol. 401b.
73. Ibid., 32,888, fol. 275.
74. T29:33, p. 243.
75. General Stanwix borrowed of Pennsylvania (Pitt, *Correspondence, 2,* 130-31, 135). General Monckton borrowed from officers on the ships, and General Murray threatened to issue paper money in Quebec (ibid., pp. 182-83).
76. T29:32, p. 445. At Braddock's request his soldiers were paid at the rate of 4s. 9d. to the Spanish dollar (ibid., p. 254). Since the troops in Nova Scotia were paid at a different rate, he had authority to make adjustments if they came under his command. Later, on the advice of the contractors, payments were made in New England by tale with dollars rated at 4s. 8d., but in Virginia by weight with silver valued at 5s. 4½d. per ounce, and gold, £4.0.7¼ (ibid., p. 276). The establishment of a fair standard involved fluctuations in the ratio of gold to silver (Stanley Pargellis, *Lord Loudoun in North America,* New Haven, Yale Univ. Press, 1933, p. 285; "Observations on the Value and Rate of Gold and Silver to Be Provided," in *Military Affairs in North America,* ed. Stanley Pargellis, New York, Appleton-Century, 1936, pp. 245-48).

Although the Government hoped that the colonies would bear the expenses of American recruiting for the regular army as well as for provincial troops, there was too much uncertainty about their cooperation to rely on them completely. At the beginning of the French and Indian War both Shirley and Braddock received secret instructions to draw on the Paymaster General for levy money if necessary.[77] The Treasury made its own interpretation of necessity, however, accepting Braddock's but refusing Shirley's drafts for this purpose.[78] Loudoun later complained that his instructions to issue funds to the troops only according to lists of effective men interfered with recruiting, presumably because this requirement tended to eliminate the noneffective fund traditionally used for filling the ranks of established regiments.[79] During the later years of the war there was little recruiting in America for the regular army. The cost of recruiting at home was, of course, borne by the British Exchequer.[80]

Comparable in many respects to the business of supplying the army with funds was the task of seeing that it was fed. During Pelham's administration there were no extensive American campaigns by British regulars, and problems of victualing were not so grave as in later years. When he came into office there were several contracts in force for the supply of garrisons or troops on the frontiers. In making new ones he consulted the Comptrollers of the Accounts of the Army.[81] Although he did not advertise for bids, he avoided parliamentary censure.

In helping to plan for Braddock's expedition the Treasury, fol-

77. T29:32, p. 273. *Military Affairs,* p. 53.

78. T27:27, p. 174. Another reason for refusing Shirley's was the argument that Braddock should have drawn these warrants.

79. T1:365, extracts of letters to Henry Fox from Albany, Aug. 1756. A royal warrant of 1745, following an address of the House of Commons, required proofs of complete musters, thus checking use of the noneffective fund (Stock, 5, 213; T52:43, pp. 207-9). In 1758 the warrant was suspended for the duration, because officers wished their pay before going to America (T52:49, pp. 154-55).

80. Pargellis, *Lord Loudoun,* has a chapter on recruiting.

81. T29:30, p. 197.

lowing the advice of the Duke of Cumberland—which was contrary to Newcastle's judgment—relied on the colonies for food supplies.[82] Braddock's experiences were discouraging, for the lack of provisions contributed to the delay at Fort Cumberland.[83] Shirley made his own arrangements with provision merchants. In neither of these instances, therefore, was the Treasury immediately responsible for the unsatisfactory results.

During the later years of the war the Treasury concluded provision contracts in England for at least the major part of the supplies. The early rate of 6d. per man per day seemed to the Treasury an exorbitant price, but this covered the risks of transportation. When the Treasury assumed these risks, the contractors were willing to furnish food at 4¾d. per man.[84]

A question of great importance for the morale of the soldier on one hand and the cost to the Exchequer on the other was whether there should be a deduction from the soldier's pay toward the cost of his food. During the War of the Austrian Succession it was usual to deduct 4d. per man per day, and for the public to pay the balance.[85] Between the wars the public assumed the full cost of provisions for the regiments in Nova Scotia,[86] and this continued to be the practice for the regular army during the French and Indian War.[87]

The Treasury kept the contractors informed of the number of men to be victualed, arranged for the convoy of ships, and dealt with the problem of impressment from the provision ships. The secretaries corresponded constantly with commanders in America

---

82. Add. MSS 32,737, fols. 101-3; 32,995, fol. 238. *Military Affairs*, pp. 35, 48.

83. Sargent, *The History of an Expedition*, pp. 287, 291.

84. T54:37, pp. 322 ff. Under these later contracts the contractors also supplied fresh provisions, although Loudoun had obtained his own.

85. Stock, *5*, 240, for example. But in 1745 the Treasury made the extraordinary allowance of 1d. for liquor in the northern regions (T29:30, pp. 195-96).

86. Stock, *5*, 410, passim.

87. T29:32, p. 254; Add. MSS 32,996, fols. 365 ff.

with regard to the effectiveness of the contract.[88] Deficiencies might occur because of seizures by the enemy, loss due to storms, or errors in judgment. In any case the Treasury bore the brunt of complaints.

In 1757, when Newcastle was temporarily out of office, his enemies called for a committee to investigate his provision contracts.[89] He escaped unscathed. In 1760 there was sharp criticism because at one time scarcity prevailed in Quebec while food was spoiling in Guadeloupe and yet, a short time later, as it was said, Quebec had ten times as much as would be required in a year.[90] Before Pitt left office he threatened to investigate the commissariat, calling it "the Occasion of all . . . [their] Misfortunes."[91] Nevertheless, unsatisfactory as the victualing may have been at times, results were reasonably satisfactory.

Another major function of the Treasury grew out of the practice of reimbursing the colonial governments for their military expenditures. Under Pelham the Treasury relied upon the Board of Trade, sometimes in consultation with the Secretary at War and the Paymaster General, to examine and verify colonial accounts.[92] Commanders who had served in America often gave assistance. With such help John Pownall, secretary to the Board of Trade, prepared the accounts of the proposed Canadian Expedition of 1746, presented to Parliament in 1750.[93] In 1756 Newcastle also relied upon the Board of Trade to make the final allotments from the first grant during the period of the Seven Years' War.[94]

Beginning with the grant of 1757, however, the secretaries to

---

88. And the Treasury, of course, supervised the settlement of accounts. Having required a security bond from the contractors, it canceled this when the contract was terminated, the accounts were audited, and the contractors had received their quietus (T29:32, p. 371, for example).

89. *CJ, 27,* 706. Add. MSS 35,909, fols. 241-45, 258.

90. T1:401. GD 8:66, West to Pitt, 2 Sept.

91. Add. MSS 32,992, fol. 15.

92. Stock, *5,* 266.

93. T29:31, p. 183. GD 8:231; T64:44, volume of accounts. Shirley had been unable to settle them in America (HEH, HM 9717).

94. T27:27, p. 194; T29:32, pp. 370, 372.

the Treasury negotiated colonial claims directly with the colonial agents. For this purpose agents had to be properly accredited by the colonial governments and furnish security.[95] When accounts had been approved and money was available for the purpose, the Treasury usually directed the Paymaster General to issue the proper amounts to the agents. In 1756, however, the Treasury decided to have the contractors send specie to the respective governors, who gave security for its safety until disposed of by the assembly. This time payments were made promptly, and the Treasury soon heard from the governors that they had received the funds.[96]

The colonies suffered many disappointments in connection with these appropriations: in some cases because their claims were disallowed; in others because of delay in making the promised payments. When Pownall settled the accounts for 1746, he noted that Rhode Island was actually in the Crown's debt because of an earlier overpayment.[97] He also disallowed accounts of Maryland and Pennsylvania for what seemed arbitrary reasons. In 1753, however, Maryland secured replacement of arms she had supplied.[98] Rhode Island never lost her sense of injury at the way the Treasury handled her claims for provisions furnished for the campaign of 1756. The accounts arrived too late for consideration, so it was said, and the agent tried in vain to obtain compensation.[99]

As frustrating as the failure to have their claims allowed was the delay that often followed the promise of payment. Prolonged investigations or the lack of available funds in the Exchequer might be understood. The latter was the case in 1760 when the Treasury

95. During the first war Massachusetts had two agents whom the Treasury finally permitted to act jointly. In the later war it recognized Abercromby as agent for Virginia, though he was chosen only by the assembly; and in the case of North Carolina it divided the grants between the two claimants, of whom Abercromby was one.

96. T1:367; T29:32, p. 419.

97. T64:44; T29:31, p. 214.

98. Stock, *5*, 574. Earlier treasury objection, T29:32, p. 118.

99. Index 4626, p. 49. Gertrude S. Kimball, ed., *Correspondence of the Colonial Governors of Rhode Island* (Boston, Houghton Mifflin, 1902–03), *2*, 297-98 n.

suggested that the agents might invest their credit in the public loan and be assured interest.[100] The colonists, however, might seem to have a just cause of complaint when the Treasury authorized the Paymaster General to use funds ear-marked for reimbursement for what seemed to him more pressing needs.[101]

Still more arbitrary from the point of view of the colonies was the administration requirement in 1748 that the royal provinces should redeem their paper currency as a condition of reimbursement.[102] Such annoyances, resulting from the way in which the Treasury handled these parliamentary grants, offset much of the good will that might otherwise have accrued to the Government as a result of the policy of reimbursement.

The regular establishment of Nova Scotia and Georgia under parliamentary grants imposed additional responsibilities on the Treasury as well as on the Board of Trade. The latter drew up detailed plans for encouraging settlement in Nova Scotia and supervised their execution. On the other hand, in all financial respects the Board was subject to the final authority of the Treasury. Moreover, the latter made certain business arrangements. For example, the Board estimated the tools that would be required by the settlers; the Treasury directed the agent to purchase them and ordered the issue of funds for the purpose.[103] The Treasury also made contracts for the subsistence of the early settlers, referring terms to the Board for its opinion.[104] After 1752 the Governor, who had incurred expenses beyond the sum appropriated, was obliged to send plans for fortifications to the Treasury as well as to the Board.[105] The Board drew up the annual estimates, but subject to

100. Kimball, 2, 303.

101. Add. MSS 32,927, fol. 205, state of public cash, 25 Aug. 1761. Abercromby thought the whole Cabinet made the decision (Virginia State Library, Letter Book, p. 131).

102. T29:31, p. 150, a decision made at the request of merchants trading to Rhode Island.

103. Ibid., pp. 188-92; T52:44, pp. 558-62.

104. T29:31, p. 350.

105. Labaree, *Royal Instructions, 1*, 413.

treasury approval. Before answering a request for funds, the Treasury expected the Board to pass upon its propriety.[106]

The unusual status of these provinces gave rise to a new type of colonial agent, appointed by patent under the royal sign manual, countersigned by the Treasury, and paid from public funds.[107] At the outset the Treasury accepted the recommendations of the Board of Trade for appointments to both agencies.[108] The agents received and dispersed funds appropriated for their respective provinces, and were accountable according to the forms of the Exchequer. They were subject to instructions from both the Treasury and the Board of Trade.

One might suppose that the new and increased financial burdens discussed above in connection with both parliamentary grants and the administrative functions of the Treasury would have led to serious attempts to increase colonial revenues, especially those that would have augmented public funds. Pelham and Newcastle might have avoided new taxes and yet have improved the administration of the customs, but no significant changes occurred until 1758. Both brothers, not reformers or innovators by nature, followed closely in the Walpole tradition.

In spite of the continued spread of population, only five places were added to the customs establishment during this period, aside from those in the new provinces and the territories acquired from France.[109] Customs officers in the conquered islands were placed on the establishment, although the Treasury hoped that they might eventually be paid from the four-and-a-half per cent.[110]

Pelham and Newcastle reacted in characteristically different ways

106. T29:31, p. 378.

107. The commission for Corbyn Morris, an earlier agent for both Newfoundland and Nova Scotia, had been countersigned by the Secretary of State, and he was paid from crown funds (T52:43, pp. 270-1). He continued to hold the agency for Newfoundland. The agent for the Georgia trustees had given security at the Treasury for the public funds which he received (T54:34, p. 306).

108. T27:26, p. 453; T29:32, p. 90.

109. A careful survey by officers from London preceded the establishment of officers in Quebec and Montreal (T11:26, p. 326).

110. T11:27, pp. 188-89.

to the opportunities for patronage in the colonial customs: the former left nominations to the Customs Commissioners, while the latter took the initiative himself.[111] But both granted numerous leaves without suspension of salaries, and renewed them repeatedly, to the certain detriment of the service. Neither Pelham nor Newcastle was inclined to give serious attention to charges of fraud;[112] charges following an inspection of the West Indies, for example, had no results.[113]

By 1758 conditions, especially in New England, had become so notorious that they could no longer be ignored. In that year the Treasury returned to the Customs Commissioners responsibility for granting leaves, and directed them to suspend salaries unless they received a specific order to the contrary.[114] In the same year it gave directions for investigating conditions in Boston and other New England ports. In response, the Commissioners listed three main forms of illegal trade: importing rum and molasses from the French islands; direct trade between Europe and North America; and supplying the French colonies with provisions in spite of war. They suggested that high duties on molasses were the cause of smuggling, yet they questioned the expediency of changing the Molasses Act because it had been passed at the request of the sugar islands.[115] They urged their officers in America, however, to be more strict in their examination of ships' papers and cargo. If their diagnosis was correct, it was clear that revolutionary reforms would be required to eliminate illegal trade.

The midst of war was hardly the time for major changes which might have aroused American resentment; nor was Newcastle the

111. T11, passim. Add. MSS 32,886, 32,894, 32,897, 32,909, 32,992, 34,728, various letters on patronage.

112. From 1739 the Board of Trade had made numerous complaints about New England (T1:392, 10 May 1759).

113. T11:22, 23, passim. William Paterson, surveyor general in the West Indies, who held his office in trust for the poet, James Thomson, was protected by George Lyttelton, Thomson's patron (HEH, H. Grenville Correspondence, Box 1, 30 Apr. 1748; GD 8:34, 3 Sept. 1748).

114. T29:33, p. 16.

115. They also commented on the difficulty of securing impartial verdicts on overdue bonds in the regular courts (T1:392, 10 May 1759).

man to undertake them. Nevertheless, the Government did enlist the armed services in an attempt to reduce trade with the French. The navy seized vessels engaged in this trade, and the army gave information on which customs officers could base prosecutions.[116] Late in 1761 the Customs Commissioners recommended dismissal of the Boston collector, whose reputation was very unsavory, thus indicating their intention to discipline those conniving at fraud.[117] Newcastle's career was fast approaching its end, however. The reform of the colonial customs system awaited a more favorable moment and a more aggressive First Lord of the Treasury.

Nevertheless, the customs receipts were already showing the effects of attempts at reform. The year 1758 was the first in which there was a deposit in the Exchequer from the duty on molasses.[118] In 1760 were the first deposits under the separate head of fines and forfeitures.[119] Deposits from the duty on enumerated commodities varied but were seldom as much as £2,000.[120]

As for the American post office, the British authorities had probably abandoned hope for a revenue from this source. Nevertheless, thanks to a growing population and competent management, accounts were beginning to show a surplus both on the mainland and in Jamaica, and at the end of this period the deputy postmasters general were able to make small remittances to the receiver general in England.[121]

In 1753 Benjamin Franklin and William Hunter received com-

116. George Louis Beer, *British Colonial Policy, 1754–65* (New York, Macmillan, 1922), chap. 6, for discussion of subject.

117. T1:408, 18 Nov. 1761.

118. AO 1:817:1062. The sum of £10,000 was larger than in later years and was probably the accumulation of several. In 1733–50, £5,603 was collected but evidently not deposited in the Exchequer (CO 5:38, appendix 4). Receipts were customarily used for expenses in the ports.

119. Shelburne, *104*.

120. Ibid.

121. £494.4.8, balance to 10 Aug. 1761 (Albert H. Smyth, ed., *The Life and Writings of Benjamin Franklin*, New York, Macmillan, 1905–07, *10*, 175). According to the accounts of the receiver general, he received £277.11.6 from Franklin and £43.10.0 from Dismore in Jamaica during the year ending 5 Apr. 1764, but for the period of the late King—that is, before 25 Oct. 1760 (AO 1:99:1977).

missions as joint deputies for the Continent, with a yearly allowance of £600 from the profits.[122] Franklin had had considerable experience in the post office, having been postmaster at Philadelphia and also comptroller for the whole system.[123] Acting under their new authority the deputy postmasters general now made an extensive tour of inspection, improved the service, and increased the revenue. Their jurisdiction extended from New Hampshire to Georgia and included twelve subordinate offices for which they enjoyed the patronage.[124] Following the conquest of Canada, plans were made to extend the service to that territory.

On the declaration of war by France in 1744, the Cabinet recommended a renewal of the packet system to the colonies.[125] After some delay the Treasury agreed to the establishment of a packet system for the West Indies, discontinuing it as soon as the war ended, for the income had been only a fraction of the expense.[126] In 1755, soon after the news of Braddock's defeat had been received, the Treasury responded to demands for a packet system which for the first time would include direct sailings to New York, although the Postmaster General could hold out little expectation of a profit.[127] In 1761 he appointed an agent to reside in New York.[128] As expected, the packet system was not self-supporting.[129]

122. GPO, Orders of the Board, 1737–71, p. 180. In 1761 following the death of Hunter, John Foxcroft became joint deputy (ibid., p. 26). Earlier incumbents in this period were Head Lynch, 1739–43, and Elliot Benger, 1743–53: Butler, *Doctor Franklin* (above, p. 63, n. 85), p. 34. There is little evidence of their having exercised authority in the Islands, but Edward Dismore indicated that his predecessor in Jamaica had received his commission from the deputy on the Continent (Add. MSS 35,639, fol. 202). What little connection there had been was broken in 1753.

123. Butler, p. 37.

124. *Colonial Records of Pennsylvania* (Harrisburg, 1852–53), 7, 447. Franklin named three of his relatives (Butler, p. 48).

125. Add. MSS 33,004, fols. 81-82.

126. T29:30, p. 174; T54:34, pp. 321-23. AO 3:797.

127. T29:32, p. 346; T27:27, p. 179; T1:361, 25 Sept. 1755; T54:36, pp. 230-31.

128. GPO, Commission Book, p. 25.

129. As George III was guaranteed a definite sum for his civil list, he had no personal concern with the financial results of the postal system. Reasons for deficits included franks and lack of extensive patronage by merchants.

With some exceptions conditions in the period were as unfavorable for the receipt of crown revenues as for those imposed by Parliament. In the first place, Horace Walpole, auditor general, had lost his early, keen interest in his office. Peter Leheup, who had ceased to act as his deputy, continued to handle plantation papers as long as he remained at the Treasury, and he interfered in Walpole's business with seeming malice and unfortunate results.[130]

On Walpole's death in 1757 Robert Cholmondeley succeeded to the office of auditor general.[131] Cholmondeley had had no experience in government or acquaintance with the colonies, and he had little to recommend him for this position. On the other hand, he appointed as deputy James Abercromby, who had held office in America and was author of a penetrating study of the colonies with special consideration of the revenue.[132] Cholmondeley or his deputy made several suggestions for reform; but the Treasury showed little confidence in them or their proposals. The prestige of the office appeared to decline.

As far as the treasury officials themselves were concerned, the demands of the wars left little time for special attention to the crown revenues. But most detrimental to the revenue were lax administrative practices, attributable primarily to the First Lord. The system of patronage led to an increase in sinecures and to the reten-

130. For example, he withheld from his superiors Walpole's recommendation for a new receiver for the Leeward Islands, writing to Charles Dunbar, whose accounts were in a bad state, not to worry about them or a successor, since he did not expect Walpole to live long (T1:333, 7 July 1748). Robert Pennant was the London deputy, 1742–46, and was succeeded by Robert Smith (T54:34, pp. 69, 356).

131. The Earl of Cholmondeley had held the reversion of the office. In 1751 the King granted it to the surviving grandson (T54:45, pp. 426, 465).

132. There are original copies of Abercromby's manuscript in the Pennsylvania Archives in Harrisburg, HEH, and WLC. An abstract with some variations under the title "Memorial of James Abercromby to the Lords of Trade," is in T98:3. Horace Walpole spoke very highly of the manuscript and the author (Add. MSS 32,735, fol. 489). In 1754 Abercromby succeeded Leheup as agent for Virginia.

tion in office of men who were notoriously unfit.[133] There were almost no crown revenue officers on whom the Treasury could rely, and information on which it might have based decisions was seldom available. Cholmondeley proposed new instructions for receivers on the mainland; but the Treasury evidently did not trust his judgment, and after consulting the Board of Trade, which refused an official opinion, did nothing.[134] Henry McCulloh had returned from his inspection of the Carolinas and was probably available for consultation, but the Treasury had come to doubt the value of his inspection and showed no disposition to use the information which he must have had.[135] Lacking an over-all policy for improvement, the Treasury contented itself with specific remedies for a few particular ills. For example, it authorized the Carolina sheriffs to collect the quit rents, as was the practice in Virginia; and it separated the collection of crown dues in New York from the receipt of the customs.

Following Walpole's policies, the Pelhams discouraged the use of crown revenues for the colonial governments, in order that there might be a larger sum for the King's use. It seems inconsistent that at the same time that Parliament was voting funds to reimburse the colonial assemblies for their outlays, the receiver general of crown revenues in Virginia was under orders to remit from £6,000 to £7,000 a year to the King.[136] A sum nearly three times this amount

133. Henry Pelham made his personal secretary, John Roberts, joint receiver of Virginia (T64:216, p. 210). Charles Dunbar kept his office in the Leeward Islands, though inefficient and deceitful (T1:332, correspondence between Walpole and Dunbar over latter's accounts). A deputy receiver in Jamaica, probably underpaid, embezzled £20,000 (T29:32, p. 213; T1:358, letter from Gov. Knowles).

134. *N.J. Arch.*, Ser. 1, *9*, 289, 295-99, proposed instructions. T27:28, p. 201; T1:413, 23 Sept. 1761. John Pownall, secretary of the Board, thought the instructions might conflict with law. Cholmondeley wished to include in the new instructions copies of those sent to the casual receivers in 1721, giving them authority to receive fines and forfeitures for illegal trade.

135. T1:323, fol. 89, Horace Walpole's comments. McCulloh claimed large rewards. He was eventually successful, though not satisfied (*APC, Col., 4,* p. 262).

136. T52:42 ff., passim.

was derived from the four-and-a-half per cent.[137] Samuel Martin alarmed Newcastle with his opinion that the King could not legally use the surplus of this revenue because in Queen Anne's reign Parliament had excepted it from the civil list. Hardwicke and the Solicitor General both reassured him, and the practice continued.[138]

As usual, the ordinary branches of the casual revenue were comparatively insignificant,[139] although His Majesty's share of prizes taken before the declaration of war against France in 1756 amounted to a considerable sum. Many of these prizes originated in American waters.[140] A commission was appointed for the express purpose of securing and selling prizes taken in this period, and receiving and accounting for the proceeds.[141] Since prizes taken after the declaration of war became the property of the captors, the business of the commission was brief but controversial, causing numerous problems for the Treasury, to which the commission was responsible.

After some objections on the part of the Treasury, Cholmondeley, supported by the Attorney General, established his right to

137. T1:469, report for 1752–60, shows payments of £101,314.8.0 from latter fund for special services, and £39,220 from quit rents. Shirley's expenses for the defense of Annapolis came from the four-and-a-half per cent (*CTB & P*, 1742–45, p. 667), as well as the usual salaries.

138. Add. MSS 32,910, fols. 140, 170, 232; 33,030, fols. 469 ff. Their argument was that Parliament had not reserved this fund for the public then or in later acts.

139. In 1756 revenue collected in the Leeward Islands was used for barracks (T29:32, p. 414; T52:43, p. 69). In 1761 the surplus in Barbados went to the Treasury for the king's use (T29:34, pp. 104, 128).

140. In the earlier wars of this period there was no reservation of the king's share in provisions for distribution. Horace Walpole, therefore, never benefited from his right to audit prizes taken in America.

141. T52:47, pp. 637-39, including order to deposit funds in the Bank of England.

audit the accounts of prizes condemned in American courts.[142] Because the Commissioners lacked the power to prosecute commanders who had prize money in their possession, Cholmondeley undertook this business.[143] During the years 1760—62 he prepared statements of several prize accounts for the examination of the Treasury and received a warrant to determine them.[144] Such prompt action is in marked contrast to the long delays in auditing accounts of prizes taken in Queen Anne's reign.[145]

In 1761 the Commissioners were able to lend the public £630,000 from the prize revenue.[146] At the conclusion of the war the King followed precedent in transferring all proceeds to the public.[147]

For the most part the new problems connected with the collection of revenue in the conquered territories remained to be settled after the peace. But the case of Guadeloupe, returned to France by the peace of 1763, was an exception. The importance of this island in official thinking was illustrated by the attention given to the possibilities of crown revenue here. The Treasury named a receiver for the island and later approved Cholmondeley's appointment of a deputy auditor.[148] Many years of controversy followed, however,

---

142. T27:27, p. 369. He also made good his claim to a commission of 5 per cent and to collect it on the gross sums accounted for (T29:33, p. 264; T54:37, pp. 351-52; T1:407, 15 July 1761, legal opinion). In 1756 the High Court of Admiralty received authority under the great seal to try prize cases and to extend similar authority to admiralty courts in the plantations (PC 2:105, p. 180).

143. T29:34, p. 101; T1:447, Information and Answer in case of Admiral Cotes.

144. T54:37, pp. 399, 428-36; T54:39, p. 4. No provision was made for declaration before the Chancellor of the Exchequer, and no evidence has been found that this was done. On the other hand, the Commissioners' account of prizes brought into ports of the Kingdom were audited by the auditors of the imprests according to the regular procedure of the Exchequer (AO 1:-482:1820).

145. They were declared in 1755 (T52:47, p. 70; E351:2539).

146. T52:52, p. 131. There were also loans in earlier years (T52:50, 51).

147. *CJ, 29,* 669. By 1790 the total income amounted to over £700,000 ("Return of Public Income," 1868—69, Pt. I, p. 144, passim).

148. T52:50, p. 53; T54:37, p. 333.

before Cholmondeley in 1767 received permission to audit these accounts without a formal adjudication of his rights.[149] The receipts consisted mainly of duties previously owed to the French king.[150]

During the war the home government considered it indiscreet to press the colonies for grants of permanent revenue.[151] Jamaica and Virginia continued to be the only provinces with significant permanent grants. The Crown exercised its right to decide the use of the two shillings a hogshead in directing Virginia to repay from this fund the loan made by the English government early in the war. Virginia protested, and asked that the sum should be taken from the quit rents.[152] The Privy Council referred the petition to its committee, where it seems to have been buried,[153] although Virginia's grievance lived on.

As for the annual grants of the assemblies, no government office in England had accounts of such funds. In 1754 Horace Walpole acknowledged that the receipt, examination, and audit of these revenues had long ago passed out of the hands of officers of the Crown.[154] A year later the Board of Trade, in reporting on a Massachusetts law, described the method of raising taxes as "a Matter of Provincial Oeconomy, of which the Representatives of the People are the Competent Judges."[155] It is clear, therefore, that the home government not only made no progress in regaining control of these funds, but appeared resigned to the situation. At the conclusion of a war which left the English Government deep in debt,

---

149. T27:28, p. 168, expression of treasury doubt; T29:39, p. 30, 17 Nov. 1767.

150. Collections of £19,481.4.0 were paid in part to the Duke of Gloucester and part to persons for special service (T1:469, 1761—69).

151. Case of New York, PC 2:105, pp. 31, 50. In 1754 the Governor of Bermuda received permission to ignore the usual requirements for the issue of funds (*APC, Col., 4,* 230-31).

152. T1:361, 11 June 1755.

153. PC 2:104, p. 508.

154. Add. MSS 32,735, fols. 487-88.

155. *APC, Col., 4,* 295.

it was plain that no relief could be expected from the colonial assemblies.

When Newcastle left office in 1762 there came to a close a period of roughly twenty years marked by important changes in the role of the Treasury in colonial administration. As far as possible, however, the Pelhams had followed examples set by Walpole, continuing to assert the authority of the Treasury within the Government but avoiding controversy with the colonies. Changes had come about largely through the accident of war.

The fact that the ancient feud with France came to a head during the administrations of the Pelhams and that an important phase was fought out in the backwoods of America gave a special character to this period. As we have seen, the war tended to restrict the Treasury's control of financial policies, for spending large sums of money in America seemed inevitable, although contrary to long-established principle. Nevertheless, because of the necessity for administering expenditures of public funds in the colonies, because of the continued supervision of colonial revenues, and because of the political power of the First Lord, the Treasury was coming to have an unparalleled influence on relations between Great Britain and her colonies.

Compared with the years immediately following, the administrations of the Pelhams appear to be marked by a significant, negative factor. That is, in spite of numerous suggestions and provocations, the Treasury avoided resort to parliamentary taxation of the colonies for purposes of revenue. Minor colonial grievances, nevertheless, were accumulating. And the Pelhams left to their successors financial problems that would lead them to adopt the controversial and revolutionary policy of colonial taxation previously avoided.

4.

Grenville's Administration: A Turning
Point in British–American Relations

WITH NEWCASTLE'S RESIGNATION there began a new period
in the relations between Great Britain and her American colonies.
Radical changes in colonial policy produced violent reactions in
America.

The most characteristic measures of the period were incorporated
in statutes. Under the guidance of the First Lord of the Treasury,
Parliament assumed unprecedented authority in fields once dominated by the Crown or left to the colonial assemblies. This increased measure of parliamentary responsibility was to have a decisive effect upon the attitude of the colonies, to say nothing of
its influence upon the nature of the English Government.

Although George Grenville was the author or sponsor of the
colonial policies most characteristic of the period, Newcastle's immediate successor at the Treasury was the Earl of Bute, the King's
confidant and former tutor. He proved to be ill-equipped for either
political leadership or financial administration, and after less than
a year resigned in favor of Grenville.

While Bute was still head of the Government, Grenville filled in
succession two posts of cabinet rank—Secretary of State and First
Lord of the Admiralty—and was temporarily manager of the House
of Commons. During this period the Government made decisions
that either foreshadowed or influenced the policies of Grenville's
own administration.

Basic for later plans were the peace terms concluding the Seven Years' War, a subject of bitter controversy in the Cabinet. Grenville differed from Bute on these terms. The most obvious feature of the treaty as far as America was concerned was the annexation of vast territories on the mainland capable of producing little or no revenue but on the contrary requiring funds for both civil and military purposes and increasing the financial embarrassment of the Government. Grenville, apparently, would have preferred to retain Guadeloupe and St. Lucia.[1]

With respect to either trade or revenue one unfortunate result of the peace was the interruption of a profitable commerce that had developed in the neutral islands where British traders had met the French. These islands were now ceded to Great Britain and thus brought within the scope and prohibitions of English trade laws. While British forces occupied certain French islands, now returned to France, there had been opportunities for international trade that were now closed.[2] Altogether the terms of the peace had a very disturbing effect upon English trade and upon relations with the colonies.

Bute was in office too short a time to influence many of the policies relating to these new situations. During that time, however, Parliament enacted at least three new measures of considerable significance for the future of America. In spite of doubt and criticism, Parliament voted a military establishment for America that

1. William J. Smith, ed., *The Grenville Papers* (London, J. Murray, 1852–53), *1*, 493. He was said to have given up the seals rather than sign the peace terms before they were accepted by Parliament (Sheffield City Library, Rockingham, Letters 1, 13 Oct. 1762). Add. MSS 36,797, fol. 6, Bute's comments. HEH, Stowe, Box 103(c), Grenville Diplomatic Correspondence, including his own notes.

2. Add. MSS 38,200, fols. 260-64. The islands ceded to Great Britain were Dominica, St. Vincent, Tobago, Grenada, and the Grenadines. St. Lucia went to France. The British had conquered Guadeloupe and Martinique during the war and returned them to France. The most recent and thorough study of the period, still in progress, is Lawrence N. Gipson, *The British Empire before the American Revolution,* 9 vols. to date, Caldwell, Idaho, Caxton, 1936; New York, Alfred A. Knopf, 1939—.

was abnormally large for times of peace.[3] A new customs act, reported by a committee of which Grenville, then First Lord of the Admiralty, was a member, encouraged officers and seamen of ships-of-war to seize vessels engaged in smuggling by promising them shares of condemned vessels.[4] The expiring Molasses Act was renewed for only one year rather than the normal five. The Government was presumably already considering important changes. According to report, Bute also adopted the policy of making the colonies pay for the army established there.[5] He resigned in the middle of the session, however, leaving the problem of an adequate supply to his successor.

The administrative work of the Treasury was peculiarly distasteful to Bute. Yet he could place little dependence on Sir Francis Dashwood, his unfortunate choice for Chancellor of the Exchequer. Samuel Martin, who continued as secretary, and his colleague, Jeremiah Dyson, previously clerk in the House of Commons, were both able men. While there was doubt as to the political loyalty of one or more of the clerks, they would probably have served Bute well enough had he been more competent.[6] During this period the treasury staff performed routine work, but little more; and the times demanded initiative.

In spite of the unconstructive character of Bute's administration, there were evidences of a changing attitude toward America. For example, someone at the Treasury must have had defects in the American customs system in mind, for one of the secretaries wrote to the Custom House for a list of officers on leave.[7] This information was available when Grenville came to the Treasury. A new emphasis on the North American Continent, characteristic of the

---

3. Actually there were two estimates: one 25 Dec. 1762–24 Apr. 1763, and another for the remainder of the year (*CJ, 29,* 504, 506). Under the latter the number of privates and noncommissioned officers, exclusive of garrisons, was about 10,000, which remained the normal establishment for some years.

4. 3 Geo. III, c. 22.

5. Russell, *Bedford Correspondence* (above, p. 84, n. 39), *3,* 209.

6. Namier, *England in the . . . Revolution,* p. 472, for case of Milward Rowe.

7. T11:27, p. 266. Add. MSS 38,335, fol. 37.

postwar period, was evident in the continuation of the New York packet in spite of losses.[8] The West Indian run, on the other hand, was allowed to lapse temporarily.

There was no real neglect of most crown revenues. George III took a personal interest in these dues, having asked Newcastle for information before the latter left office.[9] The auditor general or his deputy kept in touch with colonial officers. And the Treasury attempted to collect dues in the conquered islands, especially those to be returned to France.[10] But there were really no long-range policies. The continued failure to decide on a revenue for Quebec proved disastrous, for the whole subject was left to the discretion of the Governor, and his decisions led to legal controversies.

Clearly the Treasury needed a strong and practiced hand. As compared with Bute, Grenville had much to recommend him for this office. Having served many years as Junior Lord under Pelham, he was familiar with treasury routine. A longer term as Treasurer of the Navy had also given him valuable financial experience. He had a reputation in this field. And judging from his own statements, he felt more at ease with moneyed men in the City than had his predecessor.[11]

Competent as far as finance was concerned, Grenville also had certain desirable personal qualities. He was a man of character and determination. He had a strong sense of duty, was better informed than many politicians of his time, and was incorruptible. On the other hand, he was extremely literal-minded and unimaginative. Ambitious, ungracious, and arrogant with regard to his own views, he intensified differences among those with whom he had to work. Even his relatives could not count on his personal loyalty if it conflicted with his own ambition.[12] Many of these characteristics affected his handling of colonial problems.

George III and Bute were not unaware of Grenville's faults, but

8. T54:39, pp. 48-52, 112-13; T29:35, p. 18.

9. Add. MSS 33,040, fols. 309, 311, 353.

10. T29:35, p. 17.

11. *Grenville Papers, 1,* 484.

12. He continued in office after the retirement of his brother, Earl Temple, and his brother-in-law, William Pitt.

among their friends at the moment there seemed to be no one else so eligible for the office of First Lord of the Treasury. It soon became evident that the King did not intend to grant him the privileges of a prime minister. Unfortunately, Grenville had never learned to play the courtier acceptably. He appeared to make demands rather than requests. He never felt that he enjoyed the King's complete favor or confidence.[13]

At first the continued influence of Bute may have affected Grenville's status adversely, but in the autumn of 1763 a combination of ministers forced the favorite to retire into the country.[14] Although Grenville's part in this measure cannot have endeared him to the King, ministerial changes in the course of the year temporarily persuaded Grenville that at last he would have the real direction of Government. Other ministers, however, were reluctant to recognize his claim to priority, and his frustration continued. At no time could he feel politically secure. Many of the faults of his administration may be ascribed to the fact that he was a man in a hurry.

Possibly because of his insecurity, Grenville's methods were comparatively formal. For example, he carried to the Privy Council a proposal for reforms in the American customs system which might have been handled through the voluntary cooperation of other departments. He normally attended meetings of the Committee on Plantation Affairs, possibly because there was no one else on whom he could rely.[15] He did not encourage the ministers to continue

13. *Grenville Papers, 3,* 142-44. He noted that he had less money for secret service than his predecessors. Bute referred to his "violence" in dealing with the King (Add. MSS 38,338, fol. 280).

14. Add. MSS 38,738, fol. 274. HEH, Stowe 7, George Grenville's Letter Books, *1,* 1 Sept. 1763. *Grenville Papers, 2,* 205. Charles Townshend's comment: "Who can hear without astonishment of Lord Bute sent into Exile by the creature of his own hand and fortune" (WLC, Townshend's Correspondence, fol. 22). Richard Pares, *King George III and the Politicians,* Oxford, Clarendon Press, 1953.

15. PC 4:2, passim. As he was not always informed as to the agenda, he occasionally missed an important session, as when certain provincial papers were put into Halifax's hands (ibid., 1 Feb. 1765). Question of fees of patentees, HEH, Stowe 7, *2,* 28 June 1765.

their convivial habit of dining together at regular intervals. It was due to the Earl of Sandwich that the practice was revived.[16]

Characteristic of a government without accepted leadership was the uncertain status of the Board of Trade. Neither Shelburne, who was First Commissioner for a few months in 1763, nor Hillsborough, his successor, could obtain a clear definition of his rights and functions.[17] As a matter of fact, the Board's powers of initiative were declining, although the development in colonial business led to an increase in the number of its reports.[18]

One might summarize the political reasons for the instability of Grenville's administration as lack of "party." Family connections formed the nucleus of most of the existing party groups; but Grenville had broken with the two most influential members of his family, Earl Temple and William Pitt, who would hardly have accepted his leadership in any case. His brother-in-law, the Earl of Egremont, who was Secretary of State at the beginning of this administration, had died in August 1763, and none of the leading ministers had any personal loyalty to Grenville. Indeed, it was perfectly clear, as Grenville rather proudly averred, that he had no party.[19]

16. The group included Halifax, the other Secretary of State, and the Duke of Bedford, President of the Council (*Grenville Papers, 2,* 256, 489; HEH, Stowe 7, 2, 16 Feb. 1765).

17. When Charles Townshend accepted the office shortly before Bute's resignation there was a rumor that he was to have the privileges accorded to Halifax (*Bedford Correspondence, 3,* 209); but the Board was limited to making reports according to the terms of reference: Stowe, Box 103(b), Grenville Diplomatic Correspondence; and Stowe 7, 2, 9 Aug. 1766. At the beginning of his term he sent the order of 1752 to the royal governors, but Shelburne hesitated to follow his example (WLC, Shelburne, *134,* fols. 17 ff., 47). Shelburne was very unhappy over the situation (Add. MSS 36,797, fols. 53-55). Hillsborough referred to "unexplained connections of departments in business" (*Grenville Papers, 3,* 295).

18. Arthur H. Basye, *The Lords Commissioners of Trade and Plantations, Commonly Known as the Board of Trade, 1748—82* (New Haven, Yale Univ. Press, 1925), p. 112.

19. *Grenville Papers, 2, 213.* Lewis M. Wiggin, *The Faction of Cousins* (New Haven, Yale Univ. Press, 1958), chaps. 8, 9, discusses the dissolution of the political connection of the Grenvilles.

Under the circumstances it is not surprising that there were disputes about the patronage. At the beginning of his ministry Grenville had an understanding with the secretaries of state for a division of the spoils of office. On the death of Egremont, however, Grenville asserted his right to patronage in order better to sustain his leadership in the House of Commons.[20] With the cooperation of George III he was fairly successful in making good his claim.

American places were increasing rapidly, especially on the mainland. Many of these were in the field of revenue, the natural domain of the Treasury. Strangely enough, Grenville did not use these opportunities for appointment as effectively as many of his predecessors. In a political sense his ideals handicapped him. He insisted on knowing that candidates were properly qualified. He refused to permit the sale of offices or to allow a resignation in favor of a particular candidate.[21] Given time, his high standards might have resulted in marked improvement in the civil service, but his time was short. He left office leaving many places unfilled.

The House of Commons, which Grenville hoped to control through his handling of the patronage, had been elected in 1761. There were, however, fifty-six by-elections during his tenure, in addition to those held for re-election following appointments to office.[22] These elections should have been of the utmost concern to Grenville, for on such matters as that of general warrants divisions were close enough to anger the King.[23] Yet on the subject of elections he was apathetic, even though most of his policies depended upon favorable action by the House of Commons.[24]

The actual management of the Commons was evidently a more congenial task than that of influencing elections. Grenville, as-

20. *Grenville Papers, 2,* 210, 212-13. His personal secretary, Charles Lloyd, a poor choice for the position, actually handled the patronage (Add. MSS 38,305, fol. 23).

21. HEH, Stowe 7, passim.

22. *Return of Members of Parliament,* ordered by the House of Commons to be printed 1 Mar. 1878, Pt. II, pp. 125-36.

23. *Grenville Papers, 2,* 495.

24. HEH, Stowe 7, *1,* 15, 28 June 1763, passim.

sisted by the secretaries to the Treasury, Charles Jenkinson and Thomas Whately, was assiduous in keeping in touch with the members, informing them if their votes were needed, and reassuring them when a crisis was past.[25] In spite of political difficulties, he managed to carry through Parliament a novel and revolutionary program in the field of colonial administration. His success was no doubt due partly to lack of unity in the opposition. Quite as important was the fact that his policy of "strict economy" was naturally popular, since it implied lower taxes.[26] And the unsettled state of the colonies following the war had created an expectation of legislation in this field.

Normally most of the legislation affecting the colonies dealt with some aspect of trade. The years 1764 and 1765 were no exception. Furthermore, the laws of these years incorporated many of the traditional principles of mercantilism: bounties on colonial products, reduced duties on imports from the colonies, additions to the list of enumerated articles, and modification of the laws to permit a wider trade in certain colonial items.[27] Such changes were natural. Grenville undoubtedly considered himself a mercantilist,[28] and from one point of view, attempts to improve administration of the acts of trade might have been planned merely to give greater protection to English merchants and manufacturers. Taken in context and carefully analyzed, however, the commercial regulations appear designed primarily to increase the revenue. In some cases they were actually in conflict with the best interests of the traders.

25. Ibid., Mar. 1764, Jan. 1765, passim.
26. *Grenville Papers, 2,* 45-46.
27. Add. MSS 38,337, fol. 236, "Advantages given to America in the last two years." Beer, *British Colonial Policy,* chap. 10, discussion of changes in the acts of trade.
28. In 1768 he wrote William Knox that England should take colonial products even if it were necessary to pay a higher price than would be paid for similar products from other countries, and that the colonies should be diverted from manufacturing by giving them encouragement to produce raw materials (HEH, Stowe 7, 2, 27 June 1768).

Financial conditions in England at this time gave some cause for alarm and inspired a sense of urgency in the quest for revenue.[29] Politically it seemed safer to levy a tax on the colonies than to increase those paid in England. But in addition to the practical reasons for proposing American taxes, Grenville's own theory that Parliament rather than the King alone was sovereign over the colonies explains the almost fanatical zeal with which he approached the legislative plans of his administration.[30]

The Sugar Act illustrates the decisive role of the Treasury in planning legislation. Grenville had been in office little more than a month when Jenkinson asked the Customs Board to explain why American customs receipts were so low, and to suggest a remedy. A general reply brought requests for more definite recommendations and finally for the draft of a bill.[31] At this time the Treasury was following the unusual procedure of considering legislation at regular board meetings.

Officials at the Treasury were trying to secure statistics to show what a duty on molasses might produce if smuggling were eliminated.[32] Several unknown factors complicated the problem. No one knew how much molasses was being smuggled. Furthermore, the various duties under the Molasses Act were treated as one revenue,

29. Ninetta S. Jucker, ed., *The Jenkinson Papers, 1760—66* (London, Macmillan, 1949), p. 203. The receipts from the recent, unpopular cider tax were so small that the Treasury was obliged to borrow from the sinking fund to meet the charges on the revenue act of 1763 (T53:50, p. 430). Objections to the cider tax may have strengthened the determination to raise a revenue in America (HEH, Stowe, Box 101, Grenville Political and Official Papers).

30. On various occasions Grenville indicated his preference for parliamentary control; for example, WLC, Knox Papers, 15 July 1768.

31. T11:27, pp. 282, 303; T1:426, 21 July, 16 Sept. 1763; T29:35, pp. 125-26, 135-36, 164. Add. MSS 38,202-4, passim, letters from Henry Saxby, deputy collector, London.

32. Nathaniel Ware estimated that foreign imports might amount to 23,625 hogsheads a year, and thought the 6*d.* might be collected if local duties were eliminated (HEH, Stowe Americana, Misc. File). According to another calculation a tax of 3*d.* a gallon from an estimated 80,000 hogsheads might produce £100,000 or somewhat less (T1:434). Beer, *British Colonial Policy*, p. 235, n. 1, comments on reports of governors.

and collectors paid the charges of management out of the total, so that it was impossible to tell from the accounts how much revenue was actually derived from the one article, molasses.[33] Nevertheless, treasury officials soon decided that additional items would be required in the tax bill to raise the desired revenue, and so informed the Customs Commissioners.[34]

Late in December "fair" copies of the bill, prepared by a treasury clerk with the aid of the solicitor to the Customs, were ready for examination by the treasury secretaries.[35] William Wood, the long-respected secretary to the Customs Board, was dubious about the proposals, and wished everything "might be deferred to another year, except continuing the Act of the 6th George 2nd for a year, or longer." He thought they did not have enough information on which to base the proposed changes.[36] In spite of his warning, treasury officials proceeded with their plans for introducing the bill in the House of Commons and easing its passage through its various stages.[37] It became law with little apparent opposition.

The title of the act of 1764 as well as the provisions for appropriating the money produced by the new measure strengthen the conviction that Grenville's primary object was revenue. Whereas the original Molasses Act expressed its purpose as "better securing and encouraging the Trade of His Majesty's Sugar Colonies in America," the act of 1764 was "for granting certain duties in

33. T1:462, account signed by R. Parsons, comptroller general.

34. T11:27, p. 332. An act permitting export of rice to foreign colonies on payment of the half subsidy otherwise collected in England (4 Geo. III, c. 27) was to have appropriated the duty to American services, but by mistake the clause was omitted (Add. MSS 38,337, fols. 1-3).

35. *Jenkinson Papers*, p. 245.

36. He concluded: "I was once young but am now old; yet ... [the plantations] are of such advantage to their Mother Country, their welfare is still uppermost in my thoughts" (ibid., p. 254).

37. Add. MSS 38,335, fols. 328 ff., indicate the various steps to be taken, the resolution to be moved, the instructions for the Committee of the Whole, and various subsequent motions. Whately reported the bill (*CJ, 29*, 934). The Commons refused to hear a petition against one of the clauses on the ground that it was a money bill (ibid., p. 986).

America ... for applying the produce of such duties ... towards defraying the expenses of defending, protecting, and securing the said colonies and plantations." Unlike the first Molasses Act, the new statute stipulated that the money raised under it was to be paid into the Exchequer and was to be disposed of by Parliament.[38]

The statute was complex. It included a clause for perpetuating the Molasses Act while reducing the duty from 6*d.* to 3*d.* a gallon, new duties on foreign goods imported into the colonies, additions to the list of goods taxed on export from the colonies to other than British ports, many administrative details for assuring the enforcement of this and earlier acts, and a hint of a new vice-admiralty court for all America. Criticisms following the passage of the act were as varied as the contents and came from England as well as America. Merchants in both countries were troubled by the disruption of their accustomed trading methods and annoyed by the new bonds and other papers making the payment of additional fees necessary.[39] The broadest and most ominous protests, however, came from colonial assemblies in Massachusetts and New York, expressing doubt as to the power of Parliament to levy duties intended for revenue.[40]

The reaction of English officials stationed in America was only a little more favorable than that expressed by other interested parties. John Temple, Surveyor General of the customs in the northern district, hoped that smuggling would soon cease, but warned that the revenue would be less than the ministers expected.[41]

38. 4 Geo. III, c. 15. According to the Attorney General the revenue under the earlier act was not to be considered unappropriated public money, but belonged to His Majesty and was subject to his disposal (Add. MSS 38,335, fol. 103).

39. HEH, Stowe, Grenville, Misc. Papers, W. Reeve to Nugent, 16 Feb. 1765; T11:27, p. 49. 4 Geo. III, c. 15 increased one difficulty by prohibiting the hovering of foreign vessels off the plantation coasts.

40. *APC, Col., 4,* 732. HEH, HM 2587.

41. He recommended lowering the duty on molasses to 2*d.* and applying it to British as well as foreign imports (HEH, Stowe Americana, Temple Correspondence, 10 Sept., 9 Dec. 1764).

Having discovered certain inadequacies in the recent act and recognizing the justice of some of the specific objections, the Treasury planned to make a few changes in the following session of Parliament.[42] Grenville trusted Jenkinson with the major responsibility for the new bill; but he depended upon Whately to find some means of satisfying those who complained of the lack of uniformity in fees. Jenkinson hoped to appease the Americans without sacrificing the principles of the earlier act. After consulting both the Board of Trade and officers at the Custom House he secured Grenville's approval for the whole draft.[43]

The new act not only granted bounties on various kinds of American lumber imported into England but extended the market for colonial lumber, iron, and rice.[44] A temporary provision regarding fees gave some satisfaction to customs officers who had complained of inequality. But merchants protested because the effect of this clause and new requirements for bonds and certificates was to increase the fees they had to pay.[45] Whately promised a more definite settlement of fees in the next session of Parliament, but by that time he was out of office. Although the title of the act of 1765 suggested that it was "to encourage American trade," it accomplished very little in that direction.

The colonists' dissatisfaction with Grenville's so-called acts of

42. Temple Correspondence, letter from Whately, 10 May 1765, and Add. MSS 38,337, fols. 1-3, outline the plan.

43. Add. MSS 38,304, fols. 135-36; 38,202, fol. 286.

44. 5 Geo. III, c. 45. For example, privilege to export rice, previously extended to Georgia and South Carolina, was now granted to North Carolina. Duties were appropriated to American defense. Small coasting vessels were exempt from the requirement of cockets, but vessels sailing "in ballast" were now required to give the molasses bond.

45. T1:486, protest. If comptrollers had had no fees, they were now allowed one-third as much as the collector. Canadian officers who had been on a salary basis interpreted the act to permit them to demand fees, too (T1:461, list of New York fees adopted at Quebec). A list of forms used in Barbados (T1:436) includes 7 kinds of bonds, 14 kinds of certificates, 6 kinds of permits, and various other papers. No one merchant would require them all, but a ship with varied cargo would require many.

trade, however, was as nothing compared to their indignation when they learned of the proposal for a stamp tax. Grenville had originally expected to make this tax a part of his program for 1764. In September of the previous year Jenkinson had instructed Thomas Cruwys, the solicitor of the Stamp Office, to consult with Henry McCulloh about a plan for a stamp act for the colonies. For several months there were consultations involving Cruwys, McCulloh, one of the commissioners of the Stamp Office, the secretaries to the Treasury, and others. Two separate drafts resulted. Unable to decide among the differing views on details, the Treasury decided to postpone the bill to the following session.[46] Whately, however, announced in the House of Commons that such a tax was a possibility for the future.[47]

Grenville gave the impression that postponement was due to a desire for further information and to allow the Americans an opportunity to make alternative suggestions.[48] He seems shortly to have developed doubts about the wisdom of consulting Americans on the question, but Jenkinson evidently thought the good faith of the Administration was involved.[49] Whately had already renewed an earlier acquaintance with John Temple for the obvious purpose of obtaining his views.[50] He also opened a correspondence

46. Among the many sources for preparation of the bill are the following: Add. MSS 35,911, fols. 18 ff., solicitor's bill for his services, giving steps in preparation; ibid., 35,910, fol. 137, list of articles to be taxed as proposed by McCulloh, and fol. 204, his preamble and clause of appropriation; T1:447, fols. 266 ff., draft based closely on the English statute; Add. MSS 35,911, fols. 15 ff., queries and remarks by the secretaries to the Treasury on the American bill with notes such as "done" or "answered."

47. *CJ, 29,* 935.

48. Edmund S. and Helen M. Morgan, *The Stamp Act Crisis* (Chapel Hill, Univ. of North Carolina Press, 1953), chap. 5, discussion of postponement; and the former in more detail, "The Postponement of the Stamp Act," *William and Mary Quarterly,* Ser. 3, 7 (July 1950), 353-92.

49. *Grenville Papers, 2,* 373.

50. Preceding Temple Correspondence, Stowe Americana, is a statement that Whately's letters were "written by the direction of the Rt. Hon: Mr. Grenville."

with Jared Ingersoll of Connecticut on the same subject, and consulted him after his arrival in London the following winter.[51] Grenville also had interviews with Americans in London, including the colonial agents.[52] In the meantime Halifax, Secretary of State, was procuring from colonial governors lists of legal documents and other items that might be taxed.[53]

In general the advice from those who knew the colonies best was discouraging. John Temple admitted that the act might raise £40,000 in his district, but warned that there would probably be that much lost in orders for English manufactures, because the colonies lacked cash.[54] McCulloh was an early advocate of the stamp tax, but on the understanding that a concurrent measure would provide a uniform system of paper currency for the colonies.[55] At a meeting of the colonial agents with Grenville, Benjamin Franklin suggested a loan office to bring in revenue and at the same time provide additional currency.[56]

In spite of criticisms and continued doubt with respect to the details of the bill, Grenville never seems to have hesitated over the principle of taxation. Like Whately he may have believed that establishing the right of Parliament to tax the colonies was the most important aspect of the measure.[57] Franklin described Grenville as "besotted with his Stamp Scheme."[58] But the Government was

---

51. T[homas] W[hately], *Letter I,* printed correspondence between Whately and Ingersoll [1766?]; Lawrence H. Gipson, *Jared Ingersoll* (New Haven, Yale Univ. Press, 1920), chap. 5.

52. "The Bowdoin and Temple Papers," Massachusetts Historical Society *Collections,* Ser. 6, *9* (Boston, 1897), 43.

53. *N.J. Arch.,* Ser. 1, *9,* 448. Replies are scattered through T1:430, 433, 434, 442. HEH, Stowe, Grenville Misc., contains a list of American newspapers and printers, 1763. Extracts from the colonial charters dealing with legislative powers may have been studied in this connection (T1:433).

54. HEH, Stowe Americana, Temple Correspondence, 10 Sept. 1764.

55. HEH, HM 1480, Townshend Papers, "General Thoughts," McCulloh to Thomas Townshend. *Grenville Papers, 2,* 374 n.

56. WLC, Franklin to Galloway, 11 Oct. 1766.

57. Temple Correspondence, 12 June 1765.

58. Franklin to Galloway, 11 Oct. 1766.

in real need of revenue. Joseph Harrison, a visitor from Boston, wrote of the bill that Grenville "did not like to hear that there should be any surmise of its not being likely to produce the sum expected."[59]

Finally, therefore, Whately's plan, as the draft had come to be known, was "approved in Conference before all the Lords of the Treasury."[60] But even after the opening of Parliament the solicitor for the Stamp Office was revising the list of taxable articles on the basis of later information from America. In spite of such careful preparation the House of Commons made other changes, both in committee and after the bill was reported. One of the last amendments extended the jurisdiction of American vice-admiralty courts to violations of this act, and laid the foundation for the establishment of several regional courts in place of one for the whole continent.[61] The bill followed the now common practice of making distinctions between the mainland and the West Indies. In this case, however, the mainland had the advantage for in several instances rates for the West Indies were higher. In its final form the act levied duties on almost every conceivable enterprise in which an American might engage.[62]

According to Jared Ingersoll, only forty members of the House of Commons were opposed to the bill, and they all had some kind of connection with America.[63] Citing a precedent of Walpole's day, the Commons refused to hear petitions against the measure.[64]

---

59. Mass. Hist. Soc., *Coll.*, Ser. 6, *9*, 43. According to Add. MSS 38,337, fol. 259, Grenville expected £80,000 to £100,000; but according to Ingersoll he expected only £40,000 to £50,000 from the stamp tax and £100,000 from all revenue measures (*Letter I*, p. 25).

60. Add. MSS 35,910, fol. 310.

61. *CJ 30*, 90-192, passim. McCulloh, who was very critical of the bill, said that when he was working on the bill with Cruwys he had eliminated the clause for vice-admiralty courts as well as others later inserted (HM 1480). Whately may have had the idea for the courts and now reverted to it.

62. 5 Geo. III, c. 12.

63. *Letter I*, p. 31. The journals show no divisions.

64. *CJ, 30*, 147.

Thus, with very little apparent opposition, Whately's "great Measure of the Sessions" became law.[65]

Another hoped-for source of revenue was the postal system. Packets were again running to the West Indies and for the first time to various southern ports on the mainland as well as to New York. But in spite of a new law providing reductions, rates were higher than charges normally made by merchant captains for carrying letters, and caused criticism in the West Indies.[66]

Several other measures passed during Grenville's administration increased colonial unrest. Not all of these originated at the Treasury, but when there is no evidence that Grenville intervened, it is probably correct to assume that he approved. As a result of the request of British merchants and the recommendation of the Board of Trade, a new law was passed extending restrictions on the issues of bills of credit.[67] A consequent shortage of paper currency combined with the necessity of paying the new duties in sterling aggravated the money problem in the colonies. In spite of numerous warnings, Grenville showed no interest in the situation, and took no steps to relieve it.

The original American Mutiny Bill was drafted at the War Office.[68] George III foresaw objections to quartering soldiers in

65. Temple Correspondence, 9 Feb. 1765. Fred J. Ericson thinks the opposition has been underestimated, "The Contemporary British Opposition to the Stamp Act, 1764–65," *Papers of the Michigan Academy of Science, 29* (1943), 489-505.

66. 5 Geo. III, c. 25. Transatlantic rates were now uniform: one shilling a single sheet in either direction, and so on in proportion for double or triple sheets. Samuel Martin's father complained that he had to pay this rate even when letters were carried by regular merchant ships (Add. MSS 41,347, 5 Aug. 1765). Inland rates were based on mileage: 4*d.* a single sheet for 0 to 60 miles; 6*d.,* 60 to 100; 8*d.,* 100 to 200; and 2*d.* for each additional 100 miles or fraction thereof. These rates were the same for shorter distances as the earlier rates, but less for longer.

67. *APC, Col., 4,* 623 ff. BT, *Journal,* 1764–67, p. 15. 4 Geo. III, c. 34.

68. General Gage had recommended such a bill and Halifax approved (Clarence E. Carter, ed., *Correspondence of General Gage,* New Haven, Yale Univ. Press, 1931–33, *1,* 49; *CHOP, 1,* 529, 534).

private houses, and warned Grenville.[69] Jenkinson then assumed responsibility for revising the bill. With Grenville's approval he consulted Franklin and Governor Pownall. As a result there were changes in the method of billeting soldiers.[70] Nevertheless, even in its final form the bill added fuel to fires that were already burning fiercely in the colonies.

Other important legislation affecting the colonies included military and civil appropriations. Both were considerably larger than in earlier periods of peace.[71] It seems clear that Grenville agreed with other ministers that a standing army of considerable size was needed in America, for his plans for revenue were closely related to the estimated charge for military forces.[72] Presumably he made no effort to secure the opinion of Americans on the need for troops. Franklin, at least, would have told him that the Indians would be more manageable since the French influence had been removed.[73]

Economy, which was supposed to be the basis of government policy, consisted for the most part of transferring to the colonies a larger part of the burden of supporting an army. Not only did Grenville plan to use the new revenue for the military forces, but he was determined to put an end to the practice of reimbursing colonial assemblies for their military expenditures. He insisted

69. *Grenville Papers, 3,* 11-12.

70. Add. MSS 38,304, fol. 134. HEH, Stowe 7, *2,* 13 and 27 Apr. 1765. Smyth, ed., *Writings of Franklin, 4,* 388. T1:455, solicitor's bill of expenses. Namier, *England in the ... Revolution,* pp. 294-95, refers to the influence of the merchants. 5 Geo. III, c. 33.

71. The estimates for 1765 for military forces and ordnance were somewhat over £300,000, and as usual there were charges for which appropriations had not been made (*CJ, 30,* 25, 41). The actual military expenditures in 1765 were £394,469.1.4 (T1:461). A contemporary comparison shows that the charge for North America alone was nearly £150,000 more than it had been in 1750, early in the War of the Austrian Succession (Add. MSS 38,339, fol. 180).

72. Of the estimate of £300,000 one-third, so it was hoped, would be raised in America (*Letter I,* p. 25).

73. *Writings, 4,* 363.

that General Amherst was not to promise repayment for colonial aid in suppressing Pontiac's rebellion.[74]

Civil expenditures for the colonies, like those for military purposes, interfered with the proposed economy. In the first place, it was necessary to ask Parliament for appropriations for the new governments of East and West Florida as well as for Nova Scotia and Georgia.[75] On the other hand, in spite of some disagreement with Halifax on the subject, Grenville refused to ask Parliament for salaries for civil officers in Quebec and the Ceded Islands,[76] hoping that revenue from these two provinces would cover the costs of their civil governments. Another new item for which Parliament began to make regular appropriations in this period, however, was that of general surveys in North America.[77]

In spite of gestures toward economy, therefore, Grenville's administration provided for increased appropriations for the colonies. The total annual amount was over £400,000, of which the greater part was for the army.

A review of the legislation during Grenville's tenure shows that it was revolutionary in character. Comparisons with earlier periods disclose the increased attention Parliament was giving to America and particularly to the North American Continent. But the greatest departure from past policies was the decision to tax the colonies.

New laws required the appointment of additional crown officials. Americans were keenly aware of the increasing number of government personnel, and it was of the greatest importance to provide tactful as well as efficient administrators. Grenville understood the importance of this phase of government, and his plans for ad-

74. Beer, *British Colonial Policy,* pp. 262-63.

75. Jenkinson directed the Board of Trade to prepare estimates (BT, *Journal,* 1764—67, p. 3; T29:35, pp. 181, 271). In 1764 the total for the civil administration of the four provinces was £20,505.3.7, and in 1765, £19,277.14.11 (T1:463, Miscellaneous Article on Establishment).

76. *Grenville Papers, 2,* 481. *CHOP, 1,* 311.

77. These were ordered by the Privy Council (*APC, Col., 4,* 619-23). In 1764 they cost £1,117.12.0; and in 1765, £2,303.11.0: HC, "Return of Public Income and Expenditure," *Accounts and Papers* (1868—69) *35,* Pt. I, pp. 151, 153.

ministration were as ambitious as his legislative program.[78] Two
years, however, are scarcely long enough for thorough reforms.
Moreover, Grenville and his secretaries were devoting much of
their time to preparing bills for Parliament. It is not surprising
that he left to his successors a variety of incomplete projects and
serious administrative problems growing out of his legislative
ventures.

Under Grenville the treasury board met frequently and attendance was excellent. Vacations were shorter than usual. But neither
secretary had had previous experience at the Treasury.[79] They
were politicians rather than administrators; both were members
of Parliament and both were pamphleteers; both retired from the
Treasury when Grenville left office, giving evidence of the political
character of their tenure. The clerks, competent as they may have
been, were used to the supervision of more experienced secretaries.
Also, there seems to have been some uneasiness in the office. This
may have been due to recent violations of the seniority rule and
to the fact that Grenville appointed his private secretary, Charles
Lloyd, to one of the under clerkships.[80] In spite of all the seeming
handicaps and a few fiascoes, however, the period was marked by
tremendous activity and considerable accomplishment.

As previously, the Crown made few grants from the civil list for
colonial purposes. Reminiscent of Queen Anne's charities was an
appropriation of £1,000 for settling French protestants in East
Florida,[81] but again the plan for the establishment of bishoprics

78. A new series of treasury office records, begun 29 Oct. 1763, indicates
the growing importance of the colonies. It was called the "America Book"
(T28) and contained copies of most documents relating to the colonies, which
had previously been distributed among other classes of papers.

79. Dyson, who entered the Treasury May 1762, left Aug. 1763 and was
succeeded by Whately. Charles Jenkinson came in at the beginning of Grenville's administration. He had served under Bute when the latter was Secretary
of State and was his private secretary when Bute was First Lord of the Treasury.
His continued friendship for Bute made his loyalty suspect. He complained
of lack of influence (Add. MSS 38,304, fols. 51-52).

80. T53:49, p. 60.

81. T29:35, p. 35.

in the colonies failed to win approval.[82] Colonial revenues continued to supplement the King's civil list, but Americans seemed curiously impervious to this fact.

The administration of parliamentary grants for the armed forces in America, though seemingly less critical than in time of war, was actually cataclysmic in its eventual effect upon imperial relations. While the Treasury, of course, was not primarily responsible for the decision to keep a sizable standing army in the colonies, Grenville apparently made no objection. Furthermore, in the controversy over the proper location of British troops in America he used his influence to have them placed in port towns, for he wanted their help, when necessary, in collecting the customs.[83] Of all the administrative decisions of this period none was more laden with disaster for the future.

Nothing in the ordinary course of supplying the army with money and provisions can compare in importance with the basic decisions with respect to the number and location of British forces in America. Nevertheless, treasury methods in performing these functions are significant in a study of colonial administration not only because they affected the efficiency of the armed services, but because they illustrate the generally literal, unimaginative, and often inept character of Grenville's government.

His methods of pursuing the unexceptionable object of economy often had deplorable results. For example, early in January 1765,

82. Grenville's attitude is uncertain, but Bedford and Halifax gave tentative encouragement. HEH, Stowe, Box 101, Grenville Political, letter from the archbishop of Canterbury to Bedford. WLC, Shelburne, *59,* fols. 63 ff. Sheffield City Library, Rockingham, American 7; Rockingham, Letters 2. The clause in the Stamp Act taxing certain papers in ecclesiastical courts may have been in anticipation of such an establishment.

83. T29:35, pp. 169-73. *APC, Col., 4,* 571. Gage forwarded copies of the treasury recommendations to other officers (Carter, *Correspondence, 1,* 2). Shelburne favored reducing troops in towns and keeping only enough on the frontier to defend it from the Indians (Lord Edmond Fitzmaurice, *Life of William, Earl of Shelburne,* 2d ed. London, Macmillan, 1912, *1,* 304). Clarence W. Alvord and Clarence E. Carter, "The Critical Period, 1763–65," Illinois *Historical Collections, 10* (1915), a discussion of the problem.

the Treasury suspended issues to the money contractors because of a dispute over accounts.[84] An extreme shortage of funds resulted, aggravated by the agents' refusal to pay out what they had on hand until they received a new supply. General Gage, therefore, was dependent on what he or the deputy paymasters could raise through the sale of bills of exchange. Under the circumstances, obtaining funds in this way was extremely difficult and expensive. When Grenville left office there was not even enough money in America for the regular subsistence of the army.[85]

Less disadvantageous in the long run was Grenville's curb on extraordinary expenditures for the army. In such cases an attempt to substitute treasury discretion for that of the commander may even have had certain good results. On November 28, 1764, the Treasury adopted an elaborate minute, which was approved by the King and then sent to the Secretary at War and the Secretary of State for them to put into effect.[86] If an emergency prevented prior consultation with the Treasury, the officer might assume responsibility and obtain funds by drawing bills directly on the Treasury. But in that case, the Treasury warned, it would consider the reasonableness of the price as well as the necessity of the service and the authenticity of the vouchers before allowing the accounts. This regulation, the interpretation of which was obscure, caused consternation in the army, and the handling of an increased number of bills at the Treasury became an administrative problem. There is no evidence, however, that the order had any disastrous results. In fact, it may have been salutary in promoting caution in the handling of public funds.

Grenville had high hopes of simplifying procedures in supplying the army with funds by using revenue raised in America. He in-

84. Some of the contractors' agents were bankrupt and a dispute arose over who was responsible for the losses (T29:36, p. 225, passim).

85. Add. MSS 38,204, fol. 304; 38,305, fol. 13.

86. T29:36, pp. 166-67; T27:29, p. 108. The preliminary step was a simple minute, forwarded to Gage, that he should draw no money without the prior approval of the Treasury except in case of necessity (T29:36, p. 55; T27:29, p. 62).

tended that customs collectors and distributors of stamps should transfer their receipts to the deputy paymasters. It was not until July 9, just before the change in administration, however, that the Treasury got around to sending appropriate instructions to both sets of officers.[87] There was, of course, little income from the Stamp Act; and unforeseen difficulties developed in carrying out the plan as it related to the customs.

Among Grenville's plans for economy was a proposal for cutting the cost to the British public of victualing the army in America. One method was to require the provincial governments to supply their own troops.[88] Another was to extend the practice whereby the colonies made allowances to the regular forces stationed there, as Antigua and Jamaica had done. But the experience in Jamaica was discouraging: a quarrel over finance had led the governor to dissolve the assembly, leaving the troops without their supplementary pay; and after some delay the Treasury had been obliged to make up the deficit.[89]

Another way of saving public funds was to make the soldier pay for his rations. Grenville decided to return to the practice of withholding 4*d*. a day if it could be done "without causing a disturbance among the troops."[90] Disorders occurred wherever it was tried. The Treasury, therefore, compromised by fixing the stoppage at 2½*d*., and only in the case of troops not in actual service.[91]

The Treasury also hoped to negotiate the new victualing con-

87. HEH, Stowe 7, 2, 11 Apr. 1765. Add. MSS 38,304, fols. 135-36. T11:28, p. 76, advising the Customs Commissioners to warn the collectors in advance of formal instructions. T29:37, pp. 161-62. The final plan differed from that of Jenkinson, who after consultation with the Paymaster General and contractors had proposed transferring funds to the contractors' agents (T29:36, pp. 323, 342).

88. T29:36, p. 43; T27:29, p. 62.

89. T1:442, fols. 135, 141; T29:36, pp. 277, 317; T29:37, p. 47.

90. T29:35, p. 76; T27:28, pp. 393-94.

91. T29:35, pp. 317, 319. Amherst had tried this plan, leaving it to the option of the soldier to draw his rations every day or not as he chose, but Gage wrote that the men had refused to submit. In Newfoundland Captain Graves had simply suspended the order.

tracts on more favorable terms. This it was able to do in a few cases. On the other hand, some loss occurred because of delay in making new contracts. In the interval Amherst was obliged to buy provisions for short terms at comparatively high prices.[92] There were also losses involved in following treasury orders to sell provisions which the army had on hand when a new contract went into effect.[93]

Another plan for saving money was to require contractors to issue provisions at designated places, leaving the army to handle provisions at the smaller posts. The Treasury temporarily failed to make the arrangments clear to Gage, and vast confusion resulted until he received a clarification of orders.[94] One is left with the impression that Grenville's plans for army economies were largely failures.

Another function that continued to devolve upon the Treasury was the administering of grants made by Parliament to reimburse the colonies for their wartime services. The final appropriation was that of 1763. But Grenville's Treasury had to make decisions with respect to claims for services in the three preceding years. The secretaries now dealt directly with colonial agents in this matter, but they took General Amherst's advice on disputed points.[95] Grenville's experiences in this connection may have crystallized his opposition to such grants.

In contrast to the Treasury's responsibility for administering army matters, its functions with respect to the Admiralty were slight. Grenville was aware of the difficulties of protecting the

92. Carter, *Correspondence, 2,* 217. Add. MSS 38,338, fols. 109-11, list of new contracts made by Grenville's Treasury, and those continuing, with notes on savings.

93. T29:37, p. 85.

94. T29:36, pp. 182-83. Carter, *Correspondence, 2,* 249. T27:29, pp. 122-23. Add. MSS 38,203, fols. 343-45. Gage complained to Amherst, then in England, that the Treasury listened to reports from the contractors' agents instead of waiting for information from the army (*Correspondence, 2,* 253-54).

95. T29:35, pp. 193, 342; T1:423, agreement of agents for distribution of fund granted for services of 1760; T1:422, petition of Pennsylvania, which was refused because Amherst did not include the service in his return.

King's woods and considered a change in the office of surveyor general, but took no action.[96] He gave definite encouragement to the expanded use of the navy in the customs service and to the plans for additional vice-admiralty courts in America, but the Treasury had little to do with the actual administration of these plans.

New parliamentary grants for civil purposes laid increased burdens on the Treasury after the estimates were approved and Parliament had voted the funds. Authorizing issues to colonial agents or the surveyors of land and supervising accounts, however, were the major functions in this field.[97]

When one turns from the handling of expenditures to the supervision of revenue, one enters the area of first concern to the Grenville administration. He had been in office only a matter of weeks when he undertook reforms in the customs system. Although these administrative measures were aimed at enforcing the acts of trade, their primary object was to realize a larger income from this source. Certain improvements could be made by the Treasury's own revenue officers; others required the full cooperation of other departments.

The first step was to improve that part of the administration for which the Treasury was responsible—that is, the customs system itself. Because of the growing importance of colonial trade and revenue the Treasury approved the appointment of a special clerk at the Custom House for this branch of the business. He was to receive dispatches from America, prepare replies, and supervise the conduct of colonial officers.[98] The Treasury showed an unusual interest in accounts and other information passing through this

96. HEH, Stowe, Grenville Misc., 29 Mar. 1763; Temple Correspondence, 10 May 1765. In 1743 the Treasury, on the advice of the Board of Trade, had appointed the Governor of New Hampshire as surveyor general, who acted through deputies (T29:29, p. 361; T54:34, pp. 191-92; T52:42, pp. 325-26).

97. The Treasury occasionally settled such subsidiary questions as how funds should be transferred from one agent to another, and what should be done about the pay of a suspended officer (T29:35, p. 222; T29:36, pp. 93, 301).

98. T1:426, report from Customs Board, 28 Sept. 1763; T11:27, p. 359.

officer's hands, and required quarterly reports.[99] When suggestions of illegal trade reached the Treasury from other sources, the secretary notified the commissioners and directed them to investigate.[100]

The Treasury also gave attention to the port officers, whose neglect of duty had become notorious. It ordered that all officers who were absent from their stations should return immediately on pain of dismissal.[101] It now handled requests for leaves, granted them sparingly, and required the dismissal of officers who defied their orders.[102] New appointees learned that their salaries would not begin until they reached their ports.[103] Newly appointed officers and those on leave in England were to receive instructions in the port of London appropriate to their particular functions. The Treasury required a certificate from the Custom House when the instruction had been satisfactorily completed.[104] It also ordered the Customs Commissioners to prepare new sets of instructions for American officers, and made certain changes before giving them its approval.[105]

A general reorganization of the customs districts took place. The newly acquired territories were included in the system of surveys, and an additional surveyor general was appointed.[106] On the other hand, the Treasury favored a reduction in the number and size

99. T29:36, p. 30. The clerk had two assistants (Custom House Library, Notes and Extracts, *3*, 391).

100. T11:27, p. 481.

101. T29:35, p. 125; T11:27, p. 304. Notes and Extracts, *3*, 390. This order caused considerable consternation. The Treasury made an exception in the case of Grosvenor Bedford, who held by patent and always served by deputy (Peter Cunningham, ed., *The Letters of Horace Walpole, Earl of Orford*, London, 1857–59, *4*, 113).

102. Add. MSS 38,304, fol. 72; T11:28, p. 88; T29:36, pp. 209-10.

103. T11:27, p. 425.

104. T29:35, p. 167. Custom House Library, Notes and Extracts, *3*, 391. T1:423, 429, 441, and T64:138: examples of certificates.

105. T1:426, 16 Sept. 1763; T29:35, p. 164; T11:27, pp. 331-32, 424-25, more meticulous instructions, emphasizing detailed reports.

106. T11:28, pp. 151, 153, 164, 167. There were now five districts, but Bermuda was not mentioned in the old or new scheme.

of the port areas, although few changes seem to have been made.[107] In spite of increased business, it agreed to the appointment of only a few additional port officers.[108] A decision to enforce the acts of trade in Newfoundland, hitherto considered a "fishery" and outside their regular scope, illustrates the new attitude toward these laws.[109] As long as Grenville was in office, the Treasury retained its interest in every detail of customs administration.

For the most effective enforcement of the acts of trade the Treasury realized that it would have to secure the cooperation of other branches of the government. Early in the autumn of 1763, therefore, it sent a lengthy memorial to the King in Council, in which it outlined its administrative plans and asked for royal orders to all civil and military officers to aid in suppressing contraband trade. It specifically recommended a stronger sea guard and a uniform plan for condemning seizures.[110] The Council approved and gave orders accordingly.

Although the Secretary of State had already been in touch with the governors concerning illicit trade, in the summer of 1764 the Treasury asked him to give new orders for detailed information about such trade.[111] With his help and that of English agents in European ports, the Treasury also devised a more elaborate net for the apprehension of illicit traders. These European agents were to make full reports of ships sailing for America, because with few exceptions masters were supposed to land European goods in Eng-

107. T29:36, p. 318; T11:28, p. 78, following suggestion of Governor Sharpe of Maryland. On his own initiative Governor Wright of Georgia made Sunbury a port (T29:35, p. 358), approved in a later administration (T1:415, 18 Nov. 1766).

108. A comptroller for New Haven, with a collector on the establishment for the first time (T11:28, p. 228); and a surveyor and searcher for the Bay of Gaspé (T29:35, p. 314). The surveyor general thought more waiters were required, but it is impossible to trace appointments of such "incidental officers" (T1:429, 25 June 1764).

109. T29:36, p. 286; T11:28, p. 82. Custom House Library, Notes and Extracts, *3*, 396.

110. *APC, Col., 4*, 569 ff.

111. T29:36, p. 30; T27:29, p. 50. *CHOP, 1*, 475, 516.

land before going to the colonies. Customs officers in English ports were to make reports on all ships and goods involved in trade with the colonies. Clerks in the London Custom House were to examine and compare all such reports with comparable information from America, looking for discrepancies. If they discovered evidence of fraud, they were to notify customs and naval officers who might be able to apprehend the law-breakers.[112]

The Admiralty played a decisive part in making this plan effective. By request it stationed additional cruisers at strategic points along the coast of New England and Canada where smuggling was notorious.[113] Commanders of such ships received deputations as customs officers.[114] Even though officers of His Majesty's ships-of-war felt that hunting for smugglers was beneath their dignity, in succeeding years they made a major contribution to the unusual number of seizures and, consequently, to the revenue.

The admiralty plan for a vice-admiralty court with jurisdiction covering the North American Continent stemmed from the Treasury's memorial to the Privy Council. The Treasury later gave its approval to a specific proposal: the new court was to have concurrent jurisdiction with other vice-admiralty courts, but not the power to hear appeals.[115] The purpose was to make it possible for officers to prosecute outside the localities where prejudice was so strong as to prevent condemnation. But Halifax, where the new court was established, was so remote from most of the colonies that it was impractical to try cases there. The Treasury therefore recommended substituting three courts at widely separated points for the single one at Halifax, with appellate as well as original jurisdiction.[116] But no change occurred until after Grenville left office.

---

112. T29:36, pp. 27-30; T27:29, p. 50. SP 44:414, pp. 34-37.

113. T29:35, pp. 213, 248; T27:28, p. 462; T29:36, pp. 18, 27-28.

114. T1:402, copy of instructions. In 1763 there were 53 ships in American waters with 112 officers having deputations from the Customs Commissioners (WLC, Sydney, *10*).

115. T29:33, p. 355; T1:429, copy of memorial from Admiralty. *APC, Col.,* *4,* 663. Adm. 1:3884, authority for the Admiralty to establish the court and commission to Dr. Spry. T28:1, pp. 16-17.

116. T29:37, pp. 14-16; T27:29, p. 165; T54:39, pp. 470-72, referring to clause in the Stamp Act.

Finally, Grenville secured the promise of help from the army in protecting officers of the revenue. Gage reported that he had given orders to every officer on the Continent.[117]

While in theory many of these reforms in administration must have appeared reasonable at the time, experience revealed their defects. Grenville may have expected too much of the administrative personnel from his own secretaries on down through the ranks of the customs officers. Both Grenville and his secretaries evidently lacked the intimate knowledge of colonial geography and the people which might have prevented them from expecting the impossible. For example, they should have known that distances were too great and traveling too difficult to make a single vice-admiralty court effective. And had they given more weight to American advice, they might have realized how difficult it would be to change long-established custom.

The basic defects in the customs system were of long standing. Over the years many customs officers had received appointments who were ignorant of their duty or had learned to live in peace with their neighbors by closing their eyes to illegal trade. The Treasury could not obtain proper records from the former or full cooperation from the latter.

Of fundamental importance in explaining problems of law enforcement in America was the lack of harmony among crown officers, jointly responsible but representing different departments in the English Government. Even in the royal provinces where one might have expected greater cooperation the governor was often at odds with the revenue officers.[118] And for years governors and naval commanders had quarreled over their respective authority.[119]

Among the complaints of customs officers, supported by English merchants, was the very serious and valid charge that the navy

117. Carter, *Correspondence, 1*, 2.

118. The situation became acute in Massachusetts. Treasury papers are filled with the running quarrel: T1:429, 10 Sept. 1764, for example.

119. HEH, Stowe, Grenville Misc., letter from Gov. Lyttelton, 11 Jan. 1763. The Admiralty was afraid that governors as well as lawyers and judges would prevent them from getting the benefit of seizures (T1:442, 11 Jan. 1765).

was destroying the valuable trade in bullion between Spanish possessions and British islands, carried on in Spanish vessels. According
to practice under the Act of 1660, Spanish vessels had long been
permitted to bring bullion into the colonies, although the Act of
1696 made no such exception to the general prohibition of trade
in foreign vessels. In exchange Spaniards bought provisions or
British manufactures.[120] Taking their new instructions literally,
officers of the king's ships were now seizing all such vessels. As a
result the British islands were short of cash, and manufactures were
unsold.[121]

A diplomatic problem developed because the navy was seizing
foreign vessels coming into port for refreshment, which was contrary to international practice. Halifax obtained a royal order
against such seizures.[122] But Grenville only vaguely encouraged
Jenkinson to do all that he could to prevent "inconvenience" to
Spanish trade.[123] Consequently the Customs Board now instructed
their officers to permit Spanish vessels to enter British ports for
refreshment if there was "no attempt to trade in contraband."[124]
The larger question of trade in British manufactures remained
unsettled. It confronted Rockingham, Grenville's successor, as one
of the major issues of his administration.

As a result of Grenville's management and new legislation there
was a marked increase in customs remittances from America.[125]
He used all the available machinery of government to force col-

120. T1:430, 30 May 1764, from collector and comptroller in Jamaica. Later
legal opinion held that the later act did not repeal the former (WLC, Sydney,
10, fols. 32-36).

121. Ibid., fols. 10-36, collection of letters and documents on the subject.
Frances Armytage, *The Free Port System in the British West Indies* (London,
Longmans Green, 1953), pp. 24-26, handles the subject a little differently, em-
phasizing the effects of 3 Geo. III, c. 22, and 4 Geo. III, c. 15, the hovering act.

122. WLC, Sydney, *10*, fols. 12-13.

123. *Jenkinson Papers* (above, p. 116, n. 29), p. 291.

124. Index 4639, p. 59. WLC, Sydney, *10*, fols. 12-13.

125. The receipts in 1765 were roughly six times what had been remitted
the previous year (WLC, Shelburne, *104*). The Declared Accounts of the Audit
Office are not comparable because they do not regularly cover the calendar year.

lectors to remit what was due. Yet receipts fell far short of what had been expected. For example, Parliament appropriated £60,000 from anticipated revenues of the Sugar Act, whereas the actual income available was only £3,223.8.10.[126] According to Grenville's own criterion, therefore, his reforms of the customs system were far from successful. And he would not have taken into account the disruption of English trade in the West Indies or the rising spirit of opposition to English law and its administration in the colonies.

Like the customs system, the American post office had always presented the possibilities of revenue and had recently shown increasing profits.[127] This information must have been very welcome to Grenville. The Treasury encouraged Halifax to sound out the governors as to their opinions of the postal system. Without exception their replies seem to have been favorable.[128]

In 1763 and 1764 the deputy postmasters general on the Continent were making extensive investigations of their growing district. Franklin visited Quebec and established offices there, naming a subdeputy for the province.[129] Evidently thinking the continental

126. HC, "Return of Public Income and Expenditure" (above, p. 23, n. 49), Pt. II, pp. 402-3. Even the following year the income from this source was only £22,226 (Shelburne, *104*). Between Michaelmas 1764 and Michaelmas 1765 the income from the old and new duties plus the King's share of seizures was estimated at £42,000, whereas the costs of management (salaries and incidents), excepting the islands where such items were taken from the four-and-a-half per cent, were £14,500 (Sheffield City Library, Rockingham, American 44). Such over-all estimates of costs are very rare. This estimate of income was exaggerated.

127. The colonial accounts were included in the general accounts of the English office covering two years of Grenville's administration, but not declared until 1783. The first showed North American receipts to June 1761 and charges to 10 Aug. 1761; and Jamaican receipts and charges to 24 Dec. 1762. Both purported to be from the establishment of the offices. Franklin's showed a surplus in round numbers of £494, and Dismore's, £118 (AO 1:2001:183). The account for the following year showed a surplus of £2,070 from North America, and £234 from Jamaica (AO 1:2002:184).

128. *CHOP, 1*, 466, passim.

129. "Hugh Finlay," DNB. There were offices at Three Rivers and Montreal as well as Quebec.

system too large for effective supervision, and possibly interested in additional opportunities for patronage, the Postmaster General divided the Continent into two districts. The southern district included all the provinces south of Virginia and also the Bahamas.[130] With the appointment of a deputy postmaster for the Ceded Islands there were now three such officers in the West Indies, directly responsible to the London office.[131]

These island deputies were the more necessary because early in 1764 the Treasury approved a plan for the revival of the packet system to the West Indies and its extension to the southern part of the Continent.[132] Understanding that the packets would not be self-supporting, Grenville showed a greater awareness of their administrative value than his predecessors.

Unlike the customs duties and the postal rates, the new stamp tax had only one material object, and that, of course, was revenue. In this case the Treasury had the advantage of being able to lay the foundations of a new system. Unfortunately, however, the act was passed so late in Grenville's administration and he was so involved in politics during those last weeks that much of the work of preparing for the beginning of the tax on the first of November was neglected.

The English Stamp Commissioners were to supervise the colonial system; but at this stage they could do little without the approval of the Treasury. On April 27 they wrote to the Treasury indicating the changes that would be required in their own office to handle the additional business. But it was not until July 9, the last day of official business for Grenville's board, that Whately replied, approving a minimum number of these recommendations.[133]

130. Benjamin Barons was the deputy postmaster general (GPO: Orders of the Board, p. 126; Instructions Book, pp. 53-56).
131. Commission Book, pp. 40, 45: Edward Dismore for Jamaica; Henry Falkingham for Barbados and the Leeward Islands; Alexander Medleton for the Ceded Islands.
132. T54:39, pp. 250-51. Information regarding the captains is in the Commission Book and Instructions Book.
133. Both letters are by chance in T1:439.

In spite of an original warning from the Stamp Office on March 30—just eight days after the King had given his assent to the bill—and a reminder on April 25, there were delays in naming the twenty-four distributors and nine inspectors for America.[134] In fact Grenville left office with the places of two distributors and two inspectors unfilled.[135] A principal cause of delay may have been his determination to name only colonists of property who were particularly recommended.[136] Whatever the reason, this procrastination was peculiarly unfortunate, for the Stamp Office often had to correspond with the distributors several times regarding their securities and then wait to receive their bonds before they could send them the stamped paper.[137] Most of the stamps were not shipped until some time after Grenville left office. Rockingham found a good deal of unfinished business connected with the introduction of the new law as well as mounting hostility to the very concept of such a tax.

As compared to his zeal for taxes levied by Parliament, Grenville's interest in crown dues was rather mild, if one excepts those which the King transferred to the public. And George III made notable contributions to the public funds, encouraged no doubt by his First Lord of the Treasury as well as a series of precedents.

The Virginia quit rents did not belong to the latter class of exceptions, but remained strictly under crown control. The auditor general and his deputy eagerly formed plans for improvement, made definite recommendations to the Treasury, and reported on colonial legislation affecting this revenue.[138] But the attitude of the Treasury was so discouraging that Abercromby threatened to resign. In one respect the Treasury was diligent, and that was in

134. T1:440, list of steps taken in preparation; T54:39, pp. 438-39, 478, warrants for deputations.

135. It was not until the last moment that the Treasury announced that the distributors would be allowed 8 per cent and the inspectors £100 a year plus 20s. a day when traveling (T27:29, pp. 175-76).

136. Add. MSS 38,305, fol. 12. HEH, Stowe 7, 2, 11 Apr. 1765.

137. T1:439, 25 Apr. 1765.

138. Add. MSS 38,337, fols. 314-23; 38,204, fols. 9-10. T1:423, 30 June 1763; T1:430, 26 Mar., 11 July 1764.

demanding prompt payment of receipts. The results, however, were rather unsatisfactory.[139]

The Treasury's plan for revenue from the islands recently acquired from France included both quit rents to be reserved on land when it was sold and the four-and-a-half per cent export duty, customarily a substitute for rents. It advised the Privy Council to follow the precedent set in the case of St. Christopher and impose the latter duty by an order under the great seal.[140] Scarcely had the order been issued, however, when Jenkinson informed Grenville that there was doubt as to its legality.[141] According to a theory, eventually supported by the Court of King's Bench, an earlier proclamation by the King providing for a legislative assembly in the islands prevented him from using his prerogative to tax the inhabitants.[142] Grenville, however, refused to interfere with the collection of these duties even after the Commons had called for the pertinent papers.[143] Later administrations had to unscramble the confusion resulting from the decision that the duty was unconstitutional.

In the meantime, it seemed that Grenville had succeeded in securing from these islands a revenue sufficient for the support of Government and under the control of the Crown or Parliament. The islanders were subject to parliamentary taxes on trade, the four-and-a-half per cent duty, a poll tax on negroes, quit rents on their lands, and the payment of casual revenues.[144]

In addition to the income from these supposedly permanent

139. Out of more than £18,000 due, the only receipt in England seems to have been £7,420 paid to Jenkinson (T1:450, fols. 75-79, account of warrants).

140. Plan of procedure, Grenville Misc. T29:35, p. 246; T54:39, pp. 231-32. *APC, Col., 4*, 616-17; T28:1, pp. 52-53, copy of letters patent.

141. HEH, Stowe 7, *1*, Grenville's reply, 19 Aug. 1764.

142. Case of Campbell v. Hall, 1774 (W. P. M. Kennedy, ed., *Documents of the Canadian Constitution, 1759–1915,* Toronto, Oxford Univ. Press, 1918, pp. 79 ff.).

143. *CJ, 30,* 164. HEH, Stowe 7, *1,* 19 Aug. 1764. HEH, HM 220, Grey's Reports, pp. 33-35, report of 1764.

144. The poll tax had been collected by the French sovereign and was thus based on rights acquired by conquest.

taxes there was a temporary but sizable revenue from the sale of land in the islands. In planning for these sales Grenville seems to have had in mind Walpole's methods of disposing of land on St. Christopher.[145] Although the Board of Trade prepared a plan for the sales, the Treasury apparently supplied detailed suggestions, and later made important changes in the Board's draft, designed to encourage settlement, speed the collection of revenue, and assure treasury control.[146] The Privy Council approved the plan, which was then proclaimed by the King.[147]

The Treasury appointed the Commissioners and their subordinates, prepared their instructions, continued to advise them, and supervised their work rather closely.[148] Following a general survey, the Commissioners, acting with the Governor General, were to divide the islands into districts or parishes, fix the location for a town in each parish, and lay out roads. They were then to set aside a certain amount of land for poor settlers and give special consideration to the claims of French residents.[149] With these exceptions, land was to be sold to the highest bidder above a certain minimum, though no sale was final until approved by the Treasury. An annual quit rent of 6*d.* an acre was first reserved on all cleared land but later on only half of such land.[150]

The sales began to produce a revenue fairly quickly. Grenville was pleased.[151] A few years later there was a different story, when

145. Grenville Misc., plan of 1726.

146. HEH, Stowe, Box 103(c), Grenville Diplomatic, draft of a minute. BT, *Journal,* 1759—63, p. 402; ibid., 1764—67, p. 23. T29:35, pp. 260-69; T54:39, pp. 240-50. At Grenville's request William Young, later head of the commission, made suggestions for revising the Board's plan (Add. MSS 38,200, fol. 215).

147. *APC, Col., 4,* 580 ff. "British Royal Proclamations Relating to America, 1603—1783," ed. Clarence S. Brigham, American Antiquarian Society, *Transactions and Collections, 12* (Worcester, Massachusetts, 1911), pp. 218-23.

148. T29:35, p. 349; T28:1, pp. 31-49.

149. Under certain conditions Frenchmen who had occupied land contrary to the treaties might lease it, paying a quit rent of 1*s.*6*d.* an acre. They were restricted in transferring it.

150. T29:36, pp. 174-77.

151. HEH, Stowe 7, 2, 8 Aug. 1765.

revenues fell far short of the estimates.[152] Yet before 1782 sales had netted £139,000.[153] This sum accrued to public funds, for George III followed the example set by his great grandfather, sacrificing what might have been a welcome addition to the civil list.[154] Unlike Horace Walpole in the earlier period, however, Cholmondeley failed to receive authority to audit these accounts. The receiver's instructions directed him to deliver his accounts to the auditor of the imprests.[155]

The outlook for securing revenue from the newly acquired territories on the mainland was less promising. The population of the Floridas was too small to make the necessary provisions for their government, and Parliament accepted this responsibility. After some neglect of the financial problem in Quebec, the Treasury evidently concluded from Governor Murray's report that the revenues formerly collected by the French would be sufficient, but prudently referred the question of the King's right to the law officers.[156] Their cautious answer was to the effect that such duties could be collected "by a proper authority from his Majesty."[157] After several months of seeming negligence, the Treasury submitted the subject of raising a revenue in Quebec to the Privy Council.[158] Just before the change in administration the Treasury signed a commission for a receiver of crown dues in Quebec.[159] But there was as yet no authority for the collection of specific duties.

152. Add. MSS 38,340, fol. 350.

153. "Return of Public Income and Expenditure" (above, p. 23 n.), Pt. I, pp. 156 ff.

154. *CJ, 29,* 669.

155. T28:1, p. 43. William Young, the first receiver, never secured his quietus. In 1806 his accounts, which were still "depending," because he was in debt to the Government, were declared "desperate and obsolete" (T64:130; AO 3:1280).

156. T29:35, p. 378.

157. T1:430, 6 Aug. 1764. HM 220, same date; read 28 Nov. (T29:36, p. 165). They were doubtful whether the King by his prerogative could raise other taxes, possibly having in mind the four-and-a-half per cent in the Ceded Islands.

158. T29:37, p. 29; T54:39, p. 456.

159. T28:1, p. 67.

Both practical and legal complications resulted. In the absence of an assembly Gage did not know how to procure funds for quartering his troops according to the Mutiny Act.[160] Governor Murray raised money for the government under his own authority.[161] Later administrations inherited the resultant problems.

For sales of land on the Continent or anywhere outside the Ceded Islands the Treasury had comparatively little responsibility. The Proclamation Line of 1763, fixing a boundary west of which governors were to make no grants of land, made it necessary to procure a royal license for purchases in that area. Elsewhere on the Continent, as in the past, either the Privy Council, usually advised by the Board of Trade, or colonial governors made grants.[162]

Whether the fines and forfeitures for illegal trade were part of the King's casual revenues had long been a subject of dispute. The Sugar Act of 1764 attempted to resolve this difficulty by making collectors of the customs responsible for these dues rather than the King's receivers. With this provision another item was added to those dues which the King in this period yielded to the public: revenue from prizes and from the sale of land in the Ceded Islands.[163] Although there were clearly established precedents for

160. Carter, *Correspondence, 1,* 75.

161. Sheffield City Library, Rockingham, box of rough notes, letter from Board of Trade with extract of letter from Murray. T1:442, account of Richard Murray, deputy receiver; CO 42:87, pp. 129-33.

162. The Board of Trade encouraged the latter method (*Journal,* 1764–67, pp. 176-77). Under earlier instructions, lands in Bermuda previously held for their income, which was used for the support of government, were now being sold, and salaries of certain officials were paid from the revenue (T52:57, pp. 230-31; T28:1, pp. 68, 73; T29:36, pp. 220-21). An entry in a volume dated 1761–69 states: "In Bermuda there are no lands to be granted" (CO 5:216).

163. The King announced his intention with respect to prizes just four days after Grenville became First Lord (*CJ, 29,* 666). In 1764 this revenue was regularly appropriated to the service of that year (T52:56, p. 242; T53:49, p. 369). The amount available was £659,500, not distinguishing American sources. In later years smaller sums accrued, amounting in 1790 to a total of £701,504.1.3 ("Return of Public Income," Pt. I, p. 28).

such transfers, it seems peculiarly in keeping with Grenville's views of the prerogative and the power of Parliament that they should have been made while he was at the Treasury. The King's resignation of control over such colonial revenues is also consistent with the general shift in power in colonial affairs from the Crown to Parliament, characteristic of this period.

The growing power of Parliament, important as it proved to be, was only one of several features giving a distinctive character to Grenville's administration. When he turned over the Government to his successor, the Marquis of Rockingham, he had been in office only a little over two years, but during that short time there had been such a profound change in relations between the mother country and her colonies that attempts at conciliation could only allay surface irritations. Grenville's administration had moved the whole colonial world, and had shaken the older colonies on the mainland to their foundation.

There were many reasons for the critical character of these two years following the close of the Seven Years' War. Most obvious were the greatly increased size of the empire, the underdeveloped character and financial weakness of the territories acquired from France, the shift in emphasis from the islands to the Continent, and finally the costs of administering the new territories in the aftermath of an expensive war. These new conditions required action and presumably new policies.

Grenville supplied a dynamic approach to the problems of his time. The startling contrast between his aggressive handling of colonial administration and the more unobtrusive policies of his predecessors may have been the most important factor in the evolving crisis.

In considering his administration, however, one cannot ignore his errors in judgment. The policies that led to the interruption of Spanish trade in the West Indies, for example, or left the regular forces in America without an adequate supply of funds, or disregarded the colonial lack of specie, were the result of ignorance, reluctance to take advice, or an unimaginative quality in his mind. Such mistakes would prevent one from describing his administration as successful regardless of other features that have attracted more attention from historians.

The most revolutionary aspects of his administration were the laws for raising a revenue in America and the introduction of more efficient administrative measures to enforce them. As a practical matter, if Americans were to contribute effectively to the defense of the empire, Grenville had no sure alternative to parliamentary taxation. Nevertheless, he was departing from precedent, and precedent was a vital element in the British Constitution. While the constitutional issue was debatable, it had tremendous value in propaganda.

Nevertheless, the most important feature of these revolutionary measures was not the constitutional question which they raised but their effect upon American thinking. Hitherto, Americans for the most part had been content to be English colonists, although the more acute Englishmen might sense that a change was in process. Grenville helped to transform the specter of American nationalism into a reality. The emergence of this reality, which no conciliatory measures of later years could dispel, marks the turning point in the history of relations between Great Britain and her American colonies.

5.

A Brief Interlude: the Administration
of the Marquis of Rockingham

To MANY CONTEMPORARY observers in the summer of 1766 Rockingham's Government appeared to have made a permanent settlement of the awkward and dangerous controversy between England and her colonies which Grenville had evoked. In perspective, however, it seems merely to have provided a pause following the upheaval connected with the Stamp Act before the next provocation and renewed acts of violence.

Rockingham was not the King's first choice for a successor to George Grenville. George III had been trying for some time to secure the services of William Pitt. Failing in this attempt he permitted the Duke of Cumberland to conclude an arrangement with Newcastle, the titular head of his party group, and the young Marquis of Rockingham.[1] The latter became First Lord of the Treasury and real leader of his branch of the Whigs. He remained in office little more than a year.[2]

Rockingham was only thirty-five years of age when in July 1765 he kissed hands for the office of First Lord. Having been Lord of the Bed Chamber for nine years, he knew the court from the inside. Otherwise he had an amazing lack of political and administrative experience for one who was to have the responsibilities of the highest post in government.

1. Pares, *King George III* (above, p. 112, n. 14), pp. 113-14, for negotiations.
2. 13 July 1765—2 Aug. 1766.

Like Grenville he lacked the full support of the King, who now had his own "Friends" in various offices, and did not compel them to accept Rockingham's leadership. George III and his first minister differed as to their proper relations.[3] Moreover, Rockingham was too sincere to feign a respect he did not feel.[4] On several occasions George III appeared ready to bring the Administration to a close, and finally did so in August 1766.

When Rockingham succeeded Grenville, the time seemed ripe to bring together a ministry consisting of men of similar principles, not merely personal connections, but William Pitt, though generally agreeing with the ministers, elected to remain outside the Government.[5] Shelburne followed his example, refusing the post of First Commissioner of the Board of Trade,[6] and there were unsympathetic elements remaining from previous administrations.[7] Consequently the Government lacked the strength and unity necessary for complete assurance.

Lack of experience also characterized the Secretaries of State, Conway and Grafton, as well as the young First Lord of the Treasury. Among those who held high office, only the Duke of Newcastle, who became Lord Privy Seal, had previously enjoyed great responsibility, and now he was not really of the inner circle. This situation helps to explain both the practice of frequent consultations in large and small groups, and the long passage of time before the ministers were ready to announce their legislative plans.

Although there were suggestions for increasing the importance of the First Commissioner of the Board of Trade, the Earl of

3. Sheffield City Library, Rockingham, American 19, note to effect that the king in his "public capacity" was "wholly a Creature of Political Compact," seeming to represent Rockingham's views.

4. Rockingham, box of loose papers, an anonymous letter evidently written when Rockingham was again under consideration for first minister, explaining reason for the King's objection.

5. His decision was based at least in part on his hostility to the Duke of Newcastle (Add. MSS 32,973, fols. 55, 127-28).

6. WLC, Lacaita–Shelburne, 11 July 1765.

7. Pares, pp. 84 n., 171.

Dartmouth, his Board remained weak and unsure of itself.[8] As under Grenville, therefore, the Treasury took the lead in most measures affecting the colonies.

Parliament, of course, was the place where colonial questions had finally to be settled, for Americans were casting doubt upon the power of Parliament to tax them.[9] In the House of Lords, Rockingham faced an embarrassing opposition. In the Commons, responsibility for the government program was divided between William Dowdeswell, Chancellor of the Exchequer, and Conway, Secretary of State for the Southern Department.[10] Grey Cooper, secretary to the Treasury, and Edmund Burke, Rockingham's private secretary and recently elected to Parliament, gave valiant support to their superiors.

Patronage, so necessary for management of the House of Commons, was not completely centralized. Newcastle received directly from the King permission to recommend to preferments in the Church.[11] Nevertheless, the Treasury was generally recognized as the chief dispenser of places. Newcastle urged Rockingham to reinstate army officers who had been removed under the previous administration, and also to dismiss some of Bute's friends.[12] Rock-

8. Newcastle protested because Dartmouth was not called into consultation on American affairs (Rockingham, Letters 2, 17 Oct. and 10 Dec. 1765). When Richmond was about to become Secretary of State on Grafton's resignation, he agreed that Dartmouth should be added to the circulation list (ibid., 3, 19 May 1766).

9. The Board of Trade and the Treasury sent American papers to the Council. The latter concluded they were too important to be handled there and ordered the Secretary of State to lay them before Parliament (PC 4:2, 3 and 18 Oct. 1765).

10. Records investigated do not reveal who presided at the Cockpit and read the draft of the King's speech. John Roberts, with a long knowledge of precedents, suggested it would be appropriate for either Dowdeswell or Conway to do so (Rockingham, Letters 0, 6 Dec. 1765).

11. Thomas Pelham-Holles, Duke of Newcastle, *A Narrative of the Changes in the Ministry, 1765–1767,* ed. Mary Bateson (London, 1898), p. 33.

12. Rockingham, Letters 0, 6 July 1765; Rockingham, English 2, 26 July 1765, with comments on people previously removed for whom warrants had not yet been signed.

ingham agreed to restitution, but refused to act in what he called "a spirit of retaliation."[13]

Although patronage was important as a means to an end, Rockingham's real concern was with policy. And in spite of political and governmental weaknesses described above, he succeeded in accomplishing most of what he set out to do. That is, as he later declared, he "relieved the Country from [Grenville's] errors."[14] In the summer of 1765, when Rockingham took office, purely English questions such as the use of general warrants and the Cider Act appeared to demand most attention. But in succeeding weeks, and especially as the opening of Parliament in December approached, American affairs became of paramount importance. Rockingham was convinced that changes should be made in recent commercial legislation. Furthermore, he thought it a mistake to try to secure revenue from the colonies at the expense of trade, believing as he did that their chief value was commercial.[15] But just when he made up his mind that the Stamp Act should be repealed rather than amended is uncertain.

Early in September a member of the Wentworth family who had returned from America in 1763, writing at Rockingham's request, advised him that the colonists could not afford to pay the taxes imposed upon them.[16] Before the middle of October Newcastle was evidently ready for repeal.[17] By the end of November the opposition was suspecting that the ministry had come to this decision.[18] But Rockingham may not yet have made up his mind. He hoped "to avoid the discussion of the Stamp Act till good Principles [were]

13. Add. MSS 32,790, fols. 226-27, quoted by Namier, *England in the ... Revolution,* p. 483. Of 63 removed 1762–63, 56 were restored in 1765 (Rockingham, English 2).

14. Rockingham, Letters 4, 15 Sept. 1767.

15. Rockingham, American 19, Notes for Procedure in Parliament; ibid., 48, undated.

16. Ibid., 7, 1 Sept. 1765. He explained that their wealth was in land, not money; local taxes were in arrears because of lack of cash; and there was heavy public debt.

17. Rockingham, Letters 2, 12 Oct. 1765.

18. HEH, Stowe 7, 2, 27 Nov. 1765.

laid down for easing and assisting North America."[19] That is, he wanted to propose commercial changes first.

The news from America, however, and the pressure of public opinion in England soon showed that it would be impossible to postpone action on the Stamp Act long after Parliament had assembled. Early in December associations of British merchants, encouraged by the Government, were beginning to organize propaganda in favor of repeal.[20] By this time Rockingham was probably convinced that repeal was necessary, but was waiting for the situation to ripen before making an announcement.[21] In fact, Parliament, which had met on December 14, adjourned for the Christmas recess and reassembled on January 14 without the Government's definitely showing its hand. Pitt's speech in favor of repeal gave the ministry much needed assurance of support. Parliament soon had before it a fairly complete picture of American developments in the papers recently received from the colonies and those suppressed by the Grenville ministry. Meanwhile petitions for repeal multiplied.[22]

Rockingham like many others was convinced that Parliament must affirm its right to legislate for the colonies.[23] Measures to repeal the Stamp Act and to declare the right of Parliament over the colonies proceeded, therefore, almost simultaneously. On February 24 in the House of Commons the committee considering American papers made both recommendations.

19. Rockingham, American 19, 27 Nov. [1765].

20. L. Stuart Sutherland, "Edmund Burke and the First Rockingham Ministry," *English Historical Review, 47* (1932), 46-72. Dora Mae Clark, *British Opinion and the American Revolution* (New Haven, Yale Univ. Press, 1930), pp. 40-43.

21. Carl B. Cone, *Burke and the Nature of Politics* (Louisville, Univ. of Ky. Press, 1957), pp. 86-87, suggests that the ministers "veered toward repeal" during the recess, but does not refer to Rockingham specifically. He concludes that "Burke had decided, earlier than the Rockingham chieftains, in favor of repeal of the Stamp Act." E. S. and H. M. Morgan, *The Stamp Act Crisis,* p. 277, accept the view that the ministers came to an agreement January 17.

22. *CJ, 30,* passim.

23. Rockingham, American 19, passim.

George III caused consternation by letting it be known that he preferred modification.[24] Nevertheless, the bill for repeal passed both houses and was signed by the King.[25]

Although the Declaratory Act was less controversial, various alternatives had been under consideration, such as a resolution censuring the conduct of the colonies and a proposal to declare it treason to write or print articles casting doubt on the right of the British Parliament. Rockingham evidently objected to labeling the colonists "rebels," a word which would imply the necessity for using force against them. He also wished to avoid a distinction between internal and external taxes. The final decision was for an act declaring the power of Parliament "in general words."[26] Consequently the statute asserted the right of Parliament "to bind the colonies and people of America . . . in all cases whatsoever."[27]

Having corrected the mistake of trying to secure a revenue from America by direct means, Rockingham now felt free to deal with the complex commercial problems he had inherited from Grenville's administration. One of his principal objects was to restore by law and under careful protection the international trade which had flourished in the Caribbean until prohibited by Grenville. In addition to bullion there were products such as raw cotton and silk, drugs and dye-woods produced in the foreign islands, especially the French, for which English merchants would have liked to exchange British manufactures. But British ships were excluded from most of these islands, as were foreign ships from the British.

Spain had been experimenting with a free port on the island of Santo Domingo, and the Dutch were using St. Eustatius for this

24. Rockingham, Letters 38.
25. 6 Geo. III, c. 11. The number of the minority in the Commons changed somewhat at different stages of the bill, but at one time was as high as 167 (Rockingham, American 21; Add. MSS 32,975, fol. 169). The motion to recommit the resolution to bring in the bill was defeated 133 to 240, and the final bill passed 250 to 122 (*CJ, 30,* 602, 626). Strong opposition caused some delay in the Lords. An act was also passed to protect those who had violated the law by carrying on business without stamped paper (6 Geo. III, c. 51).
26. Rockingham, American 19.
27. 6 Geo. III, c. 12.

purpose.[28] Merchants and other Englishmen familiar with the problems of trade in the Caribbean favored the establishment of a free port in the British islands to secure their share of the local international trade.[29] Both Rockingham and Burke gave sympathetic attention to such proposals.[30] They were practical rather than doctrinaire in their approach to the free-port question.

The groups of organized merchants, however, were divided on this issue as they had not been on the question of repealing the Stamp Act.[31] Merchants trading with North America strongly favored the idea, but some of those doing business with the West Indies feared the free port would affect other British islands adversely. Various concessions to the latter group succeeded in reconciling them. The ministers were also divided, but by the middle of April the Government had seemingly settled upon an address from Parliament to the King favoring the policy.[32] Within the next few weeks the Treasury decided on quicker action and in favor of a bill to be presented at the current session.[33]

As a matter of fact two bills were finally consolidated into the Free Port Act: one for establishing free ports, two in Dominica to catch the French trade and four in Jamaica to attract the Spaniards with their bullion; and another measure for an appropriate system of duties tailored to fit the changes brought about by the system of free ports and to protect the other British possessions.[34] Although the act was complex and difficult to enforce, the principle of the free ports persisted for many years.[35]

28. GD 8:98, letter from Admiral Cotes, 28 Feb. 1759.

29. Rockingham, American 30, letter from Francis Moore. Add. MSS 33,030, fols. 318-23, "Mr. Huske's Scheme for Free Ports in America."

30. Rockingham, English 5, various letters; Sheffield City Library, Burke's Letters, Abraham Rawlinson to Burke, 11 and 23 May 1766.

31. Armytage (above, p. 136, n. 121), *The Free Port System*, p. 39.

32. Rockingham, Letters 3, from Dowdeswell, 14 April 1766.

33. Rockingham, American 31, printed copy of the bill as received 2 June with corrections.

34. 6 Geo. III, c. 49.

35. Armytage, pp. 43-48, comments on the failure to revive the Spanish trade and on smuggling.

Another act of the same session was also the result of an agreement between North American and West Indian merchants.[36] Both groups were willing to see the tax on foreign molasses imported into the plantations reduced to 1*d.* a gallon, if this were strictly enforced; but the Treasury now took a more revolutionary step, simplifying the problem of enforcement by applying the tax to all molasses whether British or foreign.[37] To compensate the West Indian planters for their loss of preference in the North American market, the new law removed the enumerated commodities duty from their sugar exports.[38] Cotton, for which there was evidently an increasing demand among English manufacturers, also became a favored article. There was to be no duty on its export from British plantations or on its importation into Great Britain if brought in British-built ships.[39]

Although this act of 1766 relaxed certain provisions of earlier statutes, it added a restriction that affected the New England carrying trade most severely. This was the requirement, introduced at the suggestion of British merchants, that all vessels clearing from the plantations with nonenumerated commodities should give bond not to land those goods in any part of Europe north of Cape Finisterre except Great Britain.[40] This requirement, supplementing the enumerated commodities bond of 1660 and the provisions of the act of 1663 obliging traders carrying European goods to America to land first at a British port, was designed to discourage

36. 6 Geo. III, c. 52. Add. MSS 38,339, fol. 235. GD 8:97. WLC, Shelburne, *49,* fols. 521 ff.

37. Rockingham, American 29, for arguments for taxing both; 19 for evidence that Rhode Island did not have enough bullion to pay the 3*d.* duty on the foreign molasses required there.

38. Sugars imported into England from British colonies on the Continent of America were to be rated as French.

39. See below for the remission of the four-and-a-half per cent export duty on this commodity. For an analysis of duties under various acts, Harper, *The English Navigation Laws* (above, p. 16, n. 28).

40. GD 8:64, 22 Mar. 1766, Trecothick to Chatham.

all direct trade between Europe and America and thus secure for British manufactures a monopoly of the American market.

Classified as a commercial act, the statute, like those of Grenville's administration, was also designed to produce revenue. The clearest evidence of this intent was the duty on British as well as foreign molasses. The proceeds were to be placed in the British Exchequer and disposed of by Parliament.

From the point of view of the colonists and no less an authority than Blackstone, provisions of the Mutiny Act requiring the assemblies to pay for the quartering of soldiers were also a form of tax.[41] During the 1766 session of Parliament a new quartering act was passed, but whether any copies of this statute reached America is a question.[42] In any case, Rockingham's administration was not entirely free from the charge of levying taxes on America.

But had there been no such concrete reminders of the power of Parliament, there would still have been the Declaratory Act, incorporating the principle that Parliament had the right "to bind the colonies . . . in all cases whatsoever." Rockingham had provided no permanent settlement for the fundamental differences that divided the English-speaking world.

Although Rockingham when he came into office could look forward to approximately six months in which to prepare his legislative program, he was obliged to tackle immediately the many administrative problems created by his predecessor. A complete change in the personnel of the treasury board, new secretaries, and a new solicitor must have made the administrative work more difficult than otherwise. Of the two secretaries, Charles Lowndes was a career man, promoted from the place of chief clerk; the other, following an interim appointee, was the much respected

41. "Debates in Parliament" from T1:372, printed in *AHR, 17* (Oct. 1911– July 1912), 569.

42. *CJ, 30,* 690-718, passim. 6 Geo. III, c. 18. Editions of statutes by Ruffhead and Pickering give only summaries. *A Collection of the Public General Statutes,* printed by Mark Basket (London, 1766), gives the text as c. 16. On 2 Jan. 1768, Gage wrote that he had received none but the act of 1765 (Carter, *Correspondence, 2,* 447).

Grey Cooper, especially qualified to handle the parliamentary business.[43]

Although the civil list, particularly the debt on this fund, was of great concern to the Administration, there were no significant developments with respect to the colonies. The Archbishop of Canterbury and the Bishop of London agreed that the time was not propitious for promoting the establishment of a bishop.[44] The civil list continued to receive some increments from the King's American revenues.

Unlike the civil list, public funds were of increasing significance in colonial administration. Rockingham supported the decision to keep a large force of troops in America, but favored withdrawing them from the outposts in the hope of reducing expenditures.[45] On the other hand, the Treasury agreed to a few additional costs for the service.[46] In handling technical problems Rockingham's approach was very practical. The Treasury, therefore, modified several of Grenville's plans for the army. Gage was to submit advance estimates when possible, but the Treasury now appeared to be more understanding of the difficulties involved.[47] Finding flaws in Grenville's plan for transferring customs revenue to the army, Rockingham limited its application to situations in which

43. William Mellish returned to his old job as receiver general of the customs (Namier, *The Structure of Politics, 2*, 480 n.). His last letter at the Treasury was dated 30 Sept. Thomas Nuthall became the new solicitor, succeeding Philip Carteret Webb, who had been tried but declared not guilty of perjury in the case relating to the seizure of Wilkes' papers (GD 8:51, 11 July 1765; "Philip Carteret Webb," *DNB*).

44. Sheffield City Library, Rockingham, Letters 2, 30 Sept. 1765. WLC, Shelburne, *59*, fols. 1 ff., 1 Mar. 1766.

45. Rockingham, English 12, Disposition of the Forces; Letters 18, proposed motion for address to the King. GD 8:97, May 1766, recommendation from the War Office.

46. Increasing the pay of the commander at Louisburg (T27:29, p. 268); appointing a barrack master general for North America (T29:37, p. 119); erecting barracks and a hospital at Pensacola "with as little Expense as possible" (ibid., p. 265).

47. Regarding proposed engineering work: T29:37, p. 82; Carter, *Correspondence, 2*, 28; *CHOP, 1*, 580, 581, 596; T27:29, p. 199.

it was convenient.[48] After some delay the dispute with the specie contractors was settled in their favor.[49] In the meantime the use of bills of exchange increased. The Treasury, therefore, tried to systematize their use. Commanders were to draw on the Treasury for extraordinaries, and the deputy paymasters on the Paymaster General for regular subsistence.[50] After some experimentation the Treasury concentrated responsibility for drawing bills for extraordinaries in Gage on the mainland and Governor Melville in the Ceded Islands.[51] For the convenience of merchants holding bills the Treasury also arranged with the Bank of England to make payment on those previously accepted at the Treasury, avoiding delay and thus reducing the rate.[52]

With respect to the victualing contracts the Treasury now gave more discretion to General Gage. It countermanded Grenville's order to sell all stores on hand, permitting Gage to sell or not as seemed best.[53] It then arranged with the new contractors to take provisions remaining under the former contract.[54] In making new contracts it was able to improve the terms.[55]

In other fields of public expenditure the activities of Rockingham's Treasury were largely routine. Although Dowdeswell considered the increasing expense of the navy "serious," the Treasury had little to do with this item.[56] The surveyor general of the woods

48. T29:37, pp. 347, 426; T11:28, pp. 105, 111, 113, 318. Since the collectors received dues by weight and the troops were paid by tale, the Treasury directed the auditors to make allowances for deficiencies in the accounts of the Paymaster General.

49. T29:37, pp. 92, 93, 399; T27:29, p. 294.

50. T29:38, pp. 76-77.

51. T29:38, p. 81; T27:29, p. 348.

52. One of the clerks kept a book listing bills accepted according to order of the Treasury Board, and drew the proper warrants for paying the requisite sums to the Bank (T29:37, pp. 81, 151, 155-56; T52:59, pp. 21-22; T61:40, p. 289).

53. T29:37, p. 85.

54. Ibid., p. 88.

55. T27:29, p. 315, contract for West Florida.

56. Rockingham, English 10(8), 5 Dec. 1765.

continued to be the principal crown officer in the colonies connected with both the Admiralty and the Treasury.[57]

Whereas most of the administrative decisions of Rockingham's administration tended to pour oil on the troubled waters of English–American relations, there was one major exception. In 1766 Rhode Island made another effort to secure reimbursement for her expenditures in the campaign of 1756. The Treasury accepted a favorable report from the Paymaster General and the Secretary at War, but suspended payment until the assembly should have compensated sufferers from the Stamp Act riots.[58] In 1767 an inhabitant of Rhode Island condemned this decision of the Lords of the Treasury as "arbitrary and illegal," and challenged the people of the colony to prevent an almost equal amount of customs revenue from being taken to England.[59] It was becoming clear that from the point of view of many colonists the British Treasury epitomized all that was most objectionable in colonial subordination to the Government of England.

Among the most delicate problems faced by Rockingham when he came into office was that created by Grenville's order respecting foreign trade in the West Indies, because under existing law much of that trade was illegal as well as contrary to the mercantilistic policies of other countries. Publicity was undesirable.[60] After re-

---

57. In the summer of 1766 John Wentworth, a friend and relative of Rockingham, succeeded his father, Benning Wentworth (T28:1, pp. 99-102). In one case pine trees condemned at Boston were sold for £10.11.8, but the costs were nearly double this amount (T1:456, account of prosecution by John Wentworth).

58. T29:37, p. 396. Kimball, *Correspondence of the Colonial Governors of Rhode Island* (above, p. 96, n. 99), *2*, 374-75. In 1772 the assembly voted a sum for one of the sufferers to be paid when their agent had received payment due (ibid., *2*, 428 n.).

59. T1:463, copy of a Rhode Island poster "By a Father of Sons and Daughters of Liberty."

60. The law officers proposed an explanatory law, and Dowdeswell suggested instructions to the governors in the meantime (Rockingham, American 31, including note by Rockingham and other suggestions). Charles Yorke confidentially advised against public orders (Rockingham, Letters 13, 25 Oct. 1765).

ceiving legal advice that the importation of bullion in foreign ships was legal, the Treasury merely adopted a cautious minute, originally sketched by Rockingham, authorizing the Customs Commissioners to direct their officers "not to seize or molest foreign vessels bringing Bullion into the said Plantations in like Manner as ... heretofore ... any late Practice to the Contrary notwithstanding."[61] Treasury officials probably hoped that such negative instructions would permit a revival of the customary trade; but later, as we have seen, resorted to the free-port legislation.

For many months after coming into office Rockingham was in the awkward position of having to enforce revenue laws of which he in some instances disapproved and which he hoped to see changed. The changes, moreover, came so late in his administration that he could only initiate the measures for their enforcement. Nevertheless, it is possible to indicate certain characteristics of treasury methods in this field.

The Treasury seemed to defer to the experts more than had been the case under Grenville. With regard to the customs it tended to follow the strict policies of Rockingham's predecessor, but left more responsibility to the commissioners except in the matter of patronage. For the latter purpose the Treasury required weekly lists of vacancies.[62] It encouraged the commissioners to limit leaves of absence and to instruct new appointees as Grenville had insisted. In spite of accumulating evidence of weakness in the colonial customs system, Rockingham attempted no major reforms. Even for the purpose of commercial regulation, therefore, the laws were not entirely effective, and the inconsistencies in the fee system remained a major source of aggravation for the traders.[63]

61. T29:37, pp. 229-30; T11:28, p. 95. Grey Cooper worked on the minute with the Attorney General and John Roberts, but said that his draft was very similar to that originally proposed by Rockingham (Rockingham, American 31, Nov. 1765).

62. T11:28, p. 94.

63. On the recommendation of the Customs Commissioners the Treasury agreed to reduce the salaries of the Quebec officers who had begun to collect fees (T29:37, p. 300).

The free ports, introducing an entirely new principle into the customs system, called for special administrative measures. The methods by which these were adopted and put into effect are characteristic of this Administration. The Treasury consulted the collector from Dominica, adopted some of his suggestions, and referred others to the Customs Commissioners, leaving them free to decide the number of officers required, their salaries, and what instructions they should have.[64]

For developments under Rockingham's successors and later relations with the colonies the most important feature of the customs system was the inadequacy of the revenue. To be sure, as a result of Grenville's legislative and administrative measures the income was increasing.[65] Compared with the costs of administering the colonies, however, the revenue was small. This financial problem remained to trouble succeeding administrations.

The packet system continued to be an expense rather than a source of profit. But a realization of the importance of communication led the Treasury to recommend an addition to the number of boats on the West Indian run and to approve an increase in their size and also higher salaries for commanders of the packets sailing between Falmouth and New York.[66]

Most disheartening of all Rockingham's problems were those connected with the administration of the Stamp Act. Until its repeal the Treasury had to carry on with plans for its enforcement; and thereafter begin to wind up the sad affair. The change in ministers in the summer of 1765 may account in part for the delay in preparing crown officers and the American public for this novel experiment. The law was to go into effect on the first of November. As the time approached, colonial governors became alarmed because they had received no instructions with respect to

64. T11:28, pp. 123, 342-43; T29:38, p. 44; T1:453, 14 Aug. 1766, report on forms of bonds, etc.

65. The act of 1764 produced more than £22,000 in 1766 (AO 1:821:1071).

66. T29:37, pp. 259, 291-93, 323; T1:451, 25 Dec. 1765, showing approval of the Board of Trade and the Post Office for the first suggestion; T54:40, pp. 86-87.

their responsibilities.[67] Although on the fourteenth of September the Treasury wrote directly to the governors of twenty-two colonies, many of these letters did not reach their destinations until the latter part of December.[68] Instructions and copies of the act had been packed with the stamped paper.[69] They naturally suffered the same fate as the paper: destruction by rioters, storage in warehouses, or return to England.

Difficulties in America increased from day to day as public opposition snowballed. Stamp officers began to resign even before the act became effective. After November first, wherever the populace prevented enforcement business temporarily ceased in all cases where stamps were required; for example, lack of stamps prevented the customs collectors from clearing vessels. The governors hesitated to give permission for them to dispense with stamps, but in the central district at least the surveyor general of the customs assumed that authority.[70] Gradually other business revived without the benefit of stamps. In the meantime the Treasury was becoming convinced that enforcement was impossible and repeal necessary.

When the act was a thing of the past, however, the Treasury still had the unpleasant duty of winding up the experiment: securing the return of unused paper and remittances of any revenue received, considering claims, and settling accounts.[71] This business had not

67. T1:442, letter from William Franklin, 7 Sept. 1765, and others.

68. Rockingham, American 4. T27:29, p. 214.

69. Rockingham, American 19, "Memoranda for Lord Rockingham." The governors were supposed to aid the distributors, see that vacancies were filled, and that the chief distributors had given bond (T27:29, p. 214; T1:442, fol. 223). In a few cases distributors who had been in England when the Act was passed carried copies with them to America.

70. T1:452, letter of 7 Dec. 1765 and others. A list of places in which there was supposed to have been no opposition is not entirely reliable: Jamaica, Barbados, Grenada, Bahamas, East Florida, West Florida, Bermuda, Pennsylvania, Nova Scotia, Quebec (*N.J. Arch.*, Ser. 1, *9*, 554).

71. T29:37, pp. 404, 427; T27:29, pp. 297, 309-10. With regard to claims, the general rule was to pay the salaries of inspectors for the time the act was in force, but to disallow the claims of distributors who were appointed on a commission basis (T1:455, petition of 21 June 1766; T1:456, petition received 23 June 1767, endorsed "nil").

been completed when Rockingham left office, and fell on the shoulders of his successors. Receipts amounted to only £3,292.9.11. After being credited with the return of stamped paper, the distributors owed a balance of £64,155.12.5½ on their consignments.[72] The actual financial loss to the British Exchequer may have been considerably less.[73] The real injury, however, is inestimable. The colonists were now thoroughly conditioned against providing revenue for the British Exchequer, and they were questioning as never before the fundamental rights of Parliament over them.

Absorbed as treasury officials were with the problems discussed above, they had comparatively little time to devote to crown revenues. Nevertheless, Cholmondeley's reports kept them reasonably well informed. They consulted him with regard to pertinent colonial laws, and followed his suggestions in the matter of accounts.[74] Rockingham continued the now well-established policy of using surplus quit rents for the king's special service.[75]

The most significant factor with respect to the four-and-a-half per cent revenue was George III's agreement that he would forego the duty on exports of cotton from the islands.[76] This measure, combined with the repeal of the enumerated commodities duty on this product, placed cotton in an extremely favorable position. Only the King suffered from the loss of revenue. In this instance,

---

72. Accounts of the comptroller general examined in 1772 (AO 3:1086).

73. The Treasury borrowed £6,837.0.8 from the sinking fund to pay expenses (HC, "Return of Public Income and Expenditure," *Accounts and Papers*, 1868–69, Pt. I, p. 155); and the warehouse keeper deposited £4,000 in the Exchequer (AO 3:1086). The Treasury also provided for some few expenses by allowing them under the head of incidents of the English office (T29:44, p. 406, rare example of payment of part of claims of a distributor). Probably none of the distributors passed his accounts. In 1770 Jared Ingersoll secured a warrant for delivering up his bond, with no mention of accounts (T54:41, p. 120).

74. T29:37, pp. 99, 122, 135; T1:445, 30 June 1766; T28:1, p. 71; T52:57, pp. 226-27.

75. T52:57, p. 260, £7,000 to Charles Lowndes for the purpose.

76. *CJ, 30,* 835.

as in various others, Rockingham deferred to the merchants with little regard to the effect on the revenue. In 1766, however, the income from the four-and-a-half per cent was unusually large, supplying money for pensions as well as salaries.[77]

Problems connected with the particular revenues from the sales of land in the Ceded Islands, prizes taken before the declaration of the late war against France, and other casual revenues continued to occupy the Treasury. A few illustrations will suffice to indicate the variety of matters handled. In the case of the land in the Ceded Islands, one of the principal questions of policy was that of removing Indians from their lands. The Treasury took no action at this time, but referred the matter to the Board of Trade.[78] In later years the Indian problem became a subject of major proportions.

In this Administration the long legal contest over Admiral Frankland's prize accounts came to an end by means of an agreement outside of court. Cholmondeley was now able to close the accounts, netting for himself the unprecedented fee of £3,600.[79] The Treasury occasionally handled a petition for a grant of a prize condemned in America, referred to it by the Privy Council. In a New York case, for example, the judge of the vice-admiralty court and the captors, though not legally entitled to it, both asked for the condemned vessel. In this instance the Treasury followed the advice of the Advocate General and the usual custom, granting possession to the captors.[80]

With regard to the revenue from Guadeloupe, the Treasury

77. The net for 1766 was £42,504.9.6¼ (Shelburne, *104*, fols. 8 ff.). Grey Cooper's life annuity of £500 a year, which he demanded before accepting the office of secretary to the Treasury, was to come from this source (T52:57, p. 339; T64:216, pp. 15-17).

78. T29:37, pp. 208-9.

79. T54:40, pp. 133-48. Prizes not taken in America were accounted for in the usual way (AO 3:326).

80. T1:451, fols. 24-27. The case was really a contest between the King's advocate and the Admiralty for possession because of an error in procedure. In England the Admiralty would have brought suit in the name of the King.

applied £1,300, as it became available, to the king's secret or special service.[81]

The critical state of Quebec finances was of peculiar significance, for it finally led Rockingham to add this province to those supported wholly or in part from funds in the British Exchequer. The revenue problem in Canada was fraught with legal complications. In the first place Governor Murray had levied taxes on his own authority, but ceased to do so when his competence was called in question. Furthermore, even after the appointment of a receiver general the Crown had failed to give specific authority for collecting the dues formerly paid to the French king. Consequently, there was no legal basis for the collection of revenue in the province.

Early in Rockingham's administration a letter from Governor Murray with a bill of exchange for government expenses brought the situation to the startled attention of the Treasury.[82] Following a reference to the Privy Council and new advice from the law officers, the Treasury drafted the necessary instructions for the receiver general, specifying the duties formerly payable to the French king which he was to collect.[83] These were published in Canada sometime before July 7, 1766.[84]

Both legal and financial questions with regard to the collection of revenue in Quebec persisted, however. The French, so it was said, had derived a large part of their revenue from wine, but French wine could no longer be imported,[85] and Canadian importers contested the legality of the tax on British brandy.[86] They

---

81. T52:57, p. 506. Cholmondeley's claims to audit accounts of revenues in islands returned to France were still in controversy at the end of this administration. The story can be followed by reference to T29:37, pp. 213, 449; AO 3:-1102; Add. MSS 35,637, fols. 401-2; T1:450, 7 May 1766.

82. T29:37, p. 148. In 1765 Murray had published an order from England to make a refund of dues illegally collected (WLC, Shelburne, *64*, fol. 525).

83. *APC, Col., 4*, 725 ff. HM 220, Grey's reports, 2 Nov. 1765. T28:1, pp. 88-89.

84. BT, *Journal*, 1764–67, p. 329.

85. CO 42:87, fol. 152 (p. 12 of pamphlet).

86. Rockingham, American 23.

won their case in a Quebec court, leaving the question of right in doubt until a decision should have been made on appeal.

In the meantime the immediate need for funds for the civil expenses of the government led the Treasury to order an issue of £5,530 to the receiver general from funds in the Exchequer arising from duties on foreign rum and sugar imported into the plantations.[87] Rockingham thus set a precedent for the support of Quebec from funds raised by act of Parliament, thereby adding to the mounting costs of colonial administration for which Parliament acquired responsibility.

In retrospect it seems that from the point of view of the English taxpayer Rockingham had done nothing to solve the financial problems created by the addition of territory at the end of the Seven Years' War. On the contrary, the repeal of the Stamp Act had eliminated one possible source of income from America, while other measures had increased expenditures.

On the other hand, he had accomplished his objective, which was to correct "the errors" of the Grenville administration. He had, indeed, largely satisfied the English merchants. He had also gone far toward conciliating the colonists, although the legislation of this period restricted the trade of the northern colonies. Yet one major obstacle to harmonious relations between England and her colonies remained—innocuous possibly, but of tremendous potential significance. This was the Declaratory Act, expressing for the first time in statutory form the power of Parliament "to bind the colonies . . . in all cases whatsoever."

Nevertheless, had Rockingham's successors based their programs on the foundations he had laid, the history of the next ten years might have been quite different. Unhappily for the integrity of the British empire, during the next decade treasury officials carried on a succession of unfortunate attempts to obtain revenues from Americans without their consent, ending in coercion.

87. T29:37, pp. 381-82; T61:40, p. 309.

6.

The Treasury and the Loss of Thirteen Colonies: the Administrations of the Duke of Grafton and Lord North, 1766–1776

WHEN WILLIAM PITT, Earl of Chatham, finally accepted responsibility as the King's first minister, there was no thorough sweep of government offices. Rockingham did not insist that his followers resign, and there was little reason to suppose that there would be a radical change in American policies, for Chatham had opposed Grenville's schemes, had demanded the repeal of the Stamp Act, and was known as a friend of the colonies. Less than a year had passed, however, before Parliament under treasury leadership adopted a plan for colonial taxation and novel measures for enforcement, inciting the colonies to new resistance. The mother country first used milder forms of coercion and ultimately armed force in a futile attempt to establish parliamentary supremacy over the colonies. Treasury officials were primarily responsible for the legislative policies and administrative programs that supplied the immediate impulse for the American Revolution.

The restoration of a demand for American taxes while the Earl of Chatham was still Prime Minister can be explained in large part by the peculiar character of his ministry. Chatham himself took the office of Lord Privy Seal, assigning the more arduous duties of First Lord of the Treasury to the Duke of Grafton, who had little to recommend him for that post.[1] The ministry as a whole

1. He had been Secretary of State for the Northern Department 10 July 1765–14 May 1766. Augustus Henry Grafton, *Autobiography and Political Correspondence*, ed. Sir William Anson (London, 1898), pp. 89, 91, for Grafton's reluctance. John Brooke, *The Chatham Administration, 1766–1768* (New York, St. Martin's Press, 1956), a political study.

was an experiment, a combination of individuals without common loyalties or policies. Chatham was often ill and at the most strategic moments likely to be inaccessible.

During the first few months, when Chatham was nominally at the head of the Government and everyone was looking to him for leadership—usually in vain—confusion reigned in ministerial circles. With respect to colonial affairs ministers complained of a lack of system. The president of the Privy Council explained that no plan could begin in his office because he had no direct communications with colonial officials.[2] Although American affairs were important enough to be considered in the Cabinet, without a leader this group merely disputed among themselves. Not seeming to be aware of his own responsibility, Chatham wrote to Grafton of "a certain infelicity which ferments and sowers . . . the Councils of His Majesty's servants."[3] Under Hillsborough the Board of Trade took no initiative.[4] Shelburne, who was Secretary of State for the Southern Department, looked to Chatham for advice and received none.[5] Although the most immediate problems were financial, Grafton seemed unable to supply leadership even in this field. Consequently, when Charles Townshend, Chancellor of the Exchequer, sensitive because of recent slights and eager for recognition, seized the opportunity to become the irresponsible spokesman for the Government in the House of Commons and promised a revenue from America, there was no one to restrain him.[6]

By the summer of 1767 it was all too clear that Chatham could

2. Grafton Papers 11, 9 Aug. 1767.

3. Ibid., 581, 23 Jan. 1767.

4. The repeal of the order of 1752 technically reduced the efficiency of the Board (*APC, Col., 5*, 3-4). Shelburne, *53*, fols. 17, 18, a letter of interpretation from Shelburne demanded by Hillsborough.

5. GD 8:56, for example, undated letter, Shelburne to Lady Chatham.

6. Grafton, *Autobiography*, p. 89. Add. MSS 38,205, fols. 82-83. In March 1767 North refused the place of Chancellor of the Exchequer, foiling a plan to get rid of Townshend (Grafton Papers 454). Townshend was said to know of the refusal (William Stanhope Taylor and Captain John Henry Pringle, eds., *Correspondence of William Pitt, Earl of Chatham* (London, 1838—40), *3*, 233-34.

not or would not accept responsibilities. Grafton then became the recognized representative of the King and head of the Government. In October following the death of Townshend, Lord North rather reluctantly accepted the office of Chancellor of the Exchequer, which he had refused the previous spring. Gifted in finance and enjoying the confidence of the King, he brought needed strength to the Government, especially in the House of Commons where he soon took over the leadership.[7] Divisions, however, continued to characterize the King's councils. The appointment of Hillsborough as third Secretary of State with special responsibility for the colonies counteracted the more conciliatory influence of Shelburne, still Secretary for the Southern Department.[8] In September 1768 Shelburne was said to be the only member of the Cabinet opposed to colonial coercion.[9] The next month he resigned, and shortly thereafter Chatham gave up the seals.

Early in 1770, finding himself in a minority in the Cabinet on the question of retaining the tax on tea when other Townshend duties were to be repealed, Grafton left office. Lord North, becoming First Lord of the Treasury while retaining the post of Chancellor of the Exchequer, combined the two offices that Walpole had made the basis of his great political power. Lord North, however, was serving a monarch who was far more interested in all the policies and details of administration than either George I or George II, and wielded more influence. The Government of Lord North was more literally His Majesty's Government than had been the case under either Grenville or Rockingham. Nevertheless, according to the English system, North advised the King. Parliament eventually held him responsible for the disastrous effects of this advice, though not during the period covered by this chapter.

A high degree of professionalism in political management charac-

7. Grafton 309 [Apr. 1768].

8. T64:216, pp. 101-2. The King advised Hillsborough to consult with Grafton and the Chancellor before a Cabinet was summoned, so the Cabinet need not discuss, but only approve, referring to the method that had been practiced "till of late years" (Grafton 510).

9. HEH, Stowe 7, 2, 18 Sept. 1768.

terized Lord North's administration. Patronage was more centralized than under his predecessor. As usual it was distributed for
political purposes. Both Grafton and North, however, had a certain
delicacy with respect to the patronage that may have mildly foreshadowed later reforms.[10] In both the handling of elections and the
management of Parliament, Lord North found expert assistance in
the two secretaries: John Robinson, who had been election agent
for Sir James Lowther before entering the Treasury in October
1770; and Grey Cooper, who continued at the Treasury in spite
of ministerial changes. The period between elections was little
short of the maximum allowed by law, indicating from the point
of view of the ministry satisfactory behavior on the part of the
House of Commons. There were two elections in the period under
review, one in 1768 when Grafton was at the Treasury, and the
other in 1774. Although in 1767 the House of Commons had been
far from tractable, the election in the following year appeared to
give far less concern than that of 1774.[11] Considerably more money
was spent in 1774.[12] This election, however, made little change in
government strength, which continued sufficient for administration
purposes until the reverses of the war.[13]

Actually, the day-to-day nursing of majorities was probably more
effective than the management of elections. In handling the daily
problems of obtaining the passage of government measures Lord
North had the advantage of sitting in the House of Commons,
where he spoke with great effect. Moreover, during a large part
of this period two former secretaries to the Treasury, Charles Jen-

10. GD 8:33, Grafton to Chatham [1766] hesitating to appoint relatives.
T29:40, pp. 282, 353, North's opposition to buying offices; T27:30, p. 324, plan
to abolish patent offices in Quebec. In 1769 Samuel Martin wrote his brother
that he knew of no patent places that were "sold fairly & by open permission:
except a few in the Courts of Justice" (Add. MSS 41,361, 4 Aug. 1769).

11. During the preceding year, when borough elections should have been
paving the way for success in the general election, Grafton felt that Chatham
was neglecting the cause (GD 8:33, 22 Jan. 1767).

12. Sir John Fortescue, ed., *Correspondence of King George the Third*
(London, Macmillan, 1927—28), *5*, 478, 480.

13. Ibid., *3*, 137.

kinson and Jeremiah Dyson, were Junior Lords and among the most devoted of the King's Friends.[14] Dyson had also been clerk of the House of Commons. As members of Parliament their combined knowledge of parliamentary procedure and public finance contributed to the success of government measures. The secretaries were also invaluable. Cooper was becoming a skilled parliamentarian, and the Treasury depended upon him to present many of their bills. Robinson, for his part, assembled and tabulated information concerning members and correlated it with division lists for his own purposes and for the edification of the King.[15] George III stimulated them all by his interest in every detail. Until American reaction to British policies had a serious effect on individuals and the state, the leaders had little difficulty in securing a majority for their bills.

Throughout the period legislation applying to the colonies was strongly tinged with the spirit of the Declaratory Act. Among the laws sponsored by the Treasury were examples of traditional mercantilism. The critical state of public finance, however, also produced measures clearly in conflict with mercantilist theory. These were the tax laws and administrative reforms designed to increase the revenue. When their disadvantageous effect upon British commerce became apparent, the merchants could secure only a modification, not complete repeal, because American resistance created a demand for discipline regardless of the immediate effect. In spite of some overlapping of purposes, it is possible to classify the colonial laws of this period according to four principal objects: the regulation of commerce, revenue, improvements in administration, and coercion. In addition there were the usual appropriations for defense and for civil government, which had created the original excuse for colonial taxation. But these appropriations were now based in part on expectations of colonial revenue.

At this time there was no single method of drafting commercial legislation. Sometimes the Treasury directed the Customs Commis-

14. Jenkinson, 1 Dec. 1767–12 Jan. 1773; Dyson, 28 Dec. 1768–11 Mar. 1774.
15. William T. Laprade, ed., *Parliamentary Papers of John Robinson, 1774–1784*, London, the Royal Historical Society, 1922.

sioners to do so, and sometimes the Board of Trade. Neither Grafton nor North appeared to take any personal interest in mercantile policies. While Chancellor of the Exchequer, Townshend was officially responsible for such measures but was also without apparent interest. Shortly after Lord North succeeded Townshend, Charles Jenkinson became a Junior Lord. North often deferred to Jenkinson's judgment on commercial matters. Grey Cooper frequently introduced bills dealing with customs, and defended them.

These commercial acts included previously tested devices to encourage colonial enterprise and commerce, such as bounties, reduction of English import duties, and "drawbacks" on goods going from England to the colonies.[16] On the other hand, fear of American competition led Parliament to grant bounties to British and Irish fishing vessels, and to repeal the Act of 1708, under which sailors in American waters had claimed freedom from impressment.[17] The Quebec Revenue Act of 1774 provided an even stronger illustration of English jealousy of colonial development. That act discriminated against the older, commercial colonies of the mainland by placing higher duties on molasses and syrup brought in American ships than on the same products brought in British vessels; and rum from the West Indies enjoyed a preference over that from the mainland.[18] Three years later Charles Jenkin-

16. Bounties on the importation of raw silk (9 Geo. III, c. 38) and on white oak staves (11 Geo. III, c. 50); removing duties on imported hides and skins (9 Geo. III, c. 39) and on unmanufactured wood except masts, yards, and bowsprits (11 Geo. III, c. 41); drawback on coffee and cocoa nuts (7 Geo. III, c. 46); extension of the rice market for East and West Florida and the carrying privilege to ships built in the colonies and belonging to any of His Majesty's subjects (10 Geo. III, c. 31, and 11 Geo. III, c. 39). Temporary free importation of cereals and salted meats from the colonies was to relieve shortage at home (7 Geo. III, cc. 4, 30, and others, 1770, 1772, 1773). 7 Geo. III, c. 2, amended 6 Geo. III, c. 52, to permit nonenumerated commodities to be landed in Ireland as well as England.

17. 15 Geo. III, c. 31. D. M. Clark, "The Impressment of Seamen in the American Colonies," *Essays in Colonial History* (New Haven, Yale Univ. Press, 1931), for discussion of whether the 1708 act remained in effect after the close of the War of the Spanish Succession.

18. 14 Geo. III, c. 88.

son, no longer at the Treasury but retaining considerable influence, proposed that colonial ships should be restricted to the coasting trade.[19] It may be that American merchants avoided this calamity only by achieving independence.

The first important revenue act of this period, from which succeeding troubles largely stemmed, was that of 1767, sponsored by Townshend and only lightly disguised as an act of trade. As indicated above, it failed to reflect the views of leaders or the majority of the Cabinet. On the other hand, all members of the Government were aware of the problem of financing civil and military establishments in America. As a preliminary to drafting legislation both Shelburne and the Treasury undertook to obtain information from England and America with regard to current colonial expenses and how they were being met.[20] A report from the Board of Trade on the establishments of individual colonies was a blank in several cases and out of date or inadequate in others. Only payments from parliamentary sources could be stated with any degree of accuracy.[21] In planning for the future there were imponderables, including the possibility for economy in military and Indian affairs and the readiness of the colonial assemblies to accept additional obligations, such as the quartering of English soldiers. Shelburne's secretary found it impossible to make an accurate summary of annual expenses from available statistics.[22]

It was quite as difficult to estimate the revenue. Shelburne evidently hoped that the Treasury might obtain sufficient funds from crown revenues, especially the quit rents, so that parliamentary taxation would be unnecessary. Grafton appeared to support such a proposal, at least as far as New York was concerned. Townshend then demanded a declaration on this subject, presumably to be

19. Add. MSS 38,306, fol. 73.
20. WLC, Shelburne, *55,* fol. 138, 11 Dec. 1766, to governors. *CHOP, 2, 167,* to Board of Trade, and 169, to Admiralty. T28:1, p. 111, treasury letters to governors.
21. CO 5:216, pp. 21 ff. Shelburne, *50,* fols. 331-33; *51,* passim; *57,* fol. 255, an estimate of £420,453, excluding a temporary expense.
22. WLC, Shelburne, *57,* fol. 227.

obtained from the King, which he could present to Parliament.[23] Whether Grafton actually consulted George III with regard to further use of crown revenues for colonial establishments is obscure. It may be that he finally realized that existing quit rents would be totally insufficient for the immediate need.[24]

While the above investigations were proceeding, financial and political problems became more desperate. Early in the session of 1767 the opposition needled Townshend into agreeing that the colonies ought to contribute to the support of troops established there.[25] Thereafter, he considered that his honor was involved. Completely out of hand, the House of Commons voted to reduce the land tax from four to three shillings in the pound.[26] The estimated loss to the revenue from this decision was £500,000, a sum larger than Parliament's annual appropriations for the colonies.[27] Townshend's own position in the Government was now in jeopardy; but when he learned that Lord North had refused his place, he concluded that he was secure in office and became still more highhanded.

With Chatham in retirement, the spring months passed without agreement in the Cabinet as to how American expenses could be cut or how the necessary funds could be raised. Late in the session, with the passive acquiescence of the ministers, Townshend intro-

23. Grafton 441 and 445, undated. Fitzmaurice, *Life of Shelburne, 1,* 304. *Grenville Papers, 3,* 334, Whately to Grenville, ridiculing the plan.

24. The previous November the auditor general had reported that an act of Parliament would be necessary to achieve complete rent rolls in America (T1:452, 14 Nov. 1766). Carter, *Correspondence, 1,* 130-31, 5 Apr. 1767, a discouraging letter. Early in the summer of 1767, however, Shelburne was still thinking that quit rents in the new territories might provide for their governments (WLC, Shelburne, *50,* fol. 185).

25. HMC, *Stopford Sackville MSS, 1,* 119. HEH, Stowe 7, 2, 27 Jan. 1767. Add. MSS 38,205, fol. 132.

26. *CJ, 31,* 196, 197, 204, 231. Whately had suggested these tactics to Grenville (*Grenville Papers, 3,* 336).

27. Mrs. Paget Toynbee, ed., *The Letters of Horace Walpole, Fourth Earl of Orford* (16 vols. Oxford, Clarendon Press, 1903—05), 7, 87.

duced his measure for port duties.[28] The bill which passed the Commons on June 18 placed duties on glass, red and white lead, painters' colors, paper, and tea imported into America.[29] Although the act was obviously contrary to mercantilist principles and harmful to English trade, the Government was unwilling to yield to American opposition and kept it on the statute books for three years. In 1770 a combination of mercantile interests secured the repeal of most of the taxes. The Government retained the one duty on tea as a disciplinary measure, granting compensations to the East India Company.[30] The East India Act of 1773 allowed a complete drawback on tea exported from England, but the colonial duty remained.[31] This act was the signal for the Boston Tea Party.

In 1774 the Government had decided against establishing an assembly in Quebec. That government had now become dependent on the British Exchequer. Consequently Parliament passed a revenue act expressly for that province.[32] Lord North's announcement of the following year that he had no further intention of taxing America took everyone by surprise.[33] In 1778 Parliament even repealed the duty on tea and announced that there would be no future taxes for revenue.[34] But the Declaratory Act remained as a statement of the right, and the Quebec Act as an example of the practice.

The revenue acts were only one phase of the Treasury's con-

---

28. Taylor and Pringle, *Chatham Correspondence, 3,* 233-34. There were, of course, other than American questions under dispute, especially that of the East India Co.

29. 7 Geo. III, c. 46. In order to offset the tax on tea and protect the market for the E. India Co., c. 56 of the same session provided a temporary drawback on tea exported to America and a discontinuance of the excise in England.

30. 10 Geo. III, c. 17; 12 Geo. III, c. 60.

31. 13 Geo. III, c. 44.

32. 14 Geo. III, c. 88. Trading features discriminating against the other colonies of the mainland are discussed above.

33. [William] Cobbett, ed., *Parliamentary History* (36 vols. London, 1806–20), *18,* 264-65.

34. 18 Geo. III, c. 12.

tribution to American unrest. Quite as unpopular as the Townshend duties was the establishment of a separate board of customs for America, authorized by an act of 1767. Circumstantial evidence suggests that the idea originated in a conversation between Townshend and Charles Paxton, surveyor and searcher in the Massachusetts Bay port of Boston, who was in England during the winter of 1766—67.[35] Whatever the origin of the plan, Townshend was its sponsor. Before the end of January he was promoting it in connection with his proposal for port duties.[36] Like the revenue act it did not come before Parliament until late in the session. The bill, presented by Cooper on June 3, was a simple one, merely authorizing the King to place the management of the colonial customs in the hands of commissioners to be resident in America and assuring them the same authority in their jurisdiction as that previously exercised by the Board in London.[37]

Colonial hostility to the measure sprang primarily from the obvious fact that its purpose was to assure the collection of taxes. In addition, however, the colonists hated the Board and their subordinates for their own sakes. The Declaration of Independence referred to them obliquely as "swarms of Officers [sent hither] to harass our People, and eat out their substance."

Among lesser administrative provisions recommended by the Treasury was one in the Revenue Act of 1767, authorizing the supreme court in any colony to issue writs of assistance. This provision followed an opinion of the Attorney and Solicitor General that customs officers could not enter and search without such authority, and that there was no legal way of obtaining it in Amer-

35. He was directed to attend the Treasury, 23 Sept. 1766 (T29:38, p. 127). He was intimate with members of the Townshend family, and later in writing to George, Viscount Townshend, referred to Charles as his patron: Mass. Hist. Soc., *Proceedings, 56* (1923), 349-50.

36. Fitzmaurice, *Life of Shelburne, 2,* 39. *Chatham Correspondence, 3,* 185, letter from Shelburne. T1:459, 30 Apr. 1767, showing Customs Commissioners had approved.

37. 7 Geo. III, c. 41.

ica.[38] In 1768 Lord North himself presented a rather vague bill making it possible to establish several courts of vice-admiralty for America with appellate as well as original jurisdiction.[39] These various administrative measures had greater poignancy because of their application to the hated Townshend duties. The Declaration of Independence alluded to the vice-admiralty courts in the charge that the King had "combined with others" to deprive Americans "in many cases of the benefits of Trial by Jury."

In all the major laws of this period there was evidence of a hardening attitude toward America. As early as 1767 the reaction of the ministry to New York's refusal to provide quarters for English soldiers illustrated this attitude. The Cabinet was more united on this subject than on most of the issues of 1767. When admonitions to the province failed, Chatham himself advised laying the pertinent papers before Parliament, though he had no specific proposal.[40] Townshend, who was always ready with an idea, suggested an address from Parliament, advising the King to withhold approval of New York laws until the assembly had obeyed the Mutiny Act. Shelburne thought it a mistake to raise the question of the royal prerogative. The ministers in general were cool to Townshend's proposal. After considerable delay they agreed on a statute as the better method.[41] Townshend himself introduced the bill, which thus became an integral part of his colonial program. The law suspended all activities of the New York assembly until it had complied with the terms of the Mutiny Act.[42] The decision to resort to Parliament in this emergency shows a clear preference

38. T1:453, 12 Nov. 1766. Custom House Library, Opinions of Counsel, 1766–81, p. 180. The English procedure was to apply to the Court of Exchequer, but the writs of this court did not run in the colonies.

39. *CJ, 31,* 630, 633. T29:38, p. 136. 8 Geo. III, c. 22. Cooper objected strongly to this plan for new courts and advised abolishing the one at Halifax and reforming the others (WLC, Shelburne, *48,* 639 ff.).

40. Grafton 575.

41. GD 8:56, 26 Apr. 1767. Charles R. Ritcheson, *British Politics and the American Revolution* (Norman, Univ. of Oklahoma, 1954), treats the subject in considerable detail.

42. 7 Geo. III, c. 59.

for statutory authority when disciplinary action was desired. In the Declaration of Independence Americans took note of Parliament's suspension of their "own Legislatures."

Soon after the passage of the above act the Government learned that New York had given partial compliance—sufficient, so the law officers advised, to relieve the assembly of legal penalties.[43] The ministry had now established a precedent for parliamentary coercion, although several years passed before Parliament again interfered with colonial governments. In 1770 the partial repeal of the Townshend Acts gave some relief to the tension between England and her colonies. Then, following the riots over the Tea Act of 1773, Lord North's Government turned again to Parliament for disciplinary measures. The result was the three well-known acts of 1774, closing the port of Boston, revising the government of Massachusetts Bay, and changing long-established judicial procedures in that province.[44] These coercive acts represented general government policy but at the same time were the indirect result of trade or revenue laws for which the Treasury was responsible.[45]

Appropriations for defense and civil government were both cause and effect of the acts discussed above. The growing costs of colonial administration had originally created a demand for American contributions to the revenue. Colonial resistance led the Government to supplement existing British forces in the hope of subduing the revolt. Estimates of 1773 reversed an earlier trend toward reductions.[46] For Americans the evidence of these appropriations was the standing army in time of peace, a major grievance. Appropriations for civil establishments remained practically unaltered.[47] Instead of reducing expenditures for administration,

43. WLC, Shelburne, *61*, fol. 713.

44. 14 Geo. III, cc. 19, 45, 39. The following year Parliament first placed restrictions on American commerce and fishing and then prohibited all trade and intercourse.

45. Cooper defended the Boston Port Bill, saying, according to report, that it was for the protection of trade (Cobbett, *Parliamentary History, 17,* 1186).

46. *CJ, 31-35,* passim.

47. In 1777 Parliament placed St. John on a regular establishment ("Return of Public Income," 1868—69, Pt. I, pp. 157 ff.).

therefore, the Treasury actually increased them, obtaining only temporary, moderate relief from revenue raised in the colonies.

Patent in all the colonial legislation discussed above were the policies which were to bring about the separation of thirteen colonies from the British Empire. But before policies could have any material effect upon relations between England and her colonies they had to be enforced. The methods of administration, therefore, as well as the policies themselves played an important part in developing tension between Great Britain and her colonies. Since colonial administration had become a foremost political issue, it was impossible for the Treasury to ignore these laws, had it wished to do so, or return to the somewhat careless, relaxed approach to colonial administration so characteristic of Walpole's handling of colonial affairs. Because more aspects of administration were now embedded in the law, the Treasury had less room in which to maneuver. Nevertheless, some flexibility was possible, and there were some opportunities to make the laws more or less agreeable. Unfortunately, the general tendency of administration was to aggravate a situation already ripe for revolt.

By nature both Grafton and North were rather easygoing, and easily influenced, often by subordinates who had a greater zeal for efficiency and for taking steps to assure parliamentary supremacy in the colonies. Among these subordinates was Charles Jenkinson, friend of Bute and former secretary to the Treasury under Grenville. Now, as Junior Lord, he took an unusually active part in administration, helping with the budget, occasionally drafting a minute, and undoubtedly influencing decisions in more obscure ways.[48] Although many matters, especially those involving changes in policy or procedure, came before the Board, attendance was poor and approval was probably routine. It was sometimes necessary to send about town for signatures.[49]

As usual in times of stress, the secretaries bore exceptional ad-

48. He said he liked his "old Trade of Finance" (Add. MSS 38,305, fols. 30, 32; 38,206, fol. 372.

49. There was the story of the order lost for a week and finally found in a footman's box (Rockingham, box of loose papers).

ministrative burdens without relief from their political responsibilities.[50] The confidential nature of much of their work affected their appointment and tenure. It was desirable for the First Lord to have at least one of the secretaries personally loyal to him. For that reason Grafton promoted Thomas Bradshaw to supplant Lowndes. Shortly after Grafton's resignation, John Robinson took Bradshaw's place.[51] Cooper carried on the tradition of permanent tenure.

There was no major reorganization of the clerks until 1776, when changes in the distribution of business, rules of promotion, and rewards helped to remove causes of discontent in the office.[52] The First Lord, Chancellor of the Exchequer, and secretaries each used one of the under-clerks as private secretary.[53] As American disputes increased, the work of the solicitor became more burdensome. It fell on one of the joint solicitors and his assistant because the other place continued to be a sinecure.[54]

Although George III did not revive the earlier royal practice of presiding at the Treasury Board, he was interested in all its activities. Through Jenkinson and indirectly through John Robinson, both of whom were more determined and aggressive than Lord North, George III could bring his influence to bear on the First Lord of the Treasury. The King's firmness and tenacity, therefore, played a considerable part in the conduct of government.

Among the major funds for which the Treasury was responsible, the King's civil list had gradually sunk in importance for colonial

50. In 1768 Bradshaw wrote he was "hurried and tired to death" (Add. MSS 41,354, 5 Nov. 1768).

51. Bradshaw said he felt too indebted to Grafton to serve under another (Grafton 616).

52. George III approved these changes (T29:45, pp. 53 ff.).

53. William Brummell's case is especially notable, for he served Jenkinson and then Cooper while they were secretaries, then Townshend when he was Chancellor of the Exchequer, and for ten years, Lord North. On retiring, North requested a grant for him (Fortescue, *Correspondence of George the Third, 5,* 411).

54. The assistant was dependent upon his superior for an income. When in 1775 Nuthall died insolvent, he owed his assistant over £5,000 (GD 8:231).

administration. The heavy debt on this fund, relieved from time to time by special parliamentary grants, made it more than ever desirable to avoid charging it with American items.[55] When the American refugee problem became acute, however, it was necessary to make emergency payments from the civil list until Parliament appropriated funds for the loyalists.[56] At the same time that the civil list was feeling the burden of American refugees, it was losing income from some of the American crown revenues, especially the Virginia quit rents.

Unlike expenditures from the civil list for colonial purposes, those from public funds were of increasing importance. The reason, however, had little to do with the details of treasury administration or even the slightly larger amount involved. The fact that the Government used public funds to enforce unpopular laws and increase colonial dependency, that Americans were now forced to contribute to these funds, and that the British Parliament appropriated them and the British Treasury administered them account for their importance as a factor in the growing contention between England and her colonies. At the same time it may be recorded that in handling almost every branch of these funds the Treasury was becoming moderately more efficient. A few illustrations will suffice.

For example, the Treasury made it easier for Gage to acquire funds for the army by permitting him to draw on the deputy paymaster for both subsistence and extraordinaries.[57] It also arranged for contractors to supply funds for both classes of expenditures.[58]

55. *CJ, 32,* 255, 257, 265, for appropriations in 1769. The Treasury transferred the salary of the attorney general of N.Y. to the American customs until that revenue practically disappeared (AO 1:844:1137).

56. T52:64, passim; 17 Geo. III, c. 47, and later statutes. The loss of the colonies and thus a place to which to send convicts caused Parliament to appropriate funds to place offenders, otherwise qualified for transportation, at hard labor in England (16 Geo. III, c. 43). At the close of the war the Government, with the King's happy acquiescence, planned to send convicts to the former colonies, but was prevented by Congress (Fortescue, *6,* 415, 416, 418).

57. Carter, *Correspondence, 2,* 335. T29:38, p. 284; T27:29, p. 418.

58. T29:38, pp. 245-46; T54:50, pp. 304-6.

In emergencies governors might still draw on the Treasury. If they did so, Lord North was more careful than most of his predecessors to sustain their credit.[59]

Improvements are also apparent in the methods of supplying provisions. The Treasury seemed to act with greater assurance and more business acumen than had sometimes been the case. For example, in 1770 it was able to reduce expenses of forces stationed on the Illinois River by having contractors buy provisions in that region.[60] In the crisis of 1775 it took the initiative of sending coal and forage without waiting to hear from Gage.[61]

Modest improvements in administration must have had little or no effect on factors leading to the American Revolution and American independence—factors such as American dislike of a standing army and the failure of the army to suppress the revolt in its incipiency. The explanation for this dislike and this failure would have to be sought in the whole colonial situation and outlook, and to some extent in Great Britain as well, but not in the way the Treasury performed its functions of supply.

Two agencies of the Admiralty made a significant contribution to the enforcement of the trade and revenue laws, and consequently added to colonial unrest. The navy was active in apprehending smugglers, and the vice-admiralty courts heard prosecutions which often resulted in condemnation of vessels and goods. Although the Treasury had strongly recommended these methods of enforcement, it had little to do with actual procedures other than to give financial aid to officers in cases of appeal.

On the other hand, the Treasury discouraged an unusual experiment in public relations undertaken by the navy at the suggestion of Hillsborough. In 1770 and 1771 the commander of the North American fleet received directions to make Boston his constant rendezvous "and to give every aid and assistance in his power to conciliate the minds of the people." His method was that of giving

59. T29:42, pp. 272, 330, 334; T27:30, p. 442.
60. T27:30, pp. 243, 249, indicating allowance of 10d. a ration, whereas it had previously been 13½d. (T27:29, p. 487).
61. T29:44, pp. 293, 340.

"Public Entertainments."[62] Hillsborough evidently thought the results very successful. The Treasury, taken by surprise when the warrant for payment reached that office, warned against repeating the experiment without its approval. There was no repetition.

The administration of parliamentary grants for the civil governments in America was now well organized and largely routine. The colonial agents received and accounted for funds received, according to the regular establishments. In the case of extraordinary demands they still applied to the Treasury directly or through the Board of Trade. For this period of revolt, however, the details of administration were less important than the simple fact that certain provinces were dependent upon parliamentary support and that of these parliamentary protégés only Georgia joined the revolutionary movement.

The positive character of treasury administration noted in the field of public expenditures was even more conspicuous in the collection of public revenue. In the latter case, however, there does seem to have been a close relationship between the methods of administration and the development of colonial hostility. The relationship is especially clear in the administration of the customs by the American Board of Customs. From the beginning this Board was a symbol of all that the colonists hated most in English domination. When it called for military and naval aid, it set in motion a tragic train of events that culminated in American independence. Among the immediate and inciting causes of colonial revolt none was more powerful than this American Board, for which the Treasury was responsible.

The terms of the statute authorizing the Board were so general that the Treasury had many important decisions to make. In the first place, there was the question of the scope of the new Board's jurisdiction. A late but probably fortunate decision, influenced by merchants trading to the West Indies, left those islands under the supervision of the London Board. The latter followed traditional methods and there was nothing in the administration of the West

62. T52:62, p. 308; T29:42, p. 417. This instance shows that the Treasury still had occasional difficulty in controlling expenditures.

Indian customs to arouse colonial hostility. The jurisdiction of the American Board was confined to the North American Continent, Bermuda, the Bahamas, and Newfoundland. Included in this area were forty-two regular ports of entry and nine other districts where preventive officers under one designation or another were located.[63]

Boston was the final choice for the new Board's headquarters. Much might be said both for and against this location. One of the most flourishing commercial centers, the city was near enough the geographical center of the American coast to make the choice appear practical. But Boston had been and continued to be a center of hot-headed resistance to British taxation. While the commissioners temporarily secured a greater compliance with the laws, their presence in the city undoubtedly heightened antagonism to English rule.

Finally, the Treasury was responsible for deciding on the membership of the commission and the personnel of its staff. Of primary importance for success or failure was the character of these officials. From one point of view the Treasury exercised considerable discretion in selecting them: they all had had experience in the customs in America or Great Britain, and the First Commissioner, Henry Hulton, was the former plantation clerk under the London Board. Yet it was a rather undistinguished group, whose members proved unequal to the great demands upon them. Those who had previously served in the colonies had the disadvantage of having already aroused local antagonisms.[64] There was jealousy and friction within the Board and this lack of harmony made it more difficult to deal impartially with questions coming before them, to

63. PRO, Customs 21:16, gives the list. From 1771 St. John's Island was included (AO 1:844:1137). In that year there were 182 port officers (Custom House Library, General Establishment, erroneously marked "Prior to 8th. Sept. 1767," but dated from internal evidence as 1771 or 1772). In 1775 Newfoundland was transferred to the English system.

64. John Temple was a native of Boston and former surveyor general; John Robinson and Charles Paxton had been port officers in Temple's district and were now his equals; William Burch was new to the colonies, and was probably a former officer in the Scottish system.

secure the respect of their subordinates, or conciliate the Americans among whom they had to live. Later changes in personnel eliminated some of the internal dissension,[65] but in the meantime their quarrels had damaged the reputation of the agency in both England and America, and lessened its effectiveness.[66]

With a few exceptions members of the staff owed their appointments to the Treasury and consequently lacked a sense of obligation to the Board to which they were immediately responsible.[67] The London Board provided for the instruction of the new officers who were in England and supplied them with the essential forms.[68] After the American Board was organized it named two inspectors general to travel from port to port and give immediate supervision to the officers.[69]

Although the patent for the new Board passed the seals on September 8, 1767, the Commissioners were not ready to establish themselves in Boston until the middle of November. By that time they were unpleasantly aware of the rising tide of colonial ill-will. Popular hostility was never allayed and at times of crisis rose to such heights that most of the Commissioners felt their lives to be in danger. When they sought the protection of the British army and navy, they introduced two important factors in disturbing the

65. Temple lost his place in 1770. Benjamin Hallowell, former comptroller in Boston, was appointed in his place (T29:40, pp. 243-44).

66. Historical Society of Pennsylvania, Customs Papers, *12,* letters of Charles Stewart, cashier, 29 Apr., 6 June 1770. Early in their history members of the Board had started a dancing assembly in order to get acquainted with the people *(Letters of a Loyalist Lady, Being the Letters of Ann Hulton, Sister of Henry Hulton, Commissioner of Customs at Boston, 1767—1776* (Cambridge, Harvard Univ. Press, 1927), p. 10.

67. T64:216, pp. 90-95; T28:1, pp. 300, passim. Later on, the Board had an agent at the Treasury and hired a clerk at the Custom House in London to copy papers (AO 1:844:1140). Appointment by the Treasury was the exception for subordinates of the English Board.

68. T29:38, p. 459.

69. The office of surveyor general had been suppressed. The establishment of the American system brought a slight reduction in the staff of the London Custom House. Places of chief clerk and four assistants were abolished (T11:28, p. 446; T29:39, p. 192).

peace and permanently alienating the colonists, and for this step the colonists never forgave them. In 1768 following the seizure of John Hancock's ship the *Liberty,* in 1770 following the Boston Massacre, and again in 1773 after the Boston Tea Party, the Commissioners took refuge at Castle William in the harbor[70] and thereby lost whatever prestige they had formerly enjoyed. On the closing of the port of Boston in June 1774, they moved to Salem, then in September they returned to Boston for greater safety. In 1776 they were evacuated with other crown officials.[71]

By 1770 the Treasury was dubious about the competence of the Board and its eventual success. Had it not been for an unwillingness to yield to American turbulence, so it was said, the Government might have terminated the Board's commission.[72] But North's administration had its own political prestige to consider, and the Board remained in existence while the Treasury assumed many of the functions and made many of the decisions that might otherwise have been left to the American agency. On the whole the results of this arrangement were unsatisfactory.

Certainly the Treasury's more immediate connection with the colonial customs personnel had its disadvantages. It assumed greater control of the patronage.[73] But in making appointments the Treasury took more lightly than the Board the usual requirement

70. The official story is told in innumerable letters to the Treasury from the secretary to the Board and other officers, now in T1. A personal account is in *Letters of a Loyalist Lady.* D. M. Clark, "The American Board of Customs, 1767—1783," AHR, *45* (Oct. 1939—July 1940), 777-806.

71. Americans blamed them for many other unpopular measures. Hulton was also deputy receiver of the sixpenny duty for Greenwich Hospital. Since most of the Board were Anglicans, they suffered from the colonists' fear of the establishment of the Anglican Church.

72. Historical Society of Pennsylvania, Customs Papers, *12,* letters of 29 Apr., 6 June 1770 from Stewart, the cashier. In 1770 Temple and Robinson sailed for England without leave, to represent the views of the two factions (T29:40, p. 242; T1:478, letter from Robinson, 6 Nov. 1770).

73. It required port officers to send it as well as the Board notices of vacancies, so that it might fill them with its own nominees (T29:41, p. 208; T28:1, p. 356).

that officers should not be engaged in trade. It was much more liberal than the Board in granting leaves of absence. In deciding on the proper location for a port of entry it followed the advice of merchants rather than the opinion of the Board and its inspectors.[74] By such tactics the Treasury undermined the Board's discipline and made its work more difficult.

On the other hand, treasury attempts to assist the Board by securing the cooperation of other agencies were temporarily effective. The army, navy, and consular officers abroad were encouraged to form an intricate network of communication on the subject of illegal trade comparable to the system developed by Grenville. The Treasury now formed the clearing house for much of the correspondence which was supposed in time to reach the various ports where ships might be seized, assuming that the navy had not already intercepted them at sea.[75]

The Treasury also gave what assistance it could in obtaining condemnations. The common law courts as usual were uncooperative. Those authorized by recent law to issue writs of assistance generally refused to do so. According to the law officers of the Crown, because these courts lay outside the realm no writ of mandamus issued in England would have effect.[76] The customs officers were also liable to prosecution in these colonial courts for technical violations of the law. The Treasury frequently gave financial aid in their defense, and in case of appeal to England directed the solicitor to defend them.[77]

In 1768 the Treasury took the initiative in securing four courts of vice-admiralty to be located at Halifax, Boston, Philadelphia, and Charleston. They were to replace the single court located at

74. Question of moving custom house from Williamsburg (T29:40, p. 203; T28:1, p. 345); for custom house in Florida (T29:40, p. 190; T28:1, pp. 344, 393; T1:482, 26 Mar. 1771).

75. Treasury in-letters and out-letters, passim.

76. T1:465, 3 June 1768; T1:485, 31 Aug. 1771. The courts that refused were those in Connecticut, Rhode Island, Maryland, and Pennsylvania. Virginia issued an original form, and New York was very slow (T1:491, 492, passim).

77. AO 1:844:1137.

Halifax but were to have appellate as well as original jurisdiction.[78] Like the American Board of Customs these courts had no jurisdiction in the West Indies, illustrating the peculiar emphasis the Treasury was giving to law enforcement on the Continent. Following the new line of thought on official remuneration, the Government provided regular salaries for the judges instead of fees.[79] The Treasury followed proceedings in the vice-admiralty courts with concern, and encouraged appeals from adverse decisions.[80]

Many aspects of the new administration, as of legislation, suggested a particular interest in regulating trade. From the point of view of the Treasury, however, the success of the American Board was measured by the amount of revenue it produced. Had commerce and the welfare of the merchants been a primary consideration, it would seem that the Treasury would have reformed or abolished the vexatious system of port fees, simplified the complex requirements for bonds, or at least have encouraged the prosecution of merchants who failed to cancel their bonds. Yet it failed to do these things. In fact, it agreed to forego prosecutions if such legal action was likely to increase opposition to the revenue acts.[81]

The Treasury demanded monthly reports of collections from the individual ports instead of relying upon accounts from the central office in Boston.[82] Disappointed at this evidence and the cashier's failure to make the expected remittances, it demanded an explanation. In the autumn of 1769 the Board replied that the nature of the coast encouraged smuggling, that too many port

78. T29:39, pp. 156-57. *APC, Col., 5,* 151 ff.

79. T54:40, p. 463. Payment was made from the king's share of fines and forfeitures. If this was insufficient, they were paid from the fund arising from the sale of old naval stores. For examples of judges' commissions see Adm. 1: 3884 and *Penn. Archives,* Ser. 3, *10,* 381.

80. In one case legal opinion was against an appeal, although the decree was erroneous, because the officers had been partial (T27:30, p. 98; T1:472, 25 Mar. 1769).

81. T29:41, p. 206; T28:1, p. 355. The Board notified the Treasury that it had not been customary to prosecute.

82. T28:1, p. 335, 2 Dec. 1768.

officers were engaged in trade, that the recent revenue acts were unpopular, and that Americans denied that Parliament had the right to tax them.[83] Another reason for the small returns, not stated by the Board but revealed in the accounts, was the increase in the costs of management, explained in part by the salaries of Board members and their staff, and by their incidental expenses. In addition, incidental expenses in the ports tripled in the period from 1768 to 1773. Other important items included expenses of prosecutions and payment of claims for damages resulting from riots in which officers became involved. The total cost of management was more than half the gross receipts.[84]

In the years between 1769 and 1774, however, collections under most heads improved. The Townshend duties and the continuing tax on tea were important exceptions. The duties imposed by Rockingham's Trade Act of 1766 were most remunerative. The most significant increase was in returns from seizures by customs officers and ships of war. Such dependence on income from violation of law promised little for the future of the customs system. For the nine years and four months covered by the first account submitted for audit, the cashier reported £115,317.8.7 in remittances to England and payments to civil officials in the colonies. In addition there was outstanding £45,000, part of which was probably never recovered.[85] The potential net revenue of £160,000 was far less than what the Treasury had led the House of Commons to expect from the new laws. In 1767 alone the estimate of revenue to be applied to public service was £110,000, whereas the actual payments into

83. T1:471, 14 Nov. 1769. The same letter threw light on the financial problem by stating that most of the receipts came from ten ports, and that many of the others were not even self-supporting.

84. AO 1:844: 1137 and 1138.

85. AO 16:105, Draft Journal of Insupers, no. 13, has some names from the accounts of Charles Stewart, the cashier. London Custom House, Plantation Ledger, shows balances of various American collectors in 1783. Grenville's plan for transferring revenue to the army in America had evidently been abandoned. At one time, however, the cashier loaned £3,000 to Commander Hood of the Royal Navy (T29:40, p. 69; T28:1, p. 342).

the Exchequer for that year were only a little over £24,000.[86] In succeeding years the Treasury's optimism waned, but still tended to exceed the actual receipts.

By 1790 the final accounts of the American Board of Customs had been audited and declared "even and quit." For the first time in the history of the American customs the comptroller general had been able to include the accounts of individual collectors in his general account.[87] Thus the disastrous experiment involving a separate customs system for North America came to a business-like end. Whether the Treasury was able to take any satisfaction from this achievement does not appear in the records. The younger William Pitt, who was in office in 1790, might well have included in the costs of management an item that does not figure in the accounts—that is, the loss of thirteen colonies.

In the postal system as in the customs these were dynamic years, characterized by reorganization, more centralization of authority in England, limited expansion, and concern for revenue. In 1772 the Postmaster General authorized the establishment of a central office in New York and the appointment of Hugh Finlay, post-master at Quebec, as riding surveyor.[88] Two years later, on Frank-lin's dismissal from his post of deputy postmaster general, Finlay succeeded him but continued his surveys. In 1775, on the death of the New York postmaster, it was possible to effect a certain amount

86. *CJ, 31,* 318; Add. MSS 38,340, fol. 350. Very little came from the West Indies; in 1781 only £4,676.17.6¾ (Molleson and Lane, *Reports of the Commissioners, 3,* 335).

87. AO 1:843:1134, an account of James Porter covering the years 1767–77, declared in 1784. His successor, Thomas Irving, appointed in 1774, was probably unable to prepare such accounts. John Martin Leake, the Board's London agent, also declared his accounts (AO 1:844:1140). All the declared accounts taken together are invaluable for a study of the Board and its activities.

88. GPO, Orders of the Board, pp. 10-11. Hugh Finlay's *Journal of Surveyor of Post Roads on Continent of North America, during Survey of Post Offices between Falmouth in Casco Bay in the Province of Massachusetts and Savannah in Georgia, Sept. 13, 1773–June 22, 1774* (Brooklyn, 1867), is a remarkable commentary on the system of posts.

of economy by combining the local and central offices there. John Foxcroft, Finlay's colleague, was in charge of these offices and also agent for the packet system. Had there not been obstacles in the way of removing the deputy for the southern district, the whole Continent would have been united in a system comparable to that of the customs.[89]

The home office was now taking more interest in colonial patronage with respect to both subordinates in the central office and local postmasters. It also discouraged absenteeism and the use of deputies. As a rule it objected to the extension of the inland post unless the new routes would be self-supporting; but in an exceptional instance it agreed to more frequent posts between the northern and southern districts, although it was already granting a subsidy of £400 to the latter. In numerous instances it refused requests for increases in salaries, especially in the years just preceding the Revolution, when there was a decline in revenue.

At this time the English office was experiencing difficulty in securing either accounts or remittances in good bills of exchange. The secretary wrote to Foxcroft and Finlay that he dreaded the consequences if they did not comply with orders for remitting their balance.[90] The London authorities met similar difficulties in the West Indies. They even began legal proceedings against the postmaster in Jamaica, but the case was evidently dismissed.

Like the customs system the British post office in America disintegrated in the revolting colonies. Unlike the customs offices, however, the post offices and postal routes quickly came under patriot control and furnished the basis for the American postal system.

For obvious reasons the packet system was subject to less disruption than the inland post on the Continent. The increased

89. GPO, American Letter Book, pp. 1-100, passim, for above and most of what follows.

90. The American office was supposed to remit to England the total of collections on letters from overseas and draw on only the proceeds of the inland post for costs of management. It was also to use bills of exchange drawn on London merchants, as there was a loss on bills drawn on American firms.

importance of communication in these troubled years led the Treasury to agree to additions to the service on all the regular ocean routes in spite of losses to the revenue.[91] It also approved increases in the number of men per boat, higher salaries for commanders, larger victualing allowances, bigger pensions for the seamen, and in general changes tending to sustain morale and maintain as effective a service as possible under the circumstances.[92] Such additions to the cost show that in this case at least the Treasury considered service more vital than revenue.

In administering the crown dues, on the other hand, revenue was naturally the object. There was, however, less emphasis on this branch of the revenue than on duties imposed by Parliament. The reason seems clear. Politics now required that the Treasury should partly balance growing expenditures for American defense and civil government by colonial revenue. There was no such political pressure for increasing the crown dues, which were antiquated remnants of a feudal period. The enthusiasm for developing them, engendered by Shelburne, was short-lived but resulted in a more thorough investigation of these resources than had occurred for many years. The reports not only revealed earlier neglect, but probably convinced the Treasury that improvements would come slowly at best.

Shelburne had been optimistic about the quit rents in particular. The auditor general, however, was discouraging, for he believed an act of Parliament was necessary to obtain satisfactory surveys and rent rolls.[93] Had this suggestion been carried out, the quit rents, like several other prerogative dues, might have been transformed into a parliamentary revenue. But this recommendation fell on deaf ears.[94]

The measures actually taken by the Treasury were largely repe-

91. T29:39, pp. 162, 290; T54:40, pp. 459-62, 504 ff.; T54:41, pp. 121, 139, 358-60.

92. T54:42, pp. 29-40, 166-67; T29:41, p. 279; T54:40, pp. 459-61, 451-52.

93. T1:452, 14 Nov. 1766.

94. There were those who favored abandoning quit rents (WLC, Shelburne, *85*, fols. 26-35).

titions of those that had been tried earlier: filling offices temporarily neglected, requiring receivers to be in residence, exhorting them to obey the auditor general, and encouraging the governors to secure local legislation friendly to collections. The Treasury also approved plans for a new rent roll for Virginia, and allowed charges for one already made in North Carolina.[95] There was a possibility, therefore, of some improvement in collections. But difficulties persisted: defective colonial laws, absence of any system for keeping rolls up to date, lack of a court of Exchequer, and large grants of land exempt from rents.[96] In the newer settlements the Treasury found it necessary to lower rents or postpone the date for beginning collections. In addition, the popular disturbances of this period interfered with the work of the King's receivers as of all crown officials. Receipts, therefore, were far from encouraging for those who would have relied on them in lieu of parliamentary taxes.

The policy of bringing surplus revenues to England may have played an obscure part in keeping collections of the quit rents low. Like the considerably larger amounts from Virginia, surpluses from Nova Scotia and Georgia became part of the fund for special service.[97] Had Shelburne's policy been followed, the King would have had to sacrifice his income from this source.

In the collection of the four-and-a-half per cent in Barbados and the Leeward Islands the Treasury avoided many of the administrative difficulties encountered in other connections. In 1766 Cholmondeley wrote of this revenue that it was "under such good management and so well collected" that he needed to make no comments.[98] Furthermore, at this time the West Indies had less reason for opposing this duty than in earlier years. They had recently received important concessions, including the repeal of the enumer-

95. T29:39, pp. 39-40; T54:40, p. 300.

96. T1:452, Cholmondeley's general report; reports on individual colonies in T1:437, 450, 452, 455, 456. In the Ceded Islands the Treasury was trying to relate sales of land to charges on the rent rolls (T29:42, p. 220; T28:1, pp. 208, 259; T28:2, p. 88).

97. Laprade, *Parliamentary Papers,* pp. 138 ff. T52:60-63, passim.

98. T1:453, 14 Nov. 1766.

ated commodities duty on both cotton and sugar, and the elimination of the four-and-a-half per cent duty on the former. And the new revenue acts did not bear so heavily upon them as upon North America.

In the recently acquired islands, however, the inhabitants objected to the four-and-a-half per cent duty on legal grounds, for it was levied by an order under the great seal and not by act of the local government. Nor did the payment of this duty relieve them from quit rents on their land. During this period the planters successfully challenged the right of the Crown to collect the four-and-a-half per cent duty. In a case appealed from Grenada the Court of King's Bench decided against the Crown on the ground that the order for collection followed the King's promise to summon a legislative assembly.[99] As the assemblies refused to authorize collection, the Crown was obliged to forego this source of revenue.[100]

In spite of this loss, the four-and-a-half per cent duty was the most remunerative of the regular crown revenues. Like the customs it was adversely affected by depressions and war. But year in and year out it paid into the Exchequer between £22,000 and £44,000.[101] The Government yielded to the temptation of charging to this fund more than the average annual yield, with the result that in 1785 it was necessary to apply to Parliament for a special grant to cover arrears.[102] At the end of the period under consideration it must have been clear to the unprejudiced that the duty

99. T1:507, copy of Lord Mansfield's judgment in Campbell v. Hall. Kennedy, *Documents of the Canadian Constitution* (above, p. 140, n. 142), pp. 79 ff.

100. In 1773 Tortola, now separate from the Leeward Islands, passed such a levy, but there the tradition was well established (Bryan Edwards, *The History, Civil and Commercial of the British Colonies in the West Indies,* Philadelphia, 1806, 2, 187).

101. WLC, Shelburne, *104.* Custom House Library, Minutes of the Receiver General, 1773–84, p. 248. Various accounts of this revenue are hard to reconcile, because certain payments were made in the ports, others by the husband, and others out of the Exchequer.

102. HC, "Return of Public Income," *Accounts and Papers* (1868–69), *35,* Pt. I, p. 193.

was unwise on economic grounds and in conflict with more liberal views of relations between the Crown and the colonies, but many years passed before it was abandoned.

The casual revenues of Barbados and the Leeward Islands now produced a small surplus. Cholmondeley classed the former with the four-and-a-half per cent as requiring no comment.[103] Another branch of casual revenues, that arising from the sale of land on the Continent, normally accounted for with the quit rents, was adversely affected by the Government's recent policy of restraining westward expansion. Although the Treasury left decisions as to particular grants to other agencies, it fixed the purchase price and the quit rents. The royal instructions of 1774 regarding the sale of land came too late to be effective in most of the colonies to which they applied.[104]

With regard to the revenue expected from the sales of land in the Ceded Islands, promised to the public by the King, there was considerable disappointment. Having encouraged the House of Commons to vote larger supplies from this source than were available, the Treasury put pressure on the receiver general in the islands and through him on purchasers.[105] Conditions in the islands, however, were increasingly unfavorable. The Charibs were now in revolt against being moved from their land, and there was bloodshed.[106] Some purchasers complained that they had been deceived as to the worth of their land, that the price was too high.[107] And expenses of the commissioners were larger than anticipated.[108] Between 1771 and 1777 there were no deposits in the Exchequer.

103. T1:453, 14 Nov. 1766.

104. Labaree, *Royal Instructions* (above, p. 32, n. 78), 2, 533-37.

105. *CJ, 31,* 583, 591; *32,* 374. Add. MSS 38,340, fols. 349-50. T28:1, pp. 120, 152-53.

106. T28:1, p. 180. WLC, Sydney, *10* and *11,* various papers.

107. Add. MSS 41,347 [Jan. 1767?]. T28:1, p. 447.

108. In 1774 the Treasury reduced costs by putting all business in the hands of the receiver general and the Governor, but within two years found it necessary to name a special commissioner to handle business for which the receiver was not competent (T29:44, p. 48; T29:45, p. 335; T28:1, pp. 266-67).

By 1782, however, a total of nearly £139,000 had been realized.[109]

The Treasury encountered other revenue problems in the conquered territories besides those mentioned above. For example, it proved so difficult to collect the capitation tax in the Ceded Islands that the Government was obliged to pay salaries charged to that fund from the proceeds of the Sugar Act.[110] On an appeal against the decision of the Quebec court, the English Court of Common Pleas ordered the Government to repay the merchants the difference between duties levied by the French and those collected under Governor Murray.[111] Canadian opposition led the Treasury to cut the duty on British brandy to half that collected by the French.[112] In 1774 the difficulty of collecting duties on the strength of the royal prerogative finally led the Treasury to secure from Parliament the Quebec Revenue Act mentioned earlier, which included sanction for the collection of the old prerogative dues as well as new taxes.

In all parts of the empire, one might conclude, the Crown was facing obstacles of one kind or another in collecting the hereditary dues. And by arrangements with the King, negotiated by the Treasury, Parliament was constantly acquiring more authority in this field, including the disposal of several items once enjoyed by the King. By this means as well as by legislation Parliament was reducing the scope of the King's financial jurisdiction over the colonies. If one excepts the transfer of fines and forfeitures for illegal trade from crown dues to the customs, however, one discovers that there had been little or no parliamentary encroachment on the Crown's prerogative revenues in the older colonies of the mainland, those that declared their independence in 1776.

The Declaration of Independence makes no mention of crown dues, not even by inference! Popular grievances with respect to prerogative revenues were practically restricted to the parts of the

109. HC, "Return of Public Income," Pt. I, pp. 156-86 passim.
110. T29:39, p. 302; T1:497, memorial of Gov. Melville.
111. T1:469, report of Nuthall; T1:479, report on a more recent suit against the collector of the customs.
112. T28:1, p. 142.

empire that remained loyal to the Crown. This seeming anomaly has a simple explanation. From New Hampshire to Georgia there were only a few colonies in which crown revenues were at all significant. In the corporate and proprietary colonies they were practically nonexistent. They were therefore not a rallying point or a unifying cause. Nevertheless, during the Revolution these dues vanished quickly with other phases of English sovereignty.

The policies of Grafton and North with respect to that other branch of revenues subject to contention, the assembly grants, were the same as those of their predecessors. For example, in 1772 the Treasury insisted that the royal receiver in Grenada was entitled to receive the taxes levied by the legislature.[113] But the policy of crown control was no more effective in this period than in the past. As indicated above, the home government even lacked adequate information as to the costs of the colonial governments absorbed by the assemblies, and the amount and sources of local income. In 1766 the Treasury found this lack a major obstacle to planning a general revenue policy. When the returns from the questionnaire of 1766 reached the Treasury, however, there was apparently no one there or in the office of the Secretary of State who cared to use this information. Shelburne had lost influence and soon retired. In 1773 Lord Dartmouth, the Secretary, made a more thorough study of colonial finance. It is questionable whether these records ever reached the Treasury,[114] but if so, they came too late, for that office had already embarked upon its fatal course of discipline and coercion.

Had anyone then in authority studied the returns of 1766 and 1773 he might have observed that the older colonies were self-supporting and were paying the debts incurred during the last war. Of course, he might have concluded that they could, therefore, contribute to the defense of the empire and the expenses of civil government in the poorer colonies. On the other hand, he might have foreseen that such financially independent governments would not easily submit to domination and would be able to resist force

113. T27:30, p. 407.
114. Replies are in WLC, Strachey Papers, *1* and *2*.

with force. Not only revolution but complete independence was possible because, on the one hand, the colonies were economically strong, and on the other, the Treasury had failed to retain control over their government finances. Grafton and North had no responsibility for this failure. As previous chapters have indicated, there was a long tradition of colonial independence in matters of finance. Americans could claim this independence as a right based on the English principle of prescription.

As one reviews the various branches of colonial revenues in relation to the financial causes of the American Revolution, it appears that crown dues were comparatively unimportant. On the other hand, parliamentary taxes, sponsored and enforced by the British Treasury, were basic among these causes of revolt. They were, however, only one phase of narrowing restrictions on American commerce that included the elimination of direct trade with Europe and consequent dependence upon British manufactures, and invidious discriminations against the older colonies of the mainland in favor not only of Great Britain but also of other parts of the empire.

So many factors, including colonial agreements against trade with England, affected commerce in these later years that it is impossible to tell what the actual economic effects of these restraints would have been in normal times. But it seems fair to say that to some degree at least they threatened American commercial progress and economic security won in earlier years under comparatively favorable conditions. Revolutionary protests touched lightly on trade regulations, if at all, for they were a delicate subject. In 1768 the Massachusetts Circular Letter noted that it was unfair to tax the imports of British manufactures when the colonists paid duties on them in England, and there were "other advantages arising to Great Britain from the acts of trade." In 1774 the First Continental Congress restricted consent to commercial regulations to those "securing the commercial advantages of the whole empire to the mother country, and the commercial benefits of its respective members." The framers of the Declaration of Independence had other grievances which they could use with more effect than commercial regulations, and made no reference to the latter. Many of the complaints which they listed, however, referred to measures initiated by the Treasury as means for enforcing commercial regulations as well as the payment of customs.

In the years between 1766 and 1776 the Treasury bore the major responsibility for measures inciting to revolution. But Grafton and Lord North built on foundations laid by Grenville and even Rockingham, and earlier generations at the Treasury had helped to produce conditions which at the end of this period made it possible for thirteen colonies to renounce their allegiance to the King and finally make good their claim to independence.

7.

In Brief

THE PRECEDING CHAPTERS have followed the rise of the British Treasury and the development of colonial administration over a period of about seventy years. During this time political power and administrative authority became centralized in a small group of the King's ministers known as the Cabinet. Because of the growing costs of government, finance was of increasing importance, and for this reason the head of the Treasury acquired the rank of prime minister. The extent of his power depended upon the favor of the King and the support of Parliament. He used patronage and control over the issue of funds to consolidate his influence.

To obtain sufficient funds for the defense of the empire and for other expenses the Treasury relied more and more upon grants by Parliament. The Government also tended to substitute statutes for orders of the Crown in the hope of strengthening colonial administration. Thus parliamentary authority, previously restricted to the regulation of trade, extended into many other aspects of colonial administration.

The growing significance of finance in colonial administration naturally increased the responsibility of the Treasury in this field. Early in the eighteenth century the Board of Trade exercised considerable authority over colonial affairs, even in matters involving the payment of money. But its power and prestige declined. The temporary revival of the Board about the middle of the century did not restore its original importance, certainly not in questions of finance. The Secretary of State for the Southern Department, and after 1768 a third secretary for the colonies, had important functions relating to America. But the Secretary of State was subordinate to the Treasury in most financial matters. Under normal conditions, therefore, the character and personal views of a powerful head of the Treasury had a decisive effect on colonial policy. But the usual, economical principles of even a Lord High Treasurer or First Lord who had the advantage of combining his office with that of Chancellor of the Exchequer gave way when the defense of the empire was at stake. War in the colonies, by increasing the necessity for colonial expenditures, was therefore one of the chief factors in the development of colonial financial policy.

There were two major processes in connection with colonial administration: the formulation of policy and its enforcement. Throughout most of this period traditional policies prevailed. That is, the Government expected the colonies to be self-supporting but to contribute to the economic strength of England through carefully regulated trade. The King derived a small amount of income from his hereditary dues, but there was no emphasis on raising revenue in America. After the Seven Years' War, however, the Treasury introduced the revolutionary policy of forcing the colonies to make larger contributions to the costs of empire.

In enforcing financial policies, the Treasury performed or supervised three functions: the handling of expenditures, the collection of revenue, and the auditing of accounts. The Lord High Treasurer or five commissioners, with a staff of secretaries and clerks, directed all operations with regard to finance, which were carried out by subordinate revenue agencies or officers of the Exchequer.

Early in the eighteenth century English expenditures for the American colonies caused the Treasury comparatively little concern. Funds granted by the colonial assemblies supplied most local needs. The Crown, however, had no control over such grants in corporate and proprietary colonies. Even the royal provinces were not always willing to carry out English policies. Moreover, the wars of the eighteenth century increased the costs of defense beyond the ordinary resources of the assemblies. Consequently, the Treasury occasionally drew on other funds: the King's civil list, his hereditary dues, or parliamentary supplies.

The Treasury tried to avoid using the English civil list for colonial purposes. Although it drew on hereditary dues collected in America for some needs, it resisted demands on this source also, considering it the King's own property. As the financial burden of colonial defense increased, therefore, the Treasury applied to Parliament for additional supplies. With the settlement of the frontier provinces of Nova Scotia and Georgia, furthermore, it established a precedent for calling on Parliament to support civil governments in undeveloped provinces.

The Treasury did not favor such parliamentary appropriations for they were a burden on the English taxpayer. Eventually, as a result of these expenditures, there was an increased interest in colonial revenues, especially those which could be used to protect England's authority and promote her policies. At the close of the Seven Years' War, when the issue became acute, the main branches of such revenues were the customs and postal rates levied by Parliament, and crown dues—for most of the funds voted by the assemblies, contrary to theory, were not really subject to crown control. The traditional purpose of colonial customs, however, was the regulation of trade rather than revenue. The Treasury administered the trade laws through the London Board of Customs and its subordinates in the colonies, with some assistance from other crown officers. The income was insignificant, partly because of lax administration and easy evasion of the laws.

Until the latter part of the period proceeds from colonial postal rates scarcely covered the costs of management. The Postmaster General in England, acting under the Treasury, appointed one or more deputies for America who made subordinate appointments and were responsible for the collection of rates under the English statute of 1711.

Royal dues were collected by receivers appointed by the Crown, who were under the supervision of the surveyor and auditor general of His Majesty's plantation revenues. Although these revenues might have seemed very appropriate for the Crown's purposes in America, the Treasury did not think so. The amount available was reduced by its application to the King's special or secret service, by transfers of large amounts to the public, and by instances in which the assemblies assumed the right to dispose of these dues according to their own discretion. At the close of the Seven Years' War the total income from colonial revenues was inadequate for the defense of America as planned by the home government or even for all the costs of civil administration.

The third financial function of the Treasury, that of auditing accounts, was less controversial than the other two. Accounting was of considerable importance as a means of checking on expenditures and the collection of revenue. Chancellors of the Exchequer, before whom accounts were declared, differed as to the emphasis they placed on this function. In any event, accounts were usually too much in arrears to keep the Treasury informed on contemporary finances. Many colonial accounts were defective in some respect and not suitable for a regular audit. In particular, the Treasury failed to secure regular accounts from the colonial assemblies, and thus contributed to their growing independence.

Early in the century, in spite of Godolphin's business-like administration, the colonial governments and individuals were accustomed to ignoring many of their financial obligations. Neither Walpole nor the Pelhams took any very effective measures to strengthen England's financial interests in America. On the other hand, during their administrations parliamentary expenditures for the colonies greatly increased.

At the close of the Seven Years' War a situation existed which seemed to Grenville utterly wrong, and he attempted to change it. England had acquired heavy debts in a war fought largely to defend the empire. Americans, though prosperous, were contributing very little revenue for civil government and defense aside from funds subject to their own control and often used to defeat English policies. Grenville's proposed solution was to improve the administration of existing customs legislation and to levy new taxes. Colonial opposition to the resulting stamp tax was so effective that Grenville's successor, the Marquis of Rockingham, secured its repeal. At the same time, however, Parliament declared its right "to bind the colonies in all cases whatsoever." In some respects trade laws were increasingly restrictive.

Scarcely had the American revolt against the Stamp Act quieted down when the Townshend taxes, accompanied by more determined methods of enforcement, revived colonial resistance. Chief among the new and unpopular administrative agencies was a separate board of customs for North America. The army and navy collaborated with the customs officials. Clashes soon occurred between the military forces and the people. Parliament now countered American opposititon to its laws with coercive measures affecting both government and trade. Open hostility followed these disciplinary measures, and the war ended with the independence of the older colonies on the mainland of North America.

The causes of the American Revolution were not of course simply the measures introduced by the Treasury in the period following the Seven Years' War: earlier administrations had accustomed the colonies to a political and commercial way of life that made independence possible. Grenville sensed what had been happening and wished to bind the colonies more closely to England, but he chose methods that had the opposite effect. He and his successors were too much concerned with political pressures at home and with strictly financial needs to consider possible alternatives to American subjection on the one hand and outright independence on the other.[1]

Private individuals might dream of a commonwealth of nations. But among political leaders there was no one, with the possible exception of Chatham, who had the qualifications for remolding the empire along new and daring lines. His proposal of 1775 came too late to be acceptable in America, and lacked political support in England. Earlier, when there was more possibility of conciliation, he avoided responsibility and left the Treasury to pursue its fatal course.

1. Even a liberal like Sir George Savile thought that Grenville's act "only brought on a crisis 20 or possibly 50 years sooner than was necessary." He added that "in the nature of things . . . Colonies so situated must assure to themselves the rights of nature and resist those of law; which is Rebellion." Rockingham, Letters 4, 31 July 1768.

Bibliographical Notes and Lists of Selected Sources

THE FOLLOWING NOTES and lists exclude modern monographs, biographies, and other secondary works. The reader can easily discover such studies by consulting library catalogues, publishers' lists, and bibliographical guides. While my obligation to secondary writings is not negligible, I have depended more heavily on the original sources mentioned below. The footnotes contain references to a few recent works.

Manuscripts
OFFICIAL DOCUMENTS IN ENGLISH REPOSITORIES

Public Record Office

The absolutely indispensable basis for a study of the British Treasury in its relation to the American colonies is, of course, the records of that department in the Public Record Office in London. This is especially true for the many years of the eighteenth century for which these records are as yet uncalendared. Even calendars are sometimes inadequate or obscure, and in such cases reference to the original is desirable.

The most important among the treasury papers are the minutes of the Board. Comparatively slight in the early years of the century under Godolphin and Oxford, they became increasingly detailed as the years passed, indicating the growing importance of the Treasury in the field of colonial administration as well as the fact that a Board required more detailed minutes than a Lord High Treasurer. These volumes report the business and decisions of the lords of the Treasury, and are consequently an important guide to their administrative practices and policies. Rarely, on the other hand, is there information about proposed legislation.

Scarcely less necessary for this investigation is the correspondence of the Board, in-letters and out-letters. The former classification consists of bundles of original letters from official and private correspondents together with enclosures, consisting of accounts or other records. The letters are frequently endorsed with the date they were read at the Board and the disposition made of them, sometimes "nil." The contents of the bundles are in general—though not strict—chronological order. In some instances there seems to be a dual system for numbering folios, and in such cases designation by date may be clearer.

One classification of out-letters is "General." This class contains copies of many letters addressed to colonial officials or officials in England concerned with colonial administration, especially in the period before 1763. Copies of most letters to the Customs Commissioners, however, are in a special set of volumes, containing instructions, warrants for appointments, and authorization for the payment of established salaries, to mention the more important documents. In the earlier part of the period the Customs Commissioners often went to the Treasury for consultation, with the result that the correspondence for that time contains less information than later.

In 1763 the Treasury adopted a new classification of colonial records and correspondence, the "Out-Letters, America." More popularly known as the "America Book," these volumes contain most but not all colonial records and correspondence from 1763 on. Volume 1 covers the period 1763—78.

Valuable for studying treasury processes are also copies of king's warrants, treasury warrants relating to money, treasury warrants not relating to money, order books, disposition books, and accounts departmental. Accounts departmental contain various items (not necessarily for consecutive years), such as fee books, details of the civil list, auditors' statements or "states" of accounts, and registries of declared accounts. Most of the classes mentioned in this paragraph, unlike those above, have been merely sampled in order to understand practices, or searched for particular items.

There are other miscellaneous classes of papers or special collections which are of more than passing significance. The Blathwayt Journals, for example, are one of the most important sources for a study of crown revenues in the early part of the period. The first series of the Chatham Papers are also extremely valuable, containing in addition to correspondence of the first Lord and Lady Chatham, important official papers. Volume 16 of the customs series is unique, for it consists of letters from the inspector of imports and exports, who was also register general of shipping, connected with the American Board, to the port officers of that time. It throws light on the whole customs system in North America in the pre-revolutionary period.

Papers in the audit office series most often used for this investigation are the declared accounts. These records of income and expenditure are indispensable for the study of a particular revenue agency or government official whose accounts were submitted to the auditors of the imprests and were declared according to the routine of the Exchequer. A comparison of the date of the account with that of the declaration, moreover, may also show the degree of efficiency and dispatch with which this phase of treasury and exchequer business was conducted. "Accounts Various" include many preliminary statements of accounts, sometimes with vouchers, lists of fees, accounts of treasury solicitors, and so forth.

The series of declared accounts of the Pipe Office contain certain accounts not found in those of the Audit Office, for example accounts of the receiver general of the four-and-a-half per cent, account of sales of land on St. Christopher, and early prize accounts.

In addition to the above records, which were relied on most extensively, "Colonial Office Papers," "State Papers," "Admiralty Papers," and the "Privy Council Register" were used for particular phases of this study or searched for special bits of information not located elsewhere.

London Custom House

In addition to the customs papers in the Public Record Office, there are a few extremely useful records in the library of the Custom House. These include the American Custom House establishments, 1768—76; Plantation Ledger, 1768—75; "Notes and Extracts from the Minutes and Orders Issued by the Commissioners of the Customs, 1696—1869," presented to the Board of Customs by Sir William Musgrave; Minutes, Receivers General, 1716—34, 1760—65, 1773—84, including minutes of the Board relating to this office, letters from the office, and from the Treasury concerning the office; and Opinions of Counsel 1727—1814. Because the Custom House fire of 1814 destroyed so many valuable records, the "Notes and Extracts," made by a contemporary, have a peculiar value.

General Post Office

A repository for numerous postal records. Among those containing information about the inland post in America and the packet system are Orders of the Board, 1737—71; Commission Book, 1759—1854; Instructions Book, 1763—1811; and American Letter Book, 1773—83. For the earlier years one must rely mainly on the treasury records at the Public Record Office. The Treasury Letter Books in the post office collection date from the seventeenth century, but duplicate the letters and copies of letters at the Record Office.

OFFICIAL DOCUMENTS IN THE UNITED STATES

In the Library of Congress, Washington, D.C., are many reproductions of records from various English repositories. They are important in a restricted sense, for one is seldom satisfied with selections made by someone else. I have, however, made extensive use of the transcriptions of the declared accounts of the customs as well as the originals in England.

There are in this country two record books for the port of Salem, Massachusetts, covering the years 1763—75, which are invaluable for a study of the customs system in the years before the Revolution. The earlier is in the Essex Institute, Essex, Massachusetts, and is known as "Book of Records for the Custom House of Salem, 1763—1772." The other, known as the "Salem Letter Book" is in the United States Custom House in Boston in the care of the collector. It contains copies of in-letters and out-letters. In the Historical Society of Pennsylvania, Philadelphia, is a collection of valuable customs papers for that port. I made extensive use of Volumes 7—9, containing correspondence between the deputy collector of that port and the American Board and other customs officers.

PRIVATE MANUSCRIPTS IN ENGLISH REPOSITORIES

The designation "private" is somewhat arbitrary, as historians will realize, because public officials occasionally retained public records of their own administrations or copies of the same, as well as those of earlier administrations. Moreover, a collection like that of the Chatham Papers, now in the Public Record Office, includes what might be called private correspondence on public business. The collections listed below contribute somewhat less to an understanding of administration in a narrow sense than the public documents mentioned above. They are, however, necessary for a knowledge of men and their policies.

British Museum

The British Museum is the great repository for private collections of manuscripts donated to the public. With a few exceptions the papers used for this study are in the great classification "Additional Manuscripts." Of first importance for the study of the Treasury are the papers and correspondence of one-time Lords of the Treasury, secretaries, and other officials connected with that department, as, for example, Newcastle; Charles Montagu, first Earl of Halifax; the Earl of Bute; William Lowndes; John Robinson; Charles Jenkinson; James West; Samuel Martin; William Blathwayt; and Robert Cholmondeley. In not every case mentioned, however, is there a whole collection under that name. The outstanding collection, in both size and significance, is that seemingly inexhaustible source of eighteenth-century history the Newcastle Papers. Probably next in importance is that of Newcastle's friend and mentor, the Earl of Hardwicke. For a later period one would mention particularly the Liverpool Papers and the Martin

Papers, including Samuel Martin's Letter Book, 1748–76. Aside from the collections listed under the names of their former owners, there are many scattered items which—except in the case of the most recent acquisitions—can be located through the manuscript catalogues.

Sheffield City Library

The Rockingham Letters and Papers form one large class of the Wentworth-Woodhouse Muniments placed on deposit for a period of years by the owner, Earl Fitzwilliam. For my purposes the Rockingham Letters and Papers covering the period of the earlier administration of the Marquis of Rockingham were very significant. Other papers of a later period reveal Rockingham's views on government. I took advantage of the opportunity to read some of Burke's letters of the period 1744–69.

Bodleian Library

The few manuscripts used in this library were of the seventeenth century, but supplied background.

Grafton Papers

For a short period before the war this private collection belonging to the present Duke of Grafton was on deposit at the Public Record Office, where it could be used by special permission. The papers are more valuable for the political aspects of my subject than for the administrative; but the correspondence has a special flavor that reveals the political character of the third Duke and thus throws considerable light on his administration. Particularly interesting to me were the letters from Thomas Bradshaw, secretary to the Treasury. Among the papers are many accounts, including some of the civil list, showing special concern for the debt.

PRIVATE MANUSCRIPTS IN THE UNITED STATES

Henry E. Huntington Library, San Marino, California

In this country the Henry E. Huntington Library is unique for the exquisite care given to its manuscripts and rare books. The

Stowe Collection is of outstanding importance for its variety as well as for the interest attached to particular items. Taken together, the George Grenville Letter Books, his diplomatic and political correspondence, and other papers, while possibly unimpressive in quantity, are exceptionally useful in illuminating the man, his aims, and ideals. Stowe Americana contain the Temple-Whately correspondence of the period when the latter was secretary to the Treasury, including several letters not published in the *Collections* of the Massachusetts Historical Society. Correspondence of three colonial governors—William Mathew, Henry Grenville, and William Shirley—illustrate their relations with the Treasury. Shirley's letters to Henry Pelham when the latter was First Lord of the Treasury are especially interesting. The Blathwayt Papers contribute to a better understanding of crown revenues.

William L. Clements Library, Ann Arbor, Michigan

At the William L. Clements Library the Shelburne Papers form the most attractive single collection, notable for its many official or semi-official items, such as the accounts of annual deposits of revenues in the Exchequer. The letters of William Dowdeswell, Chancellor of the Exchequer under Rockingham; of Charles Townshend, Chancellor of the Exchequer under Grafton; the correspondence of William Knox; and the Germain, Lacaita-Shelburne, Sydney, and Strachey Papers all contributed directly or indirectly to the substance of my research. Of special interest were letters from Franklin to Galloway.

Library of Congress, Washington, D.C.

Selections from manuscripts in the British Museum and other English repositories have been reproduced for the convenience of American scholars. I have made occasional use of these collections, usually to verify notes taken in London.

Other Repositories

The following items have been found and used in other repositories: extracts from the letters of Robert Charles, colonial agent, in the William Smith Papers, New York Public Library; the Letter

Book of Richard Corbin, the King's receiver general of Virginia, in the Virginia Historical Society Library; and the Letter Book of James Abercromby, colonial agent and deputy of the auditor general of His Majesty's plantation revenues, in the Virginia State Library in Richmond; and the latter's "An Examination of the Acts of Parliament Relative to the Trade and Government of Our American Colonies," in the Pennsylvania State Archives at Harrisburg. There is a copy of the last-named document in the Henry E. Huntington Library, and another in the William L. Clements Library.

Printed Official or Semi-Official Sources
GENERAL

Parliament

House of Commons, *Accounts and Papers:* 1806, Vol. 7, "Reports of Commissioners appointed by 25 Geo. III, cap. 19, to enquire into the Fees, Gratuities, Perquisites, and Emoluments which are or have been lately received in the several Public Offices therein mentioned," 1786–88; 1809, Vol. 9, for account of the four-and-a-half per cent duty presented in 1740; 1868–69, Vol. 35, "Return of Public Income and Expenditure."

———— *Journals.*

———— *Parliamentary Papers,* 1878, Vol. 62, "Return of Members of Parliament."

———— *Reports from the Select Committee Appointed to Inquire into the Public Records of the Kingdom, July 4, 1800.*

———— *Reports of the Commissioners Appointed to Inquire into the Fees, Gratuities, Perquisites, and Emoluments . . . in the Several Public Offices . . . Presented to the House of Commons, June 1793,* London, 1793.

House of Lords, *Journals.*

Parliamentary History of England, a collection of debates, ed. [William] Cobbett, 36 vols. London, 1806–20.

Proceedings and Debates of the British Parliaments respecting North America, ed. Leo Francis Stock, Washington, D.C., Carnegie Institution, 1924—.

The Reports of the Commissioners Appointed to Examine, Take, and State the Public Accounts of the Kingdom, Presented to His Majesty, and to Both Houses of Parliament, ed. William Molleson and John Lane, 3 vols. London, 1783—87.

The Statutes at Large, from Magna Charta to 41 Geo. III, ed. Owen Ruffhead, a new ed. continued by Charles Runnington, London, E. Eyre and A. Strahan, 1786—1800. This edition was used to check all statutes after 1713; but *A Collection of the Public General Statutes,* 6 Geo. III, 1765—66, printed by Mark Basket, London, 1766, was used for the Mutiny Act of that year.

The Statutes of the Realm, 1101—1713, "Printed by Command of his Majesty King George the Third, London, 1810—28. Prepared by a Sub-Commission of the Record Commission." Used for period covered.

Administrative Agencies and Crown Officials (a series of calendars published by His Majesty's Stationery Office)

Acts of the Privy Council, Colonial Series, ed. W. L. Grant et al., 6 vols. 1908—12.

Calendar of Home Office Papers of the Reign of George III, 1760—75, ed. Joseph Redington and Richard A. Roberts, 4 vols. 1878—99.

Calendar of State Papers, Colonial Series, America and West Indies, Vols. 18-42, 1700—36, ed. Cecil Headlam and A. P. Newton, 1910—53.

Calendar of State Papers, Domestic Series, 2 vols. covering reign of Queen Anne, ed. Robert P. Mahaffy, 1916—24.

Calendar of Treasury Books, Vols. 9-28, 1689—1714, ed. or prepared by William A. Shaw, 1904—57. No one who has worked in this field can fail to acknowledge a great debt to the late Mr. Shaw for both his editorial work and his explanatory introductions.

Calendar of Treasury Books and Papers, 1729—45, ed. William A. Shaw, 5 vols. 1897—1903.

Calendar of Treasury Papers, 1557—1728, ed. Joseph Redington, 6 vols. 1868—89.

Journal of the Commissioners of Trade and Plantations, 1704—82, 14 vols. 1920—38. The earlier journals were published in the *Calendar of State Papers, Colonial.*

Miscellaneous

"British Royal Proclamations Relating to America, 1603—1783," ed. Clarence S. Brigham, American Antiquarian Society, *Transactions and Collections,* Vol. 12, Worcester, Massachusetts, 1911.

Finlay, Hugh, *Journal of Surveyor of Post Roads on Continent of North America, during Survey of Post Offices between Falmouth in Casco Bay in the Province of Massachusetts and Savannah in Georgia, Sept. 13, 1773—June 22, 1774,* Brooklyn, 1867.

Military Affairs in North America, 1748—1765, ed. Stanley Pargellis, New York, Appleton-Century, 1936.

Opinions of Eminent Lawyers on Various Points of English Jurisprudence, Chiefly Concerning the Colonies . . . , ed. George Chalmers, Burlington, Vermont, 1858.

Royal Instructions to British Colonial Governors, 1670—1776, ed. Leonard Woods Labaree, New York, Appleton-Century, 1935.

Walker, Sir Hoveden, *A Journal or Full Account of the Late Expedition to Canada, with an Appendix,* London, 1720.

RELATING TO PARTICULAR COLONIES

Colonial Statutes (used primarily for acts relating to the Post Office)
Acts and Resolves Public and Private of the Province of Massachusetts Bay, Vol. 1, Boston, 1869.

Laws of New Hampshire, Vol. 2, Concord, 1913.

Laws of the Colony of New York, Vol. 1, Albany, 1894.

Statutes at Large of Pennsylvania, Vol. 2, Harrisburg, 1896.

The Laws and Acts of the General Assembly of Her Magesties Province of Nova Casarea or New Jersey ... Printed by W. Bradford, 1709. A photostat supplied by the Division of the State Library, Archives and History.

Other Official Documentary Collections (used primarily for the relation of crown revenue officers to the provincial Council)

Archives of Maryland, ed. William H. Browne et al., Baltimore, 1885–1953.

Colonial Records of Pennsylvania, 1683–1790, Vol. 7, Harrisburg, 1851.

Documents of the Canadian Constitution, 1759–1915, ed. W. P. M. Kennedy, Toronto, Oxford University Press, 1918.

Documents Relating to the Colonial, Revolutionary and Post-Revolutionary History of the State of New Jersey, ed. W. A. Whitehead et al., Ser. 1, Newark, 1880–1906.

Documents Relative to the Colonial History of the State of New York, ed. E. B. O'Callaghan and Berthold Fernow, Vols. 3-8, London Documents, Albany, 1853–57.

Executive Journals of the Council of Colonial Virginia, Richmond, Virginia State Library, 1925–45.

Pennsylvania Archives, Ser. 3, *10,* ed. William Henry Egle, Harrisburg, 1896.

Printed Diaries, Memoirs, Correspondence, Etc.

Anson, Sir William, ed., *Autobiography and Political Correspondence of Augustus Henry, Third Duke of Grafton,* London, Macmillan, 1927–28.

Ashley, John, *Memoirs and Considerations Concerning the Trade and Revenues of the British Colonies in America,* 2 pts. 1740–43.

Bateson, Mary, ed., *A Narrative of the Changes in the Ministry, 1765—1767, Told by the Duke of Newcastle,* London, Royal Historical Society, 1898.

Brock, R. A., ed., "Official Records of Robert Dinwiddie, 1751—1758," Virginia Historical Society, *Collections,* new ser., Vols. 3, 4, Richmond, 1883—84.

———"The Official Letters of Alexander Spotswood, 1710—1722," Virginia Historical Society, *Collections,* new ser., Vols. 1, 2, Richmond, 1882—85.

Carter, Clarence, ed., *The Correspondence of General Thomas Gage,* New Haven, Yale University Press, 1931—33.

Cartwright, James J., ed., *The Wentworth Papers, 1705—1739,* London, 1883.

Channing, Edward, and A. C. Coolidge, eds., *The Barrington-Bernard Correspondence, 1760—1770,* Cambridge, Harvard University Press, 1912.

"Commerce of Rhode Island," Pt. I, 1726—1774, Massachusetts Historical Society, *Collections,* Vol. 69, Ser. 6; Vol. 9, 1914.

Copeland, Thomas W., ed., *The Correspondence of Edmund Burke,* Vol. 1, April 1744—June 1768, Cambridge University Press, 1958.

Coxe, William, ed., *Memoirs of Horatio, Lord Walpole,* 2d ed. 2 vols. London, 1808.

———*Memoirs of the Duke of Marlborough with His Original Correspondence,* 3 vols. London, 1847—48.

———*Memoirs of the Life and Administration of Sir Robert Walpole, Earl of Orford,* London, 1798.

Cumberland, Richard, *Memoirs,* ed. Henry Flanders, Philadelphia, 1856.

Dalrymple, Sir John, *Memoirs of Great Britain and Ireland,* 2 vols. London, 1771—73, Vol. 3, Edinburgh, 1788.

Fitzmaurice, Lord Edmond, ed., *Life of William, Earl of Shelburne,* 2d ed. 2 vols. London, Macmillan, 1912.

Fortescue, Sir John, ed., *The Correspondence of King George the Third from 1760 to December 1783*, 6 vols. London, Macmillan, 1927—28.

Hervey, John, Lord, *Some Materials towards Memoirs of the Reign of King George II*, ed. Romney Sedgwick, 3 vols. New York, Viking Press, 1931.

Historical Manuscripts Commission, *Diary of Viscount Percival, afterwards First Earl of Egmont*, 1730—38, 2 vols. 1920—23.

———*Report on Manuscripts of Mrs. Stopford-Sackville*, 2 vols. 1904—10.

———*Report on Manuscripts of His Grace, the Duke of Portland*, Vols. 3, 4, 8, 1894—1907.

———*Tenth Report, Various Collections*, App. VI (London, 1887), "The Political Correspondence of John Robinson," pp. 3-72.

Hulton, Ann, *Letters of a Loyalist Lady: Being the Letters of Ann Hulton, Sister of Henry Hulton, Commissioner of Customs at Boston, 1767—1776*, Cambridge, Harvard University Press, 1927.

Jucker, Ninetta S., ed., *The Jenkinson Papers, 1760—1766*, London, Macmillan, 1949.

Kimball, Gertrude Selwyn, ed., *The Correspondence of William Pitt when Secretary of State with Colonial Governors and Military and Naval Commanders*, 2 vols. New York, Macmillan, 1906.

———*The Correspondence of the Colonial Governors of Rhode Island, 1723—1752*, 2 vols. Boston and New York, Houghton Mifflin, 1920—23.

Laprade, William Thomas, ed., *Parliamentary Papers of John Robinson, 1774—1784*, London, Royal Historical Society, 1922.

Letters to the Ministry from Governor Bernard, General Gage, and Commodore Hood and Also Memorials to the Lords of the Treasury, from the Commissioners of the Customs with

Sundry Letters and Papers Annexed to the Said Memorials, Boston, 1769.

Montagu, Charles, Earl of Halifax, *Life and Works,* London, 1715.

Penn, William, and James Logan, "Correspondence," ed. Deborah Logan and Edward Armstrong, Historical Society of Pennsylvania, *Publications,* Vols. 9, 10, Philadelphia, 1870—72.

Russell, Lord John, ed., *Correspondence of John Russell, Fourth Duke of Bedford,* London, 1842—46.

St. John, Henry, Lord Viscount Bolingbroke, *Letters and Correspondence,* 4 vols. London, 1798.

Sargent, Winthrop, *The History of an Expedition against Fort Duquesne in 1755,* Philadelphia, Historical Society of Pennsylvania, 1855.

Smith, William James, ed., *The Grenville Papers,* 4 vols. London, 1852—53.

Smyth, Albert H., ed., *The Life and Writings of Benjamin Franklin,* 10 vols. New York, Macmillan, 1905—07.

Taylor, William Stanhope, and Captain John Henry Pringle, eds., *Correspondence of William Pitt, Earl of Chatham,* 4 vols. 1838—40.

"The Bowdoin and Temple Papers," Massachusetts Historical Society, *Collections,* Vol. 59, Ser. 6, Vol. 9, Pt. I, Boston, 1897.

Toynbee, Mrs. Paget, ed., *The Letters of Horace Walpole, Fourth Earl of Orford,* 16 vols. Oxford, Clarendon Press, 1903—05.

Walpole, Horace, *Memoirs of the Reign of King George the Third,* ed. G. F. Russell Barker, 4 vols. London, 1894; covers 1760—71.

——— *Journal of the Reign of King George the Third, from the Year 1771 to 1783,* ed. Dr. Doran, 2 vols. London, 1859.

——— *The Last Journals of Horace Walpole during the Reign of George III from 1771—1783,* with notes by Dr. Doran, ed. A. Francis Steuart, 2 vols. London, Lane, 1910.

——*Memoires of the Last Ten Years of the Reign of George the Second,* ed. Lord Holland, 2 vols. London, 1822.

W[hately], T[homas], *Letter I,* correspondence between Whately and Jared Ingersol [1766?].

Early Treatises or Special Items on the Treasury and Revenue Agencies

Chamberlayne, John, an annual publication under the title *Angliae Notitia* [and after the union with Scotland, *Magnae Britanniae Notitia*] or *The Present State of England;* includes lists of people in public offices; not always complete or accurate, but suggestive for further research.

Commissioners of the Customs, plate and copies of a deputation from the American Board of Customs, beginning "To All People ..." In the British Museum.

——Instructions to Collector in America [1734]. In BM.

——Instructions to Collectors of 4½% [1764]. In BM.

Crouch, Henry, *A Complete Guide to the Officers of His Majesty's Customs in the Out-Ports ...* , London, 1732. Information, rules, and regulations for officers.

F[anshawe], Sir T., *The Practice of the Exchequer Court,* London, 1658.

Madox, Thomas, *The History and Antiquities of the Exchequer,* London, 1711.

[Musgrave, William], *A Collection of All the Statutes Relating to the Revenue,* 2 vols. London, 1780. Index helpful, though not complete.

Saxby, Henry, *The British Customs: Containing an Historical and Practical Account of Each Branch of That Revenue,* London, 1757.

Index

Abercromby, James: colonial agent, 96 n., 97 n., 102 n.; deputy auditor general, 102 and n., 139

Acts:

trade and navigation: Plantation (*1673*), 10, 15 f.; *1696*, 16 and n.; *1660*, 16 n.; enumeration (*1705*), 16 n.; Walpole and, 46, 52; Molasses, 46 f., 48, 60, 81, 110, 118; sugar trade (*1739*), 48; various, passed under Walpole, 48 and n., 49 n.; passed under Pelhams, 81 and n.; for enforcement by navy, 110; characterization of, under Grenville, 115; *1764*, 117 f.; *1765*, 119 and n.; Hovering, 118 n.; Free Port (*1766*), 152; trade (*1766*), 153; *1663*, 153; *1766—76*, classification of, 170 and n.; *1775*, repealing non-impressment (*1708*), 170 and n.; Townshend, 171, 173; East India (*1773*), 173

for American Board of Customs (*1767*), 174

revenue: Post Office (*1711*), 5, 14, 21 and n.; postal (*1765*), 123; commercial, under Grenville, 117, and Rockingham, 154; Stamp, 119 ff., 122, 127 n., repealed, 149, 201; to protect violators of Stamp Act, 151 n.; Quebec (*1774*), 170; Townshend (*1767*), 171, 173

appropriations for defense of colonies, 11 ff., 52 and n., 82 ff., 109 f., 124 and n., 176; for colonial reimbursement, 83 f. and nn.; *see also* Colonies, assemblies in

prize: *1708*, 30; *1740*, 49 n.

for transportation of felons, 49 n.; hard labor substituted, 179 n.

making land banks illegal, 49

for recovery of debts, 49

curbing manufacture of hats, 49 n.

for surrender of Carolinas (*1729*), 50

appropriations for civil purposes: for Georgia, 50 f., 84 f.; for Nova Scotia, 84 f.; under Grenville, 125; under Grafton and North, 176 and n.; for surveys, 125

against bills of credit as legal tender: *1751*, 81 f.; *1764*, 123

applying Greenwich Hospital dues to America, 81 n.

cider tax (English), 116 n., 149

Mutiny (Quartering): *1765*, 123 and n.; question of enforcement in Quebec, 143; *1766*, a form of tax, 154 and n.; New York's refusal to comply, 175

Declaratory (*1766*), 150 f., 154

coercive: suspending New York assembly, 175; of *1774*, 176

for vice-admiralty courts (*1768*), 175 and n.

administration of, *see specific acts,* Customs, Army, Ordnance, Navy, Colonies

of colonial assemblies, *see* Colonies, assemblies in

Admiralty:

estimates, 11 and n.

High Court of: and commissions for vice-admiralty courts, 20; right to try prize cases, 105 n.

droits (perquisites): a casual revenue, 24; overlapping jurisdictions for, 27; treasury authority over, 27 n.; receiver general of, 27 n., 70 and nn.; tenths of prizes, 27; deposits in the Exchequer, 30

opposition of, to: colonial trials of prizes, 26 and n.; premiums on colonial naval stores, 48; expenditures for colonies, 58; office of surveyor of woods, 58; responsibility for appeals from vice-admiralty courts, 59

and Commissioners for Prizes, 27

First Lord of, Grenville as, 108

relation to Treasury under Grenville, 130

cruisers of, to prevent smuggling, 134

and establishment of vice-admiralty court, 134 and n.

procedure of, in prize disputes, 162 n.

See also Navy; Courts, in colonies

Advocate General, advice of, followed by Treasury, 162

Agents, colonial. *See* Colonies

Aggregate fund, customs appropriated to, 59

Albany, pension for minister at, 10

America: changing attitude of English government toward, 110; op-position to Stamp Act in, 160. *See also* North America; Colonies

"America Book," treasury records, 126 n.

American Board of Customs. *See* Customs

American nationalism, 145

American Revolution: responsibility for, 1; factors leading to, 180; causes of, 196

Americans: not consulted on need for troops, 124; doubt as to Parliament's power to tax, 148

Amherst, Sir Jeffrey, Governor General: bills of, returned by Navy, 89 n.; in war against Pontiac, 125; experiment with deductions for soldiers' rations, 129 n.; purchase of provisions by, 130; advice on colonial reimbursements, 130 and n.

Annapolis Royal, Nova Scotia: companies at, 52 n.; defense of, 83; use of four-and-a-half per cent for defense of, 104 n.

Anne, Queen of England: and Lord High Treasurer, 2 ff.; payments from civil list of, 8, 9 f.; accepts Commons' proposal for use of four-and-a-half per cent, 29

Anson, George, First Lord of Admiralty: and patronage, 78 n.; quoted on Pitt, 80 n.

Antigua, allowances by, to regular forces, 129

Army, British, in America:

estimates for: approved by Treasury, 11 f. and n.; increased under Walpole, 52 and n.; under Pelhams, 82 and n.; under Bute, 110 and n.; under Grenville, 124 and n.; under North, 176; cost of pro-

visions included in, 57 n.; ordnance, *see* Ordnance
extraordinaries: in parliamentary grants, 12; cost of recruiting included in, 56; cost of provisions included in, 57 n.; curbed by Grenville, 128; commanders to draw bills for, 156
funds for:
  policy of making colonies provide, 12, 92, 128 f.
  colonial grants of, 12, 129
  problems and method of supplying, 13, 56, 88 ff., 127 ff., 155 f., 179 f.
  use of bills of exchange for: Canadian expedition (*1711*), 52, 83 n.; accepted by Treasury, 83; under Henry Pelham, 88 f. and n.; power of commander to draw, 89; drafts for levy money, 93; dependence of army on, 128; treasury minute on, 128 n.; increase, system in, 156 and n.; Bank of England to accept, 156; by Governor Murray, 163
  bankruptcy of company agents handling, 56, 128 n.
  rate of exchange, 56, 92 and n.
  contracts and contractors for: under Walpole, 56; under Pelhams, 89; Thomlinson and Hanbury, 90; treasury order for specie for Braddock, 91; under Grenville, 128; dispute over, 128, 156; bankruptcy of agents, 56, 128 n.; under Rockingham, 156; under North, 179
  proposed use of customs and stamp revenue for, 128, 155 f.
  greater efficiency in supplying, 179

standing, in peace: an American grievance, 12, 176; Grenville's approval for, 124
victualing, 13; improvement of, under Walpole, 57 and n.; deductions from soldiers' pay for (stoppages), 57 and n., 94, 129 and n.; contracts for, 57, 93 ff., 129 f., 156, 180; under Pelhams, 93 ff.; parliamentary investigations of, 95; audit of contractors' accounts of, 95 n.; under Grenville, 129 f.; under Rockingham, 155 f.; under North, 180
recruiting for, 56; during French and Indian War, 93
commanders of, help in securing military accounts of, 95
and collection of revenue, 100, 127, 135, 183, 185, 202
location of, in port towns, 127
See also Paymaster General of the Forces; Secretary at War
Army, colonial, to be victualed by colonies, 129. *See also* Colonies, reimbursement
Ashley, John, Barbadian correspondent of Chandos, 46
Attorney General, Great Britain: report on local law, 24; drafting bill for purchase of Carolinas, 50; opinion of, on revenue from Molasses Act, 118 n.; and treasury minute, 158 n.; on right of search, 174. *See also* Law officers
Audit: of assembly funds, lost by the Treasury, 32 f., 109; responsibility of Treasury for, 34 ff., 36; of accounts of prizes, 34, 105; of crown dues, 35, 201; of Guadeloupe accounts, 105 f.; of customs, 34; of accounts under Amer-

ican Board, 188; varying emphasis on, 201. *See also* Auditor general; Auditors of the imprests; Customs, accounts and audit

Audit Office, Declared Accounts of, 34 n.

Auditor general (surveyor and auditor general of His Majesty's plantation revenues):

Blathwayt, William, as: functions of, 25 ff.; neglect of, by Oxford, 25; on use of quit rents, 29; reports of, 29 n., 32; audit of crown dues by, 35 f.; on use of crown dues, 63; compared with Horace Walpole, 64

Walpole, Horace, as: influence of, 41; connection of, with the Treasury, 63 ff.; perquisites, 64 n.; on issue of quit rents, 67 n.; audit of four-and-a-half per cent, 68; attempt to improve casual revenues, 69; and local revenues, 72; decline of interest of, in office, 102; death of, 102; comment on Henry McCulloh, 103 and n.; on loss of audit of assembly grants, 106

Cholmondeley, Robert, as: succession of, relation to the Treasury, 102; proposals for crown receivers, 103; audit of prize accounts, 105, 162; and Guadeloupe accounts, 105; contact with colonial officers, 111; plans for improving revenue, 139; lack of authority to audit accounts of sales of land, 142; reports to the Treasury, 161; on need for statute on quit rents, 172 n., 190; reports on four-and-a-half per cent, 191; on casual revenues, 193; supervision of crown revenues, 200

deputies of:
  in the colonies, 25, 66, 68, 105
  in London: Peter Leheup, 64, 102 and n.; James Abercromby, 102 and n., 139; Robert Pennant, Robert Smith, 102 n.

See also names of individual officers

Auditors of the imprests, 34 f.; loss of audit of four-and-a-half per cent, 68; audit of prize accounts, 105 n.; and accounts of sales of land, 142; treasury directions to, 156 n.

Austrian Succession, War of the, 76, 94, 124 n.

Bahamas: proprietors of, 23; purchase of, 50 n.; company in, 52 n., 57 n.; Captain General of, payment of, 69 n.; inclusion of, in southern postal district, 138; question of opposition to Stamp Act in, 160 n.; under American Board of Customs, 182

Baltimore, Lord. *See* Calvert, Charles

Bank of England: receipt of funds from prizes by, 104 n.; to make payment on bills of exchange, 156

Barbados: surveyor general for, 26 n.; appropriation of fines and forfeitures by, 31 n.; crown approval of local revenue act in, 33; petition to Privy Council, to Parliament, 46 f.; customs forms in, 119 n.; deputy postmaster in, 138 n.; question of opposition to Stamp Act in, 160 n.; four-and-a-half per cent in, *see* Four-and-a-half per cent

Barons, Benjamin, deputy postmaster, 138 n.

Barrack master general, appointment of, for North America, 155 n.

Barrington, William Wildman, 2d Viscount, Secretary at War, patron of Bradshaw, 86 n.

Beaver skins, reduction of duties on, 48 n.

Bedford, Duke of. *See* Russell, John

Bedford, Grosvenor, patent customs officer, exception to rule against leaves, 132 n.

Bermuda: salary of governor of, 10, 69 n.; army in, 12 n.; surveyor general for, 26 n.; permanent grant in, 31; placed on customs establishment, 62 n.; issue of funds by governor, 106 n.; omitted from new customs arrangements, 132 n.; sale of land in, 143 n.; question of opposition to Stamp Act in, 160 n.; under American Board of Customs, 182

Bills of credit. *See* Paper currency

Bishop of London. *See* London, Bishop of

Blackstone, Sir William, on Mutiny Act, 154

Blakeney, Colonel William, recruiting by, 56

Blathwayt, William. *See* Auditor general

Board of Trade:

varying status of: under William III and under Anne, 4; desire for executive authority, loss of power, 42; rise under Halifax, 78 f.; under order of *1752*, 78 n., 166 n.; after *1761*, 79 n.; under Shelburne and Hillsborough, 113 and n.; weakness of, 147 f.; under Hillsborough, 166; declining authority of, 198

administrative activities of: recommendation for ordnance estimates for colonies, 13; and surveyor of woods, 14, 58, 131 n.; makes recommendation for use of four-and-a-half per cent, 29; approval of local revenue acts, 30; compares philosophy of Crown and local assemblies, 33; and sale of lands, 70 f. and n., 141, 143 and n.; and colonial reimbursement, 95; and civil establishments for colonies, 97 f., 181; registers complaints against New England, 99 n.; report on Massachusetts act, 106; sends American papers to Council, 148 n.; report on colonial finance, 171

colonial policies of: for use of crown revenues in colonies, 31, 63, 67, 69; purchase of Pennsylvania, 55; expenditures by Navy, 58; nurture of acts of trade, 60; improvement of quit-rent laws in colonies, 65; parliamentary regulation of New York land grants, 65

and legislation: the Molasses Act, 46; premiums on naval stores, 48; preparation of bills, 49 n.; bills restricting issue of colonial bills of credit, 82 and n., 123

relations to the Treasury: treasury instructions for, 69, 125 n.; consulted by, 81, 119; supplies figures on colonial expenditures, 84 n.; refuses to advise, 103; approval of plan for packets, 159 n.; treasury reference of Indian troubles to, 162. *See also above,* varying status of

Bolingbroke, Viscount. *See* St. John, Henry

Bonds: in plantation trade, 15 and n., 16, 39 n., 99 n., 153; molasses, 119 n.; variety of, 119 n.; for non-enumerated commodities, 153; report on forms of, 159 n.; uncanceled, failure to prosecute, 186 and n.

Boston, Massachusetts: pension for minister at, 10; charges of customs fraud at, 99; Tea Party, 173, 184; closing port of, 176 and n., 184; rendezvous for North American fleet, 180; headquarters for American Board of Customs, 182; Massacre, 184; seat of a vice-admiralty court, 185

Bounties and premiums: on naval stores, 48; on colonial products, 115, 170 n.

Braddock, Edward, Major General: defeat and death of, 83, 91; experience with financing army, 90 f. and n.; rate of his soldiers' pay, 92 n.; his instructions on levy money, 93; plans for his expedition, 93 f.; effect of defeat of on establishment of packet system, 101

Bradshaw, Thomas: principal clerk of the Treasury, 86 n.; secretary to the Treasury, 178 and n.

Brandy, British, duty on, in Quebec, 163, 194

Bridger, John. *See* Woods, surveyor general of

British Museum, lottery for, 86

Brummell, William, treasury clerk, 178 n.

Brydges, James, Duke of Chandos: on means of securing a favor, 42 n.; appeal for support of candidate, 44 n.; on contest at Haslemere, 44 n.; and the Molasses Act, 46; land scheme of, 70 n.

Budget, under Pelhams, 88

Bullion, question of foreign trade in, 136 and n., 158 and n.

Burch, William, member of American Board of Customs, 182 n.

Burke, Edmund: private secretary to Rockingham, Member of Parliament, 148; for repeal of Stamp Act, 150 n.; and proposal for free ports, 152

Bute, 3d Earl of. *See* Stuart, John

Byng, Robert, receiver of rights and perquisites of the Admiralty, 70 n.

Cabinet: and Admiralty estimates, 3, 11; under Walpole, 41 f.; under Pelhams, 78; committee of, 78; divided over war policies, 79 f.; recommendation of packet system, 101; controversy over peace terms, 109; considers American affairs, 166; and tax on tea, 167; George III on, 167 n.; and Townshend Act, 171; reaction of, to New York's refusal to quarter soldiers, 175; center of power, 198

Calvert, Charles, 3d Lord Baltimore, proprietor of Maryland, 23

Campbell, Agatha, purchase of seigneury of, 65

Campbell, John, 4th Earl of Loudoun, complains of instructions, 93

Campbell v. Hall, 140 n.

Canada: expedition against (*1711*), 3; settlement for debt of expedition, 52, 83 n.; plan for expedition against (*1746*), 83; extension of postal system to, 101; financial problems in, 142 f.; publication of receiver general's instructions in, 163. *See also* Quebec

Canso, garrison in, 53 n.

Canterbury, Archbishop of, and American episcopate, 155

Cape Breton, regiments in, 82 n.

Capitation tax, in Ceded Islands, 194

Caribbean, problems of foreign trade in, 152. *See also* Bullion, trade in; Free ports; Trade

Carlisle, Earl of. *See* Howard, Charles

Carolinas: dues from proprietors of, 23, 28; and extension of rice trade, 48 n.; purchase of by Parliament, 50 and n., 65 and n.; company in, 52 n.; new ports of entry in, 60. *See also* North Carolina; South Carolina; Quit rents

Carteret, John, Lord (later Lord Granville), proprietor of Carolinas, 50 n.

Carthagena, expedition to, 56, 65

Castle William, refuge of American Board of Customs, 184

Casual revenues, 24, 69 ff., 104 ff., 141 ff., 193 f.; receivers of, 27, 70, 103 n.; appropriations of, by Jamaica and Barbados, 30; uses of, 104 n.; question of including fines and forfeitures in, 143. *See also* Admiralty, droits of; Fines and forfeitures; Land, sales of; Prizes

Cavendish, William, 4th Duke of Devonshire, First Lord of the Treasury, 77 n.

Ceded Islands: names of, 109 n.; question of salaries of civil officers in, 125; deputy postmaster general for, 138 and n.; duties payable in, 140, 194; trouble with Indians in, 162; objection to four-and-a-half per cent in, 192; sales of land in, *see* Land

Cereals, importation of from colonies, 170 n.

Chancellor of Exchequer. *See* Exchequer

Chandos, Duke of. *See* Brydges, James

Charles, Robert, colonial agent, quoted, 82 n.

Charleston, South Carolina, seat of vice-admiralty court, 185

Charters, colonial, reference to, 121 n.

Chatham, Earl of. *See* Pitt, William

Cholmondeley, George, 2d Earl of, 102 n.

Cholmondeley, Robert, auditor general of His Majesty's plantation revenues, 102; proposal for new instructions for receivers, 103; and audit of accounts, 105 f. and n., 142, 162, 163 n.; reports on crown dues, 161, 190, 191 and n. *See also* Auditor general

Church livings, Newcastle and, 79 n.

Civil list, 8, 10; payments from, or proposed for colonial purposes, 9 f., 15, 87 and n., 126 f. and n., 155, 178 f., 199 f.; four-and-a-half per cent included in, not included in, 29, 104; warrants for payments from, 43 n.; opposition to use of, for colonies, 55; of George III, 101 n.; relieved from charge for New York attorney general, 179 n. *See also* Secret service funds; Crown dues; Four-and-a-half per cent; Quit rents

Cockpit, meetings at, 45, 148 n.

Cocoa nuts: enumeration of, 16 n., drawback of duty on, 170 n.

Coffee, laws on, 48 n., 170 n.

Colonies:

English policies for, 1 f., 199; use of statutes to express, 49

assemblies in: appropriations of for

armed forces, 12, 129; levying four-and-a-half per cent duty, 23, 29 n., 67; question of permanent revenue acts in, 31 f., 72, 106; annual grants, Treasury's lack of control of, 32, 73, 106, 195, 199; quit rent laws in, 65; subject to Mutiny Act, 154, 171, 175 f.; Ceded Islands, refusal of, to levy four-and-a-half per cent, 192

civil establishments for, 51, 84, 97, 125 and n., 131, 164, 173

reimbursement of, 83; treasury functions in, 95 f. and n., 130 and n.; Grenville's ending of, 124 f.; Rhode Island's claims, 157

agents of: and receipt of parliamentary grants, 96 and n., 130, 181; new type of, 98 and n.; interviews of with Grenville, 121

lack of information on costs of government of, 171 and n., 195

corporate and proprietary, crown lack of financial control in, 199

See also Governors; Courts; *and names of individual colonies*

Colors, painters', duty on, 173

Commerce. *See* Trade

Commissioners. *See* Board of Trade; Land, sales of; Prizes

Compton, Spencer, Earl of Wilmington, First Lord of the Treasury, 76

Comptrollers of the Accounts of the Army, 12, 57, 93

Cone, Carl B., on repeal of Stamp Act, 150 n.

Connecticut: self-sufficiency, 14; lack of post office in, 21 n.; and Mohegan Indians, 69 n.; refusal of court of to issue writs of assistance, 185 n.

Consuls, English, aid of, in enforcing customs, 133, 185

Contracts and contractors. *See* Army, funds for, victualing

Conway, Henry Seymour, Secretary of State, 147 f. and n.

Cooper, Grey, secretary to Treasury, Member of Parliament, 148, 155, 158 n., 162 n., 168, 174, 175 n., 178 and n.

Copper, enumeration of, 49 n.

Cornbury, Lord. *See* Hyde, Edward

Cotes, Admiral Thomas, case of, 105 n., 152 n.

Cotton: enumeration of, 16 n.; removal of duty on, 153, 161; end of four-and-a-half per cent duty on, 161

Courts:

in colonies:

vice-admiralty, 20; treasury encouragement of appeals from, 59, 186; and prize cases, 105 and n., 162; new, hinted in Sugar Act (*1764*), 118; and enforcement of Stamp Act, 122 and n.; Grenville and plan for additional, 131; at Halifax, 134 and n.; treasury plan for three, 134; bill for additional (*1768*), 175 and n.: Treasury and plan for four, 185 f.; establishment of, 186 n.

ecclesiastical, existence of, implied in Stamp Act, 127 n.

common law, refusal of, to issue writs of assistance, 185 and n.

in England:

King's Bench, 192 and n.

Common Pleas, 194

See also Admiralty, High Court of; Exchequer, Court of

Crown dues, 23 ff., 63 ff., 102 ff., 139 ff., 161 ff., 190 ff., 200 f.; colonial officials of, 25, 103, 163; disposition of, 27 ff., 31, 171 f., 200; Crown's losses of, 30 f., 71, 139, 194, 195; interest of George III in, 111; treasury attempt to collect in conquered islands, 111; obstacles to collection of, 194; lack of significance of as cause of Revolution, 194 f., 196; inadequacy of income from, 201. *See also* Admiralty, droits of; Casual revenues; Four-and-a-half per cent; Quit rents; Auditor general

Cruwys, Thomas, solicitor to Stamp Office, and Stamp Act, 120, 122 n.

Cumberland, Fort, Braddock at, 91 and n., 94

Cumberland, William August, Duke of: and army appointments, 78 n.; plan of for settling Nova Scotia, 84; negotiation of with Newcastle, 146

Customs:

purpose and character of, 15 ff., 200
governors and administration of, 15, 135

duties: on enumerated commodities, 16 n., 49 n., 115; on prize goods, 19 n.; on molasses, 48, 118, 153; remission of, on cotton and sugar, 153; under Quebec Act, 170; under Townshend Act, 173

London Board of, 16, 60 f., 70 n., 99 f., 117, 120 n., 131 n., 132, 136, 158 f. and n., 174 n., 181, 183; staff of, 17 n., 131, 134, 183 n.; secretary to and Sugar Act, 117; solicitor to, and draft of bill, 117. *See* Four-and-a-half per cent for management of that duty

treasury supervision of, 17, 59 ff., 98 ff., 131 ff., 158 f., 181 ff.

patronage in, 17, 60, 99, 114, 158, 182 ff.

colonial officers: ranks and functions of, 17; instruction of, 17, 132, 183; surveyors general, 17, 60 f., 99 n., 132, 133 n., 160, 182 n., 183 n.; leaves of absence for, 17, 60, 99, 132, 158, 185; deputies for, 17, 60, 132 n.; fees of, 18, 119 and n., 158, 186; additions to establishment of, 60, 98 and n., 133, 182 n.

ports of entry, 17, 60, 98, 132 f. and n., 185

costs of administration, salaries, and incidental expenses, 18, 62 and n., 79 and n., 100 n., 137 n., 187

receipts and deposits in Exchequer, 19 and n., 62 and n., 100 and n., 136 and n., 159 and n., 187, 200

enforcement of: by Secretary of State and Admiralty, 19, 133 f.; laxity in, 61; use of army and navy for, 100, 185; in Newfoundland, 133; plans for reform in, 133 ff.

accounts and audit, 34 and n.; collectors', 62 n.; comptroller general's, 117 and n.; under American Board, final, 187 f. and n.

defects in, 110, 135, *see also above, under* colonial officers: leaves of absence, deputies, fees

officers in English ports, aid of, in enforcement, 134

stamps required for, 160

American Board of: act establishing, 174; Treasury and, 181 ff.; staff, 182; inspectors general under, 183; agent of, at Treasury, 183 n.,

188 n.; clerk of, at London Custom House, 183 n.; cashier under, 183 n., 186 f., 187 and n.; history of, 183 f.; report of, on revenue, 186 f.; comptroller general under, 188 and n.

See also Acts, trade and navigation; Courts, vice-admiralty; Free ports

Dartmouth, Earl of. *See* Legge, William

Dashwood, Sir Francis, Chancellor of the Exchequer, 110

Debenture, exchequer form, 8 n.

Debts, colonial, act for recovery of, 49 n.

Declaration of Independence, 174 f., 194, 196 f.

Declaratory Act, 150 f., 173, 201

Defense of colonies, 2, 11 ff. *See also* Acts, appropriations for defense; Army; Navy; Ordnance

Devonshire, Duke of. *See* Cavendish, William

Dismore, Edward, deputy postmaster in Jamaica, 100 n., 137 n., 138 n.

Dominica, one of Ceded Islands, 109 n.; free ports in, 152; collector of consulted, 159

Dowdeswell, William, Chancellor of the Exchequer, 148 and n., 152 n., 156, 157 n.

Downing St., Number 10, assigned to First Lord of the Treasury, 55 n.

Dues. *See* Crown

Dummer, Edward, contractor for packet boats, 22 n., 63 n.

Dunbar, Charles, casual receiver in the Leeward Islands, 47 n., 102 n., 103 n.

Dunbar, David, surveyor of the King's woods, 59

Dunk, George Montagu, 2d Earl of Halifax, president of Board of Trade, Secretary of State: importance of Board of Trade under, 78 and n.; project for settling Nova Scotia, 84; views of, on colonial taxation, 84 n.; map inscribed to, 87 n.; receipt of provincial papers, 112 n.; member of inner group of ministers, 113 n.; procures information from colonial governors, 121, 137; approval of Mutiny Act, 123 n.; disagreement with Grenville, 125; obtains royal order against seizure of Spanish ships, 136

Duquesne, Fort, Braddock's defeat and death at, 91

Dutch, free port of, on St. Eustatius, 151

Duties, English: reduction of, on imports from colonies, 115, 170 and n.; drawback of on exports to colonies, 170, 173 n. For colonial, *see* Customs; Four-and-a-half per cent

Dye-woods, enumeration of, 16 n.

Dyson, Jeremiah, secretary to Treasury, 110, 126 n.; Junior Lord of Treasury, one of "King's Friends," 169

East Florida: parliamentary appropriations for, 125; grant from civil list for, 126; question of opposition to Stamp Act in, 160 n.

East India Act (*1773*), 173

East India Company, 173 n.

East Indies, goods from, to be landed in Great Britain, 49 n.

Egremont, 2d Earl of. *See* Wyndham, Charles

Elections, 5, 43 f. and nn., 80 and nn., 114, 168 and n.

Elector Palatine, payment to, from quit rents, 29 n.

Engineers, for colonies, 13

Enumerated commodities, 16 n., 49 n., 115; bond for, 16 n. *See also* Acts; Customs, duties

Episcopate, American, proposals for, 10 n., 55, 87, 126 f. and n., 155, 184 n.

Estimates. *See* Admiralty; Army; Ordnance; Parliament

Europe, direct trade with North America, illegality of, 99, 153

Exchange, rate of. *See* Army, funds for

Exchequer:

Chancellor of: Harley as, 2 n.; and declaration of accounts, 6, 35, 201; oath of office, 7 n.; on Crown's right to four-and-a-half per cent (*1821*), 29 n.; Walpole as, 40; Pelham as, 77; Legge as, 85; Dashwood as, 109; Dowdeswell as, 148; Charles Townshend as, 166 ff., passim; importance of combination of office with that of head of Treasury, 199

Treasurer and Under-Treasurer of, 6

forms for issues from, tellers of, 8 n.

Court of, issue of writs of assistance by, 175 n.

Extraordinaries. *See* Army

Falkingham, Henry, deputy postmaster general in Barbados, 138 n.

Falmouth, England, packet from, 159

Fines and forfeitures for illegal trade: King's share of, a casual revenue, 24; appropriation of, by Barbados, 31 n.; deposits of, in Exchequer, 100; transferred to customs, 143, 194; source of judges' salaries, 186 n.

Finisterre, Cape, northern limit for trade, 48 n., 153

Finlay, Hugh, Quebec postmaster, riding surveyor, 188 and n., 189

First Continental Congress, 196

First Lord of the Treasury. *See* Treasury

Fitzroy, Augustus Henry, 3d Duke of Grafton: Secretary of State, 147; First Lord of the Treasury, 165 ff.; resignation of, 167; on Chatham's neglect of elections, 168 n.; attitude of, toward patronage, 168 and n.; and use of crown dues in America, 172; character of legislation under, 177; administration of Treasury by, 177 ff.; question of his responsibility for colonial independence, 196

Fitzwilliam, Richard, customs officer, 60 n.

Florida: inability to provide for own government, 142; custom house in, 185 n. *See also* East Florida; West Florida

Four-and-a-half per cent duty:

disposition of revenue of: for salaries of customs officers, 18, 98; for Swedish army, 31 n.; for salaries of colonial governors, 69 n., 87 n.; for defense of Annapolis, 83, 104 n.; for special service, 104 n.

origin of: in Barbados and Leeward Islands, 23 f., 29 and n.; in former French half of St. Christopher, 24, 67; in Tortola, 192 n.

management of: by London Board of Customs, 26; subordinate officers in London, 26; surveyor general, 26 n.; investigation of and new instructions, 68 f. and n.; auditor general's report on, 191 f.

question of sovereign's authority over: Queen's agreement with the Commons, 29; settled for George I, 68; raised under Newcastle, 104

receipts and deposits, 29 n., 68 n., 103 f. and n., 161 f. and n., 192 and n.

accounts and audit, 35 f., 68 and n., 192 n.

controversy over in Ceded Islands, 140, 192

renunciation of part of by George III, 161

Fox, Henry (later 1st Lord Holland), Secretary of State, 81, 84 n.

Fox, Stephen, secretary to Treasury, 54 n.

Fox, William Erdman, collector of customs for Philadelphia, 61

Foxcroft, John: deputy postmaster general, 101 n.; agent for packet system, 189

France: war with, 75 ff.; illegal trade of English with colonies of, 99; terms of peace with, 109; duties of collected in Canada, 163

Frankland, Sir Thomas, Admiral, his prize accounts, 162

Franklin, Benjamin: deputy postmaster general, 100 f. and nn., 101 and n., 137 and n., 188; on Grenville, 121; suggestion of, for loan office, 121; consulted on mutiny bill, 124; opinion of on danger from Indians, 124

Franklin, William, Governor of New Jersey, on lack of Stamp Act instructions, 160

Free ports: Spanish and Dutch and proposal for English, 151; Act (*1766*), 152; administration of, 159

French and Indian War, 76 ff. *See also* Seven Years' War

Funds, issue of. *See* Army, funds for; Treasury, head of

Furnese, Henry, secretary to Treasury, 87 n.

Fustic, enumeration of, 16 n.

Gage, Thomas, Lieutenant General: recommendation of Mutiny Act by, 123 n.; and aid for revenue officers, 127 n., 135; effect of suspension of money contracts on, 128; treasury orders to, 128 n., 156, 179; complaints of treasury methods by, 130 n.; problem of enforcing Mutiny Act in Quebec, 143; failure to receive copy of Mutiny Act, 154 n.

Gaspé, Bay of, customs establishment on, 133 n.

General warrants, in England, 149

George I: accession of, 39; confidence of in Walpole, 41; creation of important position for Walpole, 54; and meetings of the Treasury, 54 n.

George II: confidence of in Walpole, 41; and meetings of the Treasury, 54 n.; and the Pelhams, 77; and army patronage, 78 n.

George III: and Newcastle's loss of power, 78; civil list of, 101 n.; interest of, in crown revenues, 111; failure of to give Grenville full power, 113; and patronage under Grenville, 114; warning of, on American mutiny bill, 123 f.;

approval of treasury minute by, 128; contributions of to public from crown revenues, 139, 142, 143 and n.; attempt of, to secure Pitt, 146; objection of to Rockingham, 147 and n.; renunciation of four-and-a-half per cent on cotton, 161; interest of in administration, 167; advice of, to Hillsborough on cabinet methods, 167 n.; interest in division lists, 169; question as to consultation with on use of crown revenues, 172; interest of in Treasury, 178 and n.

Georgia: extension of rice trade of, 48 n.; support of from Parliament, 50 f., 84, 125, 200; regiment in, 52 n., 57 and n.; rangers in, 82 n., 85 n.; surrender of charter of and parliamentary establishment for, 85; agent for trustees of, 98 n.; post office in, 101; only parliamentary protégé to join Revolution, 181; quit rents from, 191

Glass, duty on (*1767*), 173

Gloucester, William Henry, Duke of, grant to, 106

Godolphin, Charles, brother of Earl and first commissioner of customs, 17 n.

Godolphin, Sydney, 1st Earl: Lord High Treasurer, 2 ff.; and Queen Anne, 2 ff.; as member of House of Lords, 5; character of, as administrator, 5 f.; and elections and management of Commons, 5; strictness of, in payments from civil list, 10 f.; establishment of Comptrollers of Accounts of Army by, 12; methods of supplying armed forces in America, 12 f.; and customs patronage, 17, 60; character of administration of crown dues, 25, 63; control of Commissioners of Prizes, 26; favors use of quit rents to supplement civil list, 29; emphasis of on audit, 34 ff.

Goldsworthy, Burrington, receiver of rights and perquisites of the Admiralty, 70 n.

Governors: royal, equipment of provided by Crown, 11; share of Treasury in nonenforcement of instructions, 33; instructions to, on bishops, 55 n.; responsibility for shipping lists, 61; salaries, 69 and n.; grants of land by, 71 n., 143; sympathy of, with local point of view, 73; promised pay for troops, 83; and receipt of parliamentary grants, 96; supplying information, 121, 137; orders to, on illegal trade, 133; quarrels with revenue officers, 135; lack of instructions on Stamp Act, 159 f.; duties under Stamp Act, 160 n.; consulted on colonial expenses, 170 and n.; permitted to draw on Treasury, 180

Grafton, 3d Duke of. *See* Fitzroy, Augustus Henry

Granville, Lord. *See* Carteret, John, Lord

Greenwich Hospital dues, in America, 49 n., 81 n.

Grenada: one of the Ceded Islands, 109 n.; question of opposition to Stamp Act in, 160 n.; appeal from, to King's Bench, 192

Grenville, George: Secretary of State, First Lord of the Admiralty under

Bute, 108 ff.; personal character of, 111; First Lord of the Treasury, 112 ff.; and George III, 112; in the Privy Council, 112 and n.; character of administration, 113 f.; and patronage, 114; apathy toward elections, 114; management of the Commons by, 114 f.; character of colonial legislation under, 115; his emphasis on revenue, 115, 131; his theory of parliamentary sovereignty, 116 and n.; on colonial policy, 116 n.; his reliance on secretaries, 119; postponement of stamp bill by, 120; interviews with Americans, 121; described by Franklin, 121; expectations of revenue, 121 f. and n.; warned against quartering soldiers in America, 123 f.; for standing army in America, 124, 127; economy of in financing army, 124 ff.; disagreement with Halifax over Quebec, 125; and American episcopate, 127 n.; plans for increasing revenue, 131 ff.; evident ignorance of colonies, 135; and destruction of bullion trade, 136; and expansion of postal system, 137 f.; his delays in administering the Stamp Act, 138 f.; administration of crown dues by, 139 ff.; plans for revenue in Ceded Islands, 140 ff.; effect of administration of on colonies, 145; modification of his military plans by Rockingham, 155 f.; and origin of the American Revolution, 197, 201

Grenville-Temple, Richard, Earl Temple: retirement of, 111 n.; break with Grenville, 113

Guadeloupe: surplus of provisions at, 95; crown revenue in, 105 f.; retention of, favored by Grenville, 109; conquered by British and returned to France, 109 n.; revenue from, applied to special service, 162 f.

Halifax, Nova Scotia, seat of new vice-admiralty court, 134, 185

Halifax, 1st Earl of. *See* Montagu, Charles

Halifax, 2d Earl of. *See* Dunk, George Montagu

Hallowell, Benjamin, member American Board of Customs, 183 n.

Hamilton, John, manager of American post office, 21 n.

Hampton Court, treasury meeting at, 54 n.

Hanbury, John, contractor. *See* Army, funds for

Hancock, John, seizure of his ship, the *Liberty,* 184

Hardinge, Nicholas, secretary to the Treasury, 87 and n.

Hardwicke, 1st Earl of. *See* Yorke, Philip

Harley, Robert, Earl of Oxford and Mortimer: and Queen Anne, 2; patronage and issue of funds under, 2 f.; Chancellor of the Exchequer, 2 n.; Lord High Treasurer, 2 ff.; conflict with Secretary of State, 3 f.; elections and management of Commons under, 5; as Secretary of State, 5; successor to Godolphin at the Treasury, 5; treasury administration under, 7 ff.; and payments from civil list, including money for purchase of Pennsylvania, 10, 50; comparative lack of interest in crown dues, 25; appointment of special commissioner for prizes, 27; favors using quit rents to supplement civil list, 29

Harley, Thomas, joint secretary to the Treasury, 7

Harrison, Joseph, from Boston, quoted, 122

Haslemere, election contest at, 44 n.

Hats, curb on manufacture of, 49 n.

Hides and skins, removal of duty on, 170 n.

Hill, Wills, 1st Earl of Hillsborough: First Commissioner of Board of Trade, 113 n., 166 and n.; Secretary of State for the colonies, 167; advised by George III on cabinet methods, 167 n.; and public relations, 180

Hillsborough, 1st Earl of. *See* Hill, Wills

Hood, Commodore Samuel, loan to from customs, 187 n.

House of Commons. *See* Parliament

House of Lords. *See* Parliament

Howard, Charles, Earl of Carlisle, First Lord of the Treasury, 39 n.

Hulton, Ann, on American Board of Customs, 183 n.

Hulton, Henry: first commissioner of American Board of Customs, 182; receiver of six-penny duty, 184 n.

Hunter, William, deputy postmaster general, 100 f. and n.

Huske, John, scheme for free ports, 152 n.

Hyde, Edward, Lord Cornbury, assigned dues from Carolina, 28

Impressment, of colonial seamen, 170 and n.

Indians: Franklin on danger from, 124; in Ceded Islands (Charibs), 162, 193

Indigo, premium on, 81 n.

Ingersoll, Jared, 121 f., 161 n.

Inspector of quit rents. *See* McCulloh, Henry

Ireland, nonenumerated commodities to be landed in, 170 n.

Iron: failure of attempt to restrict manufacture of, 50 and n.; free import of, 81 n.; extension of colonial market for, 119

Irving, Thomas, comptroller general of American customs, 188 n.

Issues of funds. *See* Exchequer; Treasury

Jamaica: opposition to "standing army," 12; appropriation of casual revenues by, 29 f.; lack of treasury interest in revenue act of, 32 n.; companies in, 52 n., 58; permanent revenue act in, 72, 106; refusal of supplementary pay for army, 129; Spanish trade with, 130 and n.; free port in, 152; question of opposition to Stamp Act in, 160 n. *See also* Post Office, deputy postmasters general; Quit rents

Jeffreys, John, secretary to the Treasury, 87 n.

Jenkinson, Charles (later 1st Earl of Liverpool): secretary to the Treasury and Member of Parliament, 115; investigates customs receipts, 116; responsibility for trade act (*1765*), 119; instructions for drafting stamp bill, 120; on consulting Americans, 120; responsibility for revising American mutiny bill,

124; directions to Board of Trade, 125; friend of Bute, 126; plan for transfer of customs to army, 129 n.; and Spanish trade, 136; on legality of four-and-a-half per cent in Ceded Islands, 140; in receipt of quit rents, 140; Junior Lord of Treasury and one of "King's Friends," 168 f., 177; proposal of for restricting colonial trade, 170 f.

Jersey, island of, salary of governor, 69 n.

Jerseys, proprietors of, dues of, 23

King: chair of at the Treasury, 54 n.; question of his prerogative, 142 n.; "Friends" of, 147; views on status of, 147 n.; importance of favor of, 198. *See also names of individual sovereigns*

King-in-Council. *See* Privy Council

Knowles, Sir Charles, governor of Jamaica, 103 n.

Land, sales of:
source of casual revenue, 24
on St. Christopher: revenue of, appropriated by Parliament, 51, 71 and n.; method and responsibility of Treasury for, 71 f.; management of, by commissioners, 71; terms for, 71 n.; accounts and audit of, 71 n.; precedent for sales in Ceded Islands, 141
usual procedures in, 70
in Ceded Islands: plan of Board of Trade for, 141; responsibility of Treasury for, 141 f.; history, 141, 162, 193; management of, by commissioners, 141, 193 n.; terms of, 141; disappointment over revenue of, 142; transfer of revenue to public, 142; accounts and audit, 142 n.
in Bermuda, 143 n.

Land banks, made illegal, 49 n.

Lansdowne, 1st Marquis of, and 2d Earl of Shelburne. *See* Petty, William

Law officers of the Crown: opinion on legality of bullion trade, 136 n.; report on King's rights in Quebec, 142, 163; proposal for bullion trade, 157 n.; on New York and the Mutiny Act, 176; on English writ of mandamus in colonies, 185. *See also* Attorney General; Solicitor General

Laws. *See* Acts

Lead, duty on, 173

Leake, John Martin, agent of American Board, his accounts, 188 n.

Leeward Islands: regiment in, 52 n.; casual receiver in, 102 n.; deputy postmaster general in, 138 n. *See also* Four-and-a-half per cent

Legge, Henry Bilson: secretary to the Treasury, 56, 87 n.; Chancellor of the Exchequer, 85

Legge, William, 2d Earl of Dartmouth: First Commissioner of Board of Trade, 147 f. and n.; Secretary of State, 195

Leheup, Peter: treasury clerk and deputy to auditor general of plantation revenues, 64; loss of clerkship, 86 and n.; interference in work of auditor general, 102 and n.

Lennox, Charles, 3d Duke of Richmond and Lennox, Secretary of State, 148 n.

Liberty, seizure of, 184

Liverpool, 1st Earl of. *See* Jenkinson, Charles

Lloyd, Charles: secretary to George Grenville, and patronage, 114 n.; under clerk in Treasury, 126

Lloyd, John, deputy postmaster general in America, 62 n.

London, Bishop of: commissary of, in Virginia, 28; and licenses for American school teachers, 55 n.; and American episcopate, 155

Lord High Treasurer. *See* Treasury; Godolphin, Sydney; Harley, Robert; Talbot, Charles

Lord Privy Seal: Newcastle as, 147; Chatham as, 165

Lords Commissioners of Trade and Plantations. *See* Board of Trade

Loudoun, 4th Earl of. *See* Campbell, John

Louisburg: garrison at, 82 n.; expedition against (*1745*), 83; specie for, 89; pay of commander at, 155 n.

Lowndes, Charles: secretary to the Treasury, 154; recipient of special service funds, 161 n.; supplanted, 178

Lowndes, William: secretary to the Treasury, 7; studies Virginia revenues, 25; death of, 54

Lowther, Sir James, his election agent, 168

Loyalists, civil list and parliamentary payments to, 179

Lumber: bounties on and extension of market for colonial, 119; removal of duties on, 170 n.

Lynch, Head, deputy postmaster general, 63 n.

Lyttelton, George: Junior Lord of the Treasury, 79 n.; patron of poet, 99 n.

Lyttelton, William Henry, 1st Baron Lyttelton of Frankley, Governor of Jamaica, on quarrel with navy officers,135 n.

McCulloh, Henry: inspector of quit rents, 66; claims of, 103 n.; failure of Treasury to consult, 103; and stamp bill, 120 and n., 121, 122 n.

Mansfield, Lord. *See* Murray, William

Manufactures, British, monopoly of American market for, 154

Martin, Samuel: secretary to the Treasury, 86 n., 87 and n., 110; on legal use of four-and-a-half per cent, 104; father of, on postal rates, 123 n.; on purchase of places, 168 n.

Martinique, conquered by British, returned to France, 109 n.

Maryland: local taxes, 31 f.; local revenue accounts, 32 n.; disallowance of military accounts, 96; refusal of court in, to issue writs of assistance, 185 n.

Massachusetts: credit for Newfoundland forces, 13; self-sufficiency, 14; postal law in, 21 n.; governor to aid customs officer, 61; salary of governor, 69 n.; pension for former governor, 69; agents for, 96 n.; local revenue act, 106; trouble among crown officers in, 135 n.; acts regulating (*1774*), 176; Circular Letter, 196

Mathew, William, Governor of Leeward Islands, on obtaining favors, 42 n.

Meat, salted, importation of from colonies, 170 n.

Medleton, Alexander, deputy postmaster in Ceded Islands, 138 n.

Mellish, William, secretary to Treasury, receiver general of customs, 155 n.

Melville, Brigadier General Robert, Governor of Ceded Islands: to draw bills of exchange, 156; memorial of, 194 n.

Mercantilism, traditional principles of, 115

Merchants:

British: on committee for Molasses Act, 47; petition against bills of credit, 82; and paper currency, 97 n.; laws against interests of, 115; effect of Sugar Act (*1764*) on, 118; for restricting bills of credit, 123; charges of, against navy, 135 f.; associations for repeal of Stamp Act, 150; divided on issue of free ports, 152; agreement on commercial act (*1766*), 153; for restricting New England trade, 153; their bills of exchange to be paid by Bank of England, 156; Rockingham's deference to, 162; declining influence of, 169; advice of on location of ports, 185

colonial, threat to trade of, 171

Middlesex, Newcastle and candidates for, 40 n.

Ministers: divided on issue of free ports, 152; change in (*1765*), 159. *See also* Cabinet *and names of individual officials*

Mitchell, Dr. John, map by, 87 and n.

Mohegan Indians, and Connecticut, 69 n.

Molasses: enumeration, 16 n.; duty on imported foreign, 62 and n.; illegal trade in, 99; deposits in Exchequer from duty on, 100 and n.; study of trade and duty on,

116 and n.; failure to appropriate revenue from, 118 n.; duty applied to British, 153 and n.; duties on under Quebec Act, 170

Monckton, Lieutenant General Robert, 92 n.

Money, problem of in colonies, 123. *See also* Army, funds for; Paper currency

Montagu, Charles, 1st Earl of Halifax: First Lord of the Treasury, 39; and petition on American episcopate, 55

Montagu, John, 4th Earl of Sandwich, Secretary of State, and ministerial dinners, 113

Montreal: establishment of customs officers in, 98; post office in, 137 n.

Moore, Francis, on free ports, 152

Morgan, Edmund S. and Helen M.: on Stamp Act, 120 n.; on repeal of Stamp Act, 150 n.

Morris, Corbyn, colonial agent, 98 n.

Murray, Lieutenant General James: threat to issue paper money, 92; report of, on Quebec revenues, 142; taxes on own authority, 143; question of his right to tax, 163; uses bills of exchange, 163; to refund taxes, 163 n.; court decision against, 194

Murray, Richard, deputy receiver in Quebec, 143 n.

Murray, William, Lord Mansfield, Chief Justice, judgment of, in Campbell v. Hall, 192 and n.

Mutiny Act. *See* Acts

Naval officer: deputy of governor, 15; responsibility of for shipping lists, 61

Naval stores: produced in colonies, 14; enumeration of, 16 n.; premiums on, 48; fund from sale of old, 186 n.

Navy:
Victualing Board of, supplying army, 13, 57 and n.
Board: dismissal of surveyor of woods by, 14; return of bills of exchange by, 89 n.
estimates for, 14
aid in preventing illegal trade, 20, 100, 134, 135 f., 184, 185, 202; question of right to share of seizures, 135 n.; importance of seizures by, 187
Treasurer of: ordered to pay bill, 58; Grenville as, 111
trees reserved for, 59
ships in American waters (*1763*), 134 n.
commander in, and public relations, 180 f.
See also Admiralty

Neutral islands: plans for revenue in, 65; center of trade, 109

Nevis, relief for from prize money, 30 n.

New England: and expedition against Louisburg, 83; petition of for reimbursement, 83; charges of customs frauds in, 99; restrictions on trade of, 153

New Englanders, advice of on settlement in Nova Scotia, 84

New Hampshire: postal law of, 21; new port of entry in, 60; post office in, 100; Governor as surveyor general of the woods, 131 n.

New Haven, Connecticut, on customs establishment, 133 n.

New Jersey, local postal law in, 21 n.

New York: salary of Attorney General of, 10, 87 n., 179 n.; royal grant for Indian chapel at, 10; British forces in, 12 and n., 52 n.; proposal for parliamentary tax in, 14; local use of customs receipts, 19 n.; quit rents in, 23, 28; importation of salt into, 48; pension for crown receiver in, 66; crown dues of, combined with local revenues, 67; Treasury and assembly grants, 73; assembly of, and Horace Walpole's fees, 73 n.; packet sailings to, 101, 159; separation of revenue offices in, 103; question of permanent revenue act in, 106 and n.; judge of vice-admiralty court in, requests prize, 162; assembly of, and Mutiny Act, 175 f.; court in, and writs of assistance, 185 n.; central post office in, 188

Newcastle, 1st Duke of. *See* Pelham-Holles, Thomas

Newfoundland: British forces in, 12 and n., 13, 57 and n.; agent for, 98 n.; enforcement of acts of trade in, 133; under American Board of Customs, 182; transferred to English Board, 182 n.

Newspapers, reference to list of American, 121 n.

Nicholson, Sir Francis: as Colonel to use customs for armed forces, 19; as Governor of Virginia, report on revenues, 25; commissioner to recover revenue, 27

Nonenumerated commodities: bond for, 153; permission to land in Ireland, 170 n.

North, Frederick, Lord: refuses place of Chancellor of Exchequer, 166 n.; accepts place of Chancellor of Exchequer, 167; First Lord of the Treasury, 167 ff.; his relation to the King, 167; and Parliament, 167, 168 f.; character of his administration, 167 f.; attitude toward patronage, 168; on purchase of places, 168 n.; drafting of commercial legislation under, 169 f.; character of colonial legislation under, 169; announcement against colonial taxation, 173; introduces bill for vice-admiralty courts, 175; and coercive acts, 176; administration of the Treasury by, 177 ff.

North America: trade of, protected, 47; map of, 87 n.; illegal trade with Europe, 99; new emphasis on, 110 f.; distinguished from West Indies, 122; postal accounts from, 137 n.; independence of older colonies in, 202

North Carolina: quit rents in, 66, 191; agents for, 96. *See also* Carolinas

Norwich, election trouble in, 44 n.

Nova Scotia: acquisition of, 11; British forces in, 12 and n., 57 and n., 89, 92 n.; Governor of, reimbursed, 58; quit rents in, 65, 191; free import of salt into, 81 n.; plan for settlement of, 84; parliamentary provision for civil government of, 84, 85 n., 97, 200; agent for, 98 n.; question of opposition to Stamp Act in, 160 n.

Nuthall, Thomas, solicitor to the Treasury, 155 n., 178 n., 194 n.

Oglethorpe, General James Edward: his regiment in Georgia, 57 and

n.; bills of refused by the Treasury, 89

Order, for issue of funds, 8 n.

Order in Council. *See* Privy Council

Ordnance:
Office: estimates for, 11, 13; advice of on uses of four-and-a-half per cent, 29; orders to from Privy Council, 58
stores for America, 13; paid for from quit rents, 28; increasing demands for, 58

Orford, 1st Earl of. *See* Walpole, Robert

Oxford, Earl of, and Earl Mortimer. *See* Harley, Robert

Packet system. *See* Post Office

Palatines: civil list payments for, 10; forfeiture of possessions of, 61 n.

Paper, duty on, 173

Paper currency: failure of attempt to restrict, 49 n.; restrictions on, 81 f., 123; requirement for redemption of, 97; McCulloh's plan for, 121

Parliament: importance of, 5, growth in, 144; responsibility of North to, 167; necessity of support of, 198

House of Commons: Treasury and, elections to, and management of, 5, 43 ff., 79 ff., 114 f., 168 f.; failure to provide for forces in Jamaica, 12; Committee of Secrecy, 56; investigation of solicitor to Treasury by, 86; address of, on army funds, 93; investigation of contracts by, 95; procedure in, 117 n.; refusal to hear petitions, 117, 122; Committee on American papers, 150; reduction of land tax by, 172

House of Lords: Lord High Treasurer in, 5; Walpole's use of, 45, 47; opposition in, 148, 151 n.

authority for colonial taxation, 15, *see also* Acts

interest in revenue from colonies:

crown: four-and-a-half per cent, 29, 68 f., 140; quit rents, 65 n.; from sales of land, 70 f., 193; increasing authority of over, 194

public: customs, 81, 187; stamps, 120 ff., *passim*

increasing investment of in colonies, 50 f., 52, *see also* Acts, appropriations

increased responsibility of, for colonial administration, 108

theory of sovereignty, 116

question of rights over colonies: denied, 148, 161; asserted, 150, 201

opposition, effect of on Townshend, 172

and New York papers, 175

See also Acts

Parsons, R., comptroller general of customs, 117 n.

Paterson, William, surveyor general in West Indies, 99 n.

Patronage, 2 f., 42 f., 78 f. and n., 114 and n., 148 f. and n., 168 and n., 198; King and, 78 n., 79 n., 114, 148; threat to permanent tenure at Treasury, 85 f. *See also* individual revenues

Paxton, Charles, customs surveyor in Boston: and plan for American Board, 174 and n.; member of Board, 182 n.

Paxton, Nicholas, solicitor to the Treasury, dismissed, 86 and n.

Paymaster General of the Forces: accounts of, and audit, 3 n., 34, 156 n.; subordinate to Treasury, 12; and accounts for reimbursement of colonies, 95; issues by to colonial agents, 96; using reimbursement funds for other purposes, 97

Peace: characteristic of Walpole's administration, 39; of *1763*, terms of, 109 and n.

Pelham, Henry: First Lord of the Treasury and Chancellor of the Exchequer, 76 ff.; death of, 77; quoted on the King, 78 n.; in Committee on Plantation Affairs, 78; patronage under, 78 and n.; and issue of funds, 79; and reimbursement of colonies, 83 f.; postponement of plan to settle Nova Scotia, 85; objection to establishment of Georgia, 85; creation of sinecure in solicitor's office, 86; supplying forces with cash, 89; and victualing contracts, 93; and verification of colonial military accounts, 95 f.

Pelham brothers, the younger, 44 n.

Pelham brothers, Henry and Thomas Pelham-Holles, Duke of Newcastle: comparison of, with Walpole, 77; and demand for public funds, 79; elections, and management of Commons, 80 f.; unwillingness to tax America, 85; use of money contracts, 89; following Walpole's tradition in the customs, 98; expansion of colonial postal system under, 100 f.; following Walpole's policy in crown dues, 103; casual revenues under, 104 f.; character-ization of period of, 107; and co-lonial finance, 201

Pelham-Holles, Thomas, 1st Duke of Newcastle:

and elections under Walpole, 41

Secretary of State: under Walpole, 41 and n.; under his brother, 77 ff.; and patronage, 78 f.; and plan for Canadian expedition (*1746*), 83

First Lord of the Treasury, 77 ff.; advice to, from Horace Walpole, 40 n.; temporarily out of office, 77; patronage, 78 f.; and Commit-tee on Plantation Affairs, 78; dis-pute with King over patronage, 79 n.; and issue of funds, 79 f.; resignation of, 80, 107; resistance to sugar lobby, 81; and plan for colonial tax, 84 n., 85; threat to permanent tenure at the Treas-ury, 85 f.; fear of parliamentary investigation, 88; and money con-tracts, 89; pessimism, 92; and vict-ualing contracts, 94 f.; investi-gation of his contracts, 95; allot-ment of colonial grants under, 95 f.; failure of to reform customs, 99 f.; and King's right to four-and-a-half per cent, 104

in Rockingham's administration: negotiation with Duke of Cum-berland, 146; Lord Privy Seal, 147; and patronage, 148; protest by on neglect of Dartmouth, 148 n.; and repeal of Stamp Act, 149

Penn, William: payment to for Penn-sylvania, 10; proprietor, 23

Pennant, Robert, deputy to auditor general, 102 n.

Pennsylvania: plan for purchase of, 10, 50; self-sufficiency, 14; grant

to divine and schoolmaster in, 19 n.; postal law in, 21 n.; law to import salt into, 48 n.; disallow-ance of accounts, 96; treasury re-fusal to reimburse, 130; question of opposition to Stamp Act in, 160 n.; refusal of court in, to is-sue writs of assistance, 185 n.

Pensacola, hospital for, 155 n.

Permanent revenue, question of grants by assemblies, 31, 72, 106. *See also* Jamaica; Two shillings a hogshead

Petitions: from sugar islands, 46 f., 81; from merchants on bills of credit, 82; from New England for reimbursement, 83; against Sugar Act, 117 n.; against Stamp Act, 122 and n.; for repeal of Stamp Act, 150

Petty, William, 1st Marquis of Lans-downe and 2d Earl of Shelburne: First Commissioner of Board of Trade, 113 and n.; for reduction of troops in America, 127 n.; re-fusal to accept office under Rock-ingham, 147; Secretary of State, 166 ff.; interpretation of power of Board of Trade by, 166 n.; op-position of to colonial coercion and resignation of, 167; attempt of, to obtain facts on colonial ex-penses, 171; consulting governors, 171 n.; for use of crown funds for colonies, 171 f. and n., 190; on the royal prerogative, 175; loss of in-fluence and retirement of, 195

Philadelphia: customs patent office in, 61; postmaster in, 101; seat of vice-admiralty court, 185

Pipe Office, granting "quietus" to ac-countants, 35

Pitt, William, 1st Earl of Chatham:

Secretary of State, and Newcastle, 77; and patronage, 79 and n.; blaming Newcastle for lack of funds, 92; threatens to investigate commissariat, 95; political break with Grenville, 112 n., 113 and n.; decision not to accept office, 146, 147 n.; speech in favor of repeal of Stamp Act, 150; opposition to Grenville, 165; Lord Privy Seal and head of Government, 165 ff.; character of his administration, 166 f.; on King's ministers, 166; failure to accept responsibility, 166 f.; resignation, 167; neglect of elections by, 168 n.; in retirement, 172; advice on New York, 175; colonial proposal of, 202

Placemen, influenced by constituents, 45

Placentia, companies at, 52 n.

Plantation Act (*1673*), 15 f.

Poll tax, Canadian, 140

Pontiac, rebellion of, 125

Porter, James, comptroller general of the customs, 188 n.

Post Office:
English laws and rates, 14, 21 and n., 22 n., 62 n., 123 n.
revenue: the purpose of the system, 14, 15, 20; colonial remittances, 100 and n., 137 n., 189
under private monopoly, 20
Postmaster General: acquires authority over colonial system, 20; office staff, 20 n.; contract for management, 62; division of continent, 138; establishment of central office at New York, 188
colonial laws on, 21 and n.
deputy postmasters general: on continent, 21 n., 62 and n., 63 n., 100

f. and n., 137, 188 f.; in the islands, 100, 137 n., 138 n.
extent of colonial system, 21 and n., 63, 101, 137 f. and n., 188
packet system: *1702–11*, 21 f.; contract for, 22 n.; charges, a tax, 22; Walpole's failure to restore, 63; renewal of, 101; continuation of New York, discontinuation of West Indian, 111; reduction of rates for, 123 and n.; revival of West Indian, 123, 138; extension to southern part of continent, 138; captains, 138 n.; develops in spite of financial losses, 159, 190
obligation of captains of merchant vessels, 22
accounts and audit, 34, 100 n., 137 n., 189
patronage in: in England, 79 n.; in colonies, 101 and n., 138; interest of Postmaster General, 189
riding surveyor of, 188
during American Revolution, 189

Potash, free import of, 81 n.

Poulet, John, 1st Earl, First Lord of the Treasury, 2 n.

Pownall, John: secretary to Board of Trade, preparation of colonial military accounts, 96; opinion on proposed instructions, 134 n.

Pownall, Thomas, former Governor of Massachusetts and South Carolina, consulted on mutiny bill, 124

Premiums. *See* Bounties

Prime Minister: Walpole as, 41, 77; privileges of, denied to Grenville, 112; head of Treasury as, 198

Privy Council: orders in, 4, 11 n., 24, 30, 33, 58, 72, 125 n., 140, 198; ineffectiveness in centralizing colonial administration, 20; Committee on Plantation Affairs, 39, 50, 78, 106, 115; petitions to, 46, 106; cooperation with Treasury on quit-rent laws, 65; approving sale of land on St. Christopher, 71; references by, to Treasury, 81, 162; references and memorials from Treasury to, 112, 133, 142, 148 n., 163; grants of land by, 143; president of on relation to colonies, 166

Privy Seal, Lord. *See* Lord Privy Seal

Prizes: goods, duties on in colonies, 19 n.; king's share, a casual revenue, 24; act (*1708*), 26; Commissioners of, 26, 27 n., 105; grants of to captors, 30, 104; revenue of and grants to public, 30, 104, 143 and n.; accounts and audit, 34 n., 64 n., 105 and n., 162 and n.; treasury handling of petitions for, 162; Office, *see above*, Commissioners of

Proclamation Line (*1763*), 143

Proprietors, dues from, 23, 28

Protestants: settlement of in Georgia, 71; in East Florida, 126

Public funds: contrasted with civil list and crown revenue, 9; increase of expenditures from, 56, 87, 179. *See also* Acts, appropriations

Quartering. *See* Acts, Mutiny

Quebec:
    armed forces at: shortage of funds, 91 f.; shortage and surplus of food, 95
    customs: establishment, 98 n.; fees, 119 n.; salaries, 158 n.
    revenues: Bute's failure to decide on policy for, 111; poll tax in, 140

n.; problem of, before Treasury and Council, 142; Governor Murray's report on, 142; commission for receiver general, 142; Governor's own levy, 143; contest over legality of, 163 f., 194; instructions for receiver, 163; levy by Parliament, 170, 173, 194; cut in duties by Treasury, 194

cost of civil government in: failure to provide for, 125; assumed by Parliament, 164

postal system: extended to, 137 and n.; postmaster in, 188

lack of assembly in, 143, 173

question of opposition to Stamp Act in, 160 n.

plan to abolish patent offices in, 168 n.

Queen in Council. *See* Privy Council

Quit rents:
    at various periods: 23, 25, 28, 65 ff., 103, 139 f., 190 f.
    collection and administration of, 25, 103
    receipts from: unsatisfactory in amount, 28, 66, 140 and n.; policy of crown control of, 28, 67 n.; violations of policy, 28; payments from in the colonies, 28, 66 f. and n.; payments from in England, 29 and n., 37, 64 n., 67, 103, 161 and n., 191; reasons for small returns, 191
    proposal for act of Parliament for surveys and rent rolls, 190
    See also Auditor general

Randolph, Edward, and acts of trade, 60

Rate of exchange. *See* Army, funds for

Recruiting. *See* Army

Reimbursement. *See* Acts, appropriations; Colonies

Remembrancer, Queen's (or King's), holder of accountants' bonds, 35

Revenues, colonial: classification, 14; Grenville's primary concern, 131; object of Act of *1766*, 154; King's loss of, 161; promised by Townshend, 166, 172; effect of reduction of land tax on demand for, 172; increased interest in, 200. *See also* Customs; Post Office; Stamp Act; Crown dues

Rhode Island: self-sufficiency, 14; lack of post office in, 21 n.; agent of, 96; claims of for reimbursement, 96, 157; lack of bullion for taxes, 153 n.; poster in, 157 n.; refusal of court to issue writs of assistance, 185 n.

Rhode Islanders, petition from, 82

Rice: enumeration of, 16 n.; extension of market for, 48 n., 117 n., 119 n., 170 n.

Richmond, 3d Duke of. *See* Lennox, Charles

Roberts, John, secretary to Henry Pelham: election manager, 80; joint receiver for Virginia, 103 n.; on presiding at Cockpit, 148

Robinson, John, secretary to the Treasury and Member of Parliament, 168 f., 178

Robinson, John, member of American Board of Customs, 182 n., 184

Robinson, Sir Thomas (later Lord Grantham), Secretary of State, 81

Rockingham, Marquis of. *See* Watson-Wentworth, Charles

Rum: illegal trade in, 99; West Indian, legal preference for, 170

Russell, John, 4th Duke of Bedford: Secretary of State, 79, 84; President of Council, 113, 127 n.

St. Christopher, parliamentary relief for, 30 n. *See also* Four-and-a-half per cent; Land, sales of

St. Eustatius, Dutch free port, 151

St. John, Canada: civil establishment for, 176 n.; customs establishment for, 182 n.

St. John, Henry, Viscount Bolingbroke, Secretary of State, and the Canadian expedition (*1711*), 3

St. Lucia: Grenville's wish to retain, 109; acquired by France, 109 n.

St. Vincent, one of Ceded Islands, 109 n.

Salem, temporary seat of American Board of Customs, 184

Sales of land. *See* Land

Salt, laws on import of, 48 n., 81 n.

Sandwich, 4th Earl of. *See* Montagu, John

Santo Domingo, Spanish free port, 151

Sargent, Winthrop, quoted on Braddock's expedition, 91 n.

Savile, Sir George, on colonies and "rights of nature," 202 n.

Saxby, Henry, deputy collector in London, 116 n.

Scrope, John, Baron in Scottish Court of Exchequer, secretary to the Treasury and Member of Parliament: vote on Test Act, 45; drafting legislation, 49 and n.; under Walpole, 54; under Pelhams, 87 and n.

Secret service funds: in election years, 44 and n., 80 and n., 168; American crown revenues as source for, and special service, 67, 103 f. and n., 106 n., 140 n., 161 and n., 163, 191; Grenville and, 112 n.

Secretary at War: estimates by, 88 n.; letters to from commanders, 90 n.; to put treasury minute into effect, 128; report from, 157

Secretary of State: relation of to head of Treasury, 3, 77; to put treasury minute into effect, 128; orders to governors on illegal trade, 133; functions of relating to colonies, 198. *See also* Conway, Henry; Dunk, George Montagu, Earl of Halifax; Fitzroy, Augustus Henry, Duke of Grafton; Fox, Henry; Grenville, George; Harley, Robert; Hill, Wills, Earl of Hillsborough: Legge, William, Earl of Dartmouth; Lennox, Charles, Duke of Richmond; Montagu, John, Earl of Sandwich; Pelham-Holles, Thomas, Duke of Newcastle; Petty, William, Earl of Shelburne; Pitt, William; Robinson, Sir Thomas; Russell, John, Duke of Bedford; St. John, Henry, Viscount Bolingbroke; Townshend, Charles, Viscount; Wyndham, Charles, Earl of Egremont

Secretary to Treasury. *See* Treasury

Seizures: the *Liberty*, 184; for illegal trade, 187. *See also* Fines and forfeitures

Seven Years' War: "French and Indian," 76 ff.; cost, 82 ff.; and financial planning, 88; effect on treasury control of finance, 107; terms of peace, 109; character of years following, 144; financial situation at end of, 201 f.

Sharpe, Horatio, Governor of Maryland, suggestion for port, 133 n.

Sharpe, John, solicitor to the Treasury, 86 n.

Shelburne, 2d Earl of. *See* Petty, William

Shirley, Lieutenant General William, Governor of Massachusetts: and expedition against Louisburg, 83 and n.; instructions for on recruiting, 93; arrangements of with provision merchants, 94; and military accounts, 95 n.; expenses of for defense of Annapolis, 104 n.

Shrewsbury, Duke of. *See* Talbot, Charles

Silk: act (*1750*), 81 n.; bounty on raw, 170 n.

Sinecures: office of solicitor to Treasury, 86; in crown dues offices, 102. *See also* Customs, colonial officers, deputies; Walpole, Robert, attitude toward deputies

Smith, Robert, deputy to auditor general, 102 n.

Smuggling. *See* Trade, illegal

Society for the Propagation of the Gospel, 55

Solicitor. *See* Customs, London Board; Treasury

Solicitor General: aid of in drafting bill, 50; opinion on King's right to four-and-a-half per cent, 104; report of, 140 n.; opinion on rights of search, 175 f.

South Carolina: parliamentary aid for sufferers in, 51; salary of governor of, 69; companies in, 82. *See also* Carolinas

South Sea Bubble, 40

Spain. *See* Bullion, trade in; Santo Domingo, free port

Spanish Succession, War of, 2, 11

Special service. *See* Secret service

Spotswood, Alexander: Lieutenant Governor of Virginia, recruiting by, 56; deputy postmaster general, 62, 63 n.

Spry, Dr. William, judge of vice-admiralty court, 134 n.

Stamp Act:

preparation of, 120 ff.; commissioner of Stamp Office in consultation on, 120; solicitor to Stamp Office and, 120, 122

Grenville's plan for supplying army from revenue of, 128 n.

administration of: by Grenville, 138 f.; supervision by Stamp Commissioners, 138; colonial officers, 139 and n., 160 n.; by Rockingham, 159 ff.

repeal of: readiness of Newcastle for, 149; decision of Rockingham, 150; Pitt's speech for, 150

opposition to, in America, 149 f., 160 f. and n., 201; question of, 160 n.

receipts from, 161; accounts and audit of, 161 nn.

See also Acts

Stanhope, Charles, secretary to the Treasury, 54 n.

Stanhope, James (later Earl), First Lord of the Treasury, 39 n.; plan for sales of land, 71 n.

Stanwix, Lieutenant General John, 92 n.

Statutes, tendency to substitute for crown orders, 198. *See also* Acts

Stewart, Charles. *See* Customs: American Board, cashier

Stoppages. *See* Army, victualing

Stuart, John, 3d Earl of Bute: George III's devotion to, 78; First Lord

of the Treasury, 108 ff.; and peace terms, 109; legislation under, 109 f.; distaste of, for administration, 110; and Grenville, 111; forced to leave London, 112; Jenkinson, friend of, 177

Sugar: enumeration of, 16; petitions on, 46 f., 81; encouragement of trade in, 48 and n., 153 and n.; foreign, trade of New England in, 81; act of *1764*, 117, 118, 143, 159 n.; removal of, from list of enumerated commodities, 153; use of revenue from, 194. *See also* Acts; Molasses

Sunbury, Georgia, new port, 133

Sunderland, Charles, 3d Earl of, First Lord of the Treasury, 39 n.; appeal to from Duke of Chandos, 44 n.; appointment of surveyor of woods by, 58; and New York assembly grants, 73

Surveyor and auditor general of His Majesty's plantation revenues. *See* Auditor general

Surveyor general. *See* Customs; Woods

Surveys, in North America, 125 and n.

Talbot, Charles, 1st Duke of Shrewsbury, Lord High Treasurer, 2 n.

Taxation, colonial: postal rates as, 14; views on, 84 n.; avoided by Pelhams, 85, 107; reasons for, 116; customs as, 118; avoiding distinction between internal and external, 151; Mutiny Act as form of, 154; demand for under Chatham, 163; Lord North's announcement on, 173; denial of right of Parliament, 188

Taxes: on brandy in Canada, 163 f.; land in England, 172; capitation in Ceded Islands, 194. *See also* Acts, revenue; Colonies, assemblies

Taylour, John, secretary to the Treasury, 54 n.

Tea, tax on. *See* Townshend Act

Temple, Earl. *See* Grenville-Temple, Richard

Temple, John: surveyor general of the customs, correspondent of Whately, 118 and n., 120 and n.; member of American Board, 182 n., 183, 184 n.

Tennis Courts, location of H. Walpole's offices, 64 n.

Thomlinson, John. *See* Army, contracts

Thomson, James, poet, benefit for from customs, 99 n.

Three Rivers, Canada, post office in, 137 n.

Tobacco, enumeration of, 16 n.

Tobago, one of Ceded Islands, 109 n.

Tortola, act in for four-and-a-half per cent, 192 n.

Townshend, Charles, 2d Viscount, Secretary of State, 40 n.

Townshend, Charles: views on colonial taxation, 84 n.; comment on Bute, 112 n.; head of Board of Trade, 113 n.; Chancellor of Exchequer, spokesman in Commons, 166; and North's refusal of his place, 166 n.; death, 167; demand for declaration on crown dues, 171 f.; effect of parliamentary opposition on, 172; introduction of revenue bill, 173; and origin of American Board of Customs, 174; for address to King, 175; introduction of bill suspending New York assembly, 175; his secretary at the Treasury, 178 n.

Townshend, George, Viscount, letter to from Charles Paxton, 174 n.

Townshend Act: passage and repeal of, 173; cause of colonial resistance, 176, 202; collections from, 187

Trade:

object of regulation: protection, 15; revenue, 115

New England export: protection, 47, 81; restricted, 153

illegal: forms of, 99; investigation of, 132; attempts to suppress, 133 ff., 185 f.; report by American Board, 186

international, in islands: during Seven Years' War, 109; suppressed under Grenville, 135 f.; attempts to restore, 151 ff., 157 f.; failure to revive, 152 n.

threat to American, 196

See also Acts

Transportation of felons, 49 n., 179 n.

Treasury:

colonial policies of: traditional, 1, 14, 37; new, 115 f., 186, 200; emphasis on North America, 186

and responsibility for American Revolution, 1, 165, 197, 202

importance of, 1, 40, 74

head of, Lord High Treasurer or First Lord of: relation to sovereign, 2 f., 41, 77 f., 107, 111 f., 146, 167; place of, among the other ministers and in the councils, 3 ff., 41 f., 108, 112 f., 165 ff., 198; control of issue of funds, 3, 42, 79; influence on colonial policy, 199, *see also* Patronage

organization and management of: early, 6 ff.

Board: as Treasurer of the Exchequer, 6 f.; commission, authority, oaths of office, 7 and n.; remuneration of, 8; character of in various periods, 54, 85, 126, 154, 177

First Lord, 6, 39 and n., 76 f. and n., 106, 146, 163, 167

sovereign and, 7 and n., 54, 178

headquarters, 7, 55 n.

secretary: names of, 7, 54 and n., 87 and n., 110, 126 n., 154 f., 178; functions, 8, *see also* Treasury, functions; remuneration of, 9 and n.; question of permanent tenure, 54, 85; burdens of, 177 f.

clerks: number and remuneration, 8 f., 54; functions, 8; permanent tenure and promotion, 8, 86, 126; reorganization of, 178

forms and records, 8 and n., 126 n.

directions for procedure, 55 n.

solicitor to, 9; and passage of bills, 81 n.; representing Rhode Islanders, 82; sinecure in office of, 86; dismissal, 86; accounts, 86 n.; trial, 155 and n.; increasing work, 178; and defense of customs officers, 185

functions of: administrative, 12 ff., 55 ff., 87 ff., 110 ff., 126 ff., 155 ff., 178 ff.; legislative, 45 ff., 81 ff., 109 f., 115 ff., 150 ff., 169 ff.; granting dispensations, 61 and n. *See also* Audit

ignorance of colonies, 135

growing efficiency of, 179 f.

Trecothick, Barlow, letter from to Chatham, 153 n.

"Two shillings a hogshead," local duty in Virginia and Maryland, 31 f., 72 f., 106

Vice-admiralty courts. *See* Courts, in colonies

Victualing. *See* Army

Virginia: duties in, 32 n.; agent for, 96 n.; form of writ of assistance in, 185 n. *See also* Post Office; Quit rents; "Two shillings a hogshead"

Walpole, Sir Edward, 2d son of Sir Robert, secretary to the Treasury, 54 and n.

Walpole, Horatio (Horace), 1st Baron Walpole of Wolterton (*1756*), brother of Sir Robert: offices held by, 40 f.; Member of Parliament, 40, 47, 51, 82; on Sir Robert's practices, 40 n.; member of Privy Council, 41; member of the Board of Trade, 41 f.; auditor general, 41, 64 and n., ff., 102, 104 n., 106; secretary to the Treasury, 41, 47; his characterization of Leheup, 86 n.; death of, 102; on James Abercromby, 102 n.; on McCulloh's claims, 103 n. *See also* Auditor general

Walpole, Robert, 1st Earl of Orford: observer of politics, 5; offices held by, 39 and n.; resignation of, 39, 45; First Lord of the Treasury and Chancellor of the Exchequer, 40 ff.; dependence on brother, 40 f.; position in the Government, 41 ff.; control of patronage and issue of funds, 42 f.; influence in elections, 43 f. and nn.; parliamentary methods, illustrated by passage of Molasses Act, 45 ff. and nn.; attitude toward acts of trade, 46, 48; procedure in drafting legislation, 49 and n.; colonial policies in legislation, 49–52; financial character of his administration, 53 f.; administration of the Treasury by, 54 f.; opposition to use of civil list for colonies, 55; failure to purchase Pennsylvania, 55; and Committee of Secrecy, 56; appointment of surveyor of woods, 59; on purpose of American customs, 59; use of customs patronage, 60; attitude toward use of deputies, 60 f.; failure of, to restore packet system, 63; proprietary emphasis on crown revenue, 63; protection of prerogative by, 66; special interest in four-and-a-half per cent, 68; his method of selling land, precedent for Grenville, 70 f. and n., 140 and n.; failure of to control assembly grants, 73; characterization of administration of, 74; advises King to summon Henry Pelham, 76; and colonial finance, 201

War: effect of, on Treasury, 2, 76, 107; characteristic of Pelhams' administrations, 76; factor in colonial finance, 199. *See also* Austrian Succession; Seven Years' War; Spanish Succession

War Office: draft of American mutiny bill by, 123; recommendation from, 155. *See also* Secretary at War

Ware, Nathaniel, estimate of foreign molasses in America, 116 n.

Warrant, royal and treasury, 8 n.

Watson-Wentworth, Charles, 2d Marquis of Rockingham: First Lord of the Treasury and leader of Whigs, 146 ff.; lack of experience of, 146; position in the Government, 147 and n.; his note on King as "Creature . . . of Compact," 147 n.; patronage policies of, 148; and repeal of Stamp Act, 149; and proposal for free ports, 152; colonial taxation under, 153 f.; for troops in America, 155; practical approach to problems by, 155 ff.; and problem of trade in the islands, 157 f.; combining repeal with Declaratory Act, 159 f.; administration of revenue laws by, 159 ff.; and crown revenues, 161 ff.; his deference to merchants, 162; and support of Quebec, 164; effect of administration on English–American relations, 164; failure to require his followers to resign, 165; and responsibility for the American Revolution, 197

Webb, Philip Carteret, Solicitor to the Treasury, 86 n., 155 n.

Wentworth, Benning, Governor of New Hampshire, surveyor general of the woods, 157 n.

Wentworth, John, surveyor general of the woods, 157 n.

Wentworth family, member of, letter to Rockingham, 149 n.

West, James: secretary to the Treasury, 80; manager of elections, 87 and n.

West Florida: parliamentary appropriations for, 125; contracts for army in, 156 n.; question of opposition to Stamp Act in, 160 n. *See also* Florida

West Indies: army in, 16 n.; charges of customs fraud in, 99; legally distinguished from continent, 123; deputy postmasters in, 138; preference for their rum, 170; remaining under London Board of Customs, 181; outside jurisdiction of new vice-admiralty courts, 186; postal system in, 189; concessions to, 191 f. *See also* Barbados; Ceded Islands; Guadeloupe; Jamaica; Leeward Islands; St. Christopher; Tortola

Westminster, candidates for, 40 n.

Whale fins, exempted from duties, 48 n.

Whately, Thomas: secretary to the Treasury, 115, 119 ff., passim, 126 n., 138; Member of Parliament, 115, 117 n., 120, 172 nn.

Whigs, Rockingham as leader of, 146

White oak staves, bounty on, 170 n.

White pine: restrictions on cutting of, 49 n., 59; condemnation of, 157 n. *See also* Woods

White staff, symbol of office of Lord High Treasurer, 2, 6

Wilkes, John, seizure of papers of, 155 n.

William III: and Treasury, 2, 5; grant by to William and Mary College, 19 n.; commission for prizes under, 26

Williamsburg, Virginia, custom house at, 185 n.

Wilmington, Earl of. *See* Compton, Spencer

Wolfe, Major General James, on lack of specie, 91 f.

Wolterton, 1st Baron of. *See* Walpole, Horatio (Horace)

Wood, William, secretary to Board of Customs, his opposition to Sugar Act, 117 and n.

Woods, surveyor general of, 14, 58, 131 n., 156 f.

Wright, James, Governor of Georgia, establishment of port by, 133 n.

Writs of assistance: authorized for colonies, 174; status of English in colonies, 175 n.; colonial courts and, 185 and n.

Wyndham, Charles, 2d Earl of Egremont, Secretary of State, 113

Yorke, Charles: Solicitor General, opinion of, 104; Attorney General, advice of on bullion trade, 157 n.

Yorke, Philip, 1st Earl of Hardwicke, Lord High Chancellor: friend of Newcastle, 77; defense of Newcastle's patronage, 79 n.; alarm of at American map, 87 n.; on King's right to four-and-a-half per cent, 104

Young, William: head of commission for sale of land on Ceded Islands, 141; accounts of as receiver, 142 n.